KIRSTEN A. SEAVER is an independent historian who has taught at Stanford University. She has also worked as a novelist and a translator, and her work has been published extensively in both English and Norwegian. A Fellow of the Royal Geographical Society, London, her previous publications include *Maps, Myths, and Men: The Story of the Vinland Map* and *The Frozen Echo*.

THE
LAST
VIKINGS

THE EPIC STORY OF THE
GREAT NORSE VOYAGES

KIRSTEN A. SEAVER

I.B. TAURIS
LONDON · NEW YORK

New paperback edition published in 2015 by I.B.Tauris & Co Ltd
6 Salem Road, London W2 4BU
175 Fifth Avenue, New York NY 10010
www.ibtauris.com

Distributed in the United States and Canada Exclusively by Palgrave Macmillan
175 Fifth Avenue, New York NY 10010

First published in hardback in 2010 by I.B.Tauris & Co Ltd

Cover images: Detail of the prow of the Gokstad viking longship, ninth century
© Viking Ship Museum, Oslo, Norway / The Bridgeman art library. Icebergs
off the southeast Greenland coast in late august, the time of least ice (photo:
Kirsten a. Seaver).

ISBN: 978 1 78453 057 0
eISBN: 978 0 85773 540 9

A full CIP record for this book is available from the British Library
A full CIP record is available from the Library of Congress

Library of Congress Catalog Card Number: available

Printed and bound by TJ International Ltd, Padstow, Cornwall

Contents

List of Illustrations

Timeline

Ca. 300 AD	Northern tribes threatening the Roman Empire. The Norse have clinker-built rowing ships suitable for long distances.
410	Britain ceases to be a Roman province.
597	St Augustine arrives in England and converts King Ethelbert of Kent to Christianity.
787	Viking attacks on Britain begin.
825	Dicuil *De mensura orbis terrae*, identifying Thule with Iceland and noting that it was discovered by Celtic hermits in the eighth century.
855	The first permanent Norse settlements in Britain.
866–78	Concerted Norse efforts to conquer Northumbria, Mercia, East Anglia and Wessex.
Ca. 870	The Norse Settlement of Iceland begins.
879	The Treaty of Wedmore marks the start of the Danelaw, a Norse-controlled part of Mercia.
Ca. 880–90	The North Norwegian chieftain Ohthere visits King Alfred's court, and King Alfred writes down the visitor's report on a voyage around the North Cape to the White Sea.
899	King Alfred dies; succeeded by Edward the Elder.
Ca. 911	The Norse gain their hold on what was to become the Duchy of Normandy.
924	Edward dies; succeeded by Æthelstan.
930	The initial wave of Icelandic settlement ends. King Harald the Fairhaired of Norway dies.
937	Æthelstan victorious at Battle of Brunanburgh. The future King Hákon of Norway fostered at Æthelstan's court.
940	Æthelstan dies; succeeded by Edmund.
946	Edmund assassinated; succeeded by Eadred.
954	Danelaw collapse of Kingdom of York; henceforth under the overlordship of West Yarrow kings.

1296	Scotland becomes, temporarily, a dependency of England.
1341	Ívar Bárdsson sails to Greenland as the Bergen bishop's representative.
1348–49	The Black Death in England.
1349–50	The Black Death in Norway.
Ca. 1360	The *Inventio fortunata* is written by an English monk who went beyond Greenland.
1364	Ívar Bárdsson returns to Norway from Greenland and reports on his stay.
1377–78	Bishop Alf, the last resident Gardar bishop, dies at his post.
1397	The Kalmar Treaty unites Norway, Denmark and Sweden under Queen Margrethe.
	English fishermen visit the Westman Islands in Iceland.
1401	The English Parliament passes the act 'De heretico comburendo'; the first Lollard heretic is burned in England, by royal order.
1402–04	The Black Death reaches Iceland.
1405	Thorstein Olafsson, Björn Einarsson 'Jerusalem-Farer' and their companions leave Iceland for royal wedding in Norway.
1406	After attending the wedding of King Eirik of Pomerania to Philippa (daughter of Henry IV of England), Thorstein Olafsson and his companions sail from Norway to Greenland. In Florence, Jacopo Angelo da Scarperia completes translation of Ptolemy's *Geography* into Latin.
1407	A Norse Greenlander named Kollgrim is accused of black arts and is burned at the stake.
1408	Thorstein Olafsson and Sigrid Björnsdaughter are married at Hvalsey Church in Greenland.
1410	Thorstein Olafsson, Sigrid Björnsdaughter and their friends sail from Greenland to Norway.
1411	Thorstein Olafsson, Sigrid Björnsdaughter and many of their friends return home to Iceland.
1413	Henry IV dies, succeeded by Henry V.
	A house in Bergen belonging to Englishmen from Kings Lynn burned by the Hanse. More than thirty English fishing doggers off Iceland.
	The English arrive in North Iceland that year.
1422	Henry V dies; succeeded by Henry VI.
1425	King Eirik's men in Iceland, Hannes Pálsson and Balthazar von Damminn, are captured by the English in the Westman Islands and taken to England.

1440	King Eirik of Pomerania deposed in Denmark and Sweden, no longer rules Norway after 1442.
1453	The fall of Byzantium.
1455	The Wars of the Roses begin.
1467	Men from Kings Lynn kill the Icelandic chieftain Björn Thorleifsson in his home country, further exacerbating Anglo-Danish relations.
1468, 1469	Christian I of Denmark and Norway pawns Orkney and Shetland to the Scottish king as a dowry for his daughter.
1473	A two-year peace treaty between Edward IV and Christian I is reached in Utrecht.
1485	Henry VII is crowned; unites the rival houses of York and Lancaster.
1490	The Piningsdómur (Pining's Judgment) passed in Iceland.
1492	Christopher Columbus sails across the Atlantic to the Caribbean.
1497	John Cabot sails from Bristol to the Labrador-Newfoundland region.
1498	Vasco da Gama sails around the Cape of Good Hope and finds the sea route eastwards to India.
1501	An Anglo-Azorean syndicate for northern exploration is formed in Bristol.
1507	The map maker Martin Waldseemüller draws a world map on which the name 'America' appears for the first time.
1509	Henry VIII becomes king of England.
1514–16	The Norwegian archbishop, Erik Valkendorf, plans a 'rescue' expedition to the Norse Greenlanders. The expedition never took place.
1519–22	Magellan's circumnavigation.
1547	Henry VIII dies; succeeded by Edward VI.
1558	Elizabeth I becomes queen of England.
	The Venetian Nicolò Zeno publishes a map and descriptions of the North Atlantic purporting to reflect fourteenth-century voyages. The documents' fake nature eventually exposed.
1576–78	Martin Frobisher's three voyages to Baffin Island.
1596	Willem Barentsz discovers Spitzbergen.
1603	Queen Elizabeth I dies; succeeded by James I.
1605	King Christian IV sends three navy ships to Greenland, under the command of the Scot John Cunningham, to assert Danish sovereignty over the Norse Greenlanders.

1606	Christian IV sends five ships on a second expedition to Greenland.
1607	Christian IV sends a third expedition to Greenland, this time with specific instructions to land on the east coast to look for the Norse.
1630	The Skálholt Cathedral in Iceland burns; archives lost.
1652	David Danell undertakes the first of three trade voyages to Greenland for the Danish Customs Department.
1721	The Norwegian missionary Hans Egede arrives in Greenland, hoping to convert the Greenland Norse to Lutheranism.
1786	Two ships from the Danish Navy are sent to East Greenland to look for the Norse Eastern Settlement.
1822	William Scoresby proves that it is possible to make one's way inside the ice belt and lands on Greenland's east coast at 70° 31'N.
1828	Lieutenant W. A. Graah in the Danish Navy goes to Greenland, spends two years looking for the Norse in vain.
1837	Publication of *Antiquitates Americanae*.
1839	A Danish commercial assistant digs up a large part of the Norse churchyard at Herjolfsness in Greenland.
1883–85	The belief in an east coast Eastern Settlement is finally put to rest by the two Danish naval officers Gustav Holm and V. Garde.

Note on sources

In the fine tradition of historical teases, early written sources concerning Greenland in the Middle Ages are few and far between and, to make matters worse, some of them are not what they purport to be, because documentary fakes are not a modern invention. Not a single Norse document actually written in Greenland survives among the authentic materials, and primary source material written elsewhere about Norse Greenland events is not only scant, but often ambiguous to modern scholars. Much of that ambiguity comes from vague geographical notions such as those found in the earliest known document to mention Greenland by name, a bull issued by Pope Leo IX on 6 January 1053. The pope describes Archbishop Adalbert of Hamburg-Bremen and his successors as 'episcopus in omnibus gentibus Suenonum seu Danorum, Noruechorum, Islant, Scrideuinnum, Gronlant et uniuersarum septentrionalium…' (with episcopal authority over the Swedes, Danes, Norwegians, Icelanders, Skridefinners, Greenlanders and all people towards the north).[1] Four centuries later, geographical notions about the Far North remained uncertain in Rome, as demonstrated by two papal letters about Greenland, which were written in 1448 and 1492 respectively, under circumstances that will be discussed in Chapter Ten.

We are indebted to a canon of Bremen, one of Archbishop Adalbert's admirers, for the oldest surviving written mention of Norse activities in Iceland, Greenland and North America as well as for a detailed description of northern geography as perceived in the eleventh century. The *History of the Archbishops of Hamburg-Bremen* was composed during 1072–85, and its author, Adam of Bremen, was anxious to credit the Bremen archbishopric with christianising the Far North and therefore spent much labour on describing the geography of that part of the world.

Having carefully noted the spherical nature of the earth, Adam explained that in the northern ocean there were two islands named Thule, one of them lately renamed Iceland and the other a barely known island somewhere in the impenetrable and icy Polar darkness, beyond the islands of Vínland and Greenland which had recently been discovered by the Norse. Adam imagined both countries located in the distant northwestern Atlantic and therefore just east of an unexplored Eurasian *east* coast.[2] He also wrote:

> In the ocean there are very many other islands of which not the least is Greenland, situated far out in the ocean opposite the mountains of Sweden and the Rhiphaean range. To this island they say it is from five to seven days' sail from the coast of Norway, the same as to Iceland. The people there are green from the salt water, whence, too, that region gets its name. The people live in the same manner as the Icelanders except that they are fiercer and trouble seafarers by their piratical attacks. Report has it that Christianity of late has also winged its way to them.

Naturally, those rough Greenlanders' conversion to Christianity was credited to the influence of the Roman Church.

The seeds to Adam's doubts about the Norse Greenlanders' Christian commitment were probably planted by his friend King Svein Estrithsson of Denmark, who had told him about Iceland and Greenland as well as about 'yet another island...called Vinland because vines producing excellent wine grow wild there. That unsown crops also abound on that island we have ascertained not from fabulous reports but from the trustworthy relations of the Danes. Beyond that island...no habitable land is found in that ocean, but every place beyond is full of impenetrable ice and darkness.'[3]

Throughout the Middle Ages and later, Adam's *History* was so influential that its footprints are clearly discernible in the *Vinland Map*, a modern fake that supposedly indicates the approximate location of Vínland, the southernmost of three North American regions which Norse explorers reached in the early eleventh century. It was also used by the Icelandic historian Ari 'the Learned' Thorgilsson (1068–1148) who, in the 1120s, complied with a request by the bishops of Skálholt and Hólar to write a history of the Icelandic people. Segments of Ari's writing also appear in two other early descriptions of the Norse Greenlanders' settlement and of their first encounters with North American natives – the 'Saga of Eirik the Red' and the 'Saga of the Greenlanders'. The two sagas are often referred to jointly as the Vínland sagas.

Other sagas besides the Vínland sagas provide glimpses of life in Greenland. Iceland is also home to a series of annals based on Bede's chronological system, written by various compilers and begun at the end of the thirteenth century, which drew upon both foreign and domestic sources. They are such an invaluable research tool that they were edited by the Norwegian historian Gustav Storm and published as *Islandske Annaler* (*Icelandic Annals*) in 1888. That title should not be confused with the

Grænlands annáll (*Greenland Annals*), a collection of miscellaneous information about Greenland, first compiled anonymously around 1623. The collection was extensively copied a couple of decades later by the autodidact Icelander Björn Jónsson from Skarðsá (1574–1655), who inserted reflections of his own, some of which are certainly eyebrow-raising, and all of which are fascinating examples of the ideas that were circulating in Björn's own day. *Islandske Annaler* and the *Grænlands annáll*, together with the *Annálar 1400–1800* (often called the *New Annals*), are all crucial to the history of the medieval Norse in the North Atlantic, and so are the *Diplomatarium Islandicum*, the *Diplomatarium Norvegicum* and other document collections published over the years.

From Norwegian writers come two other important sources: the *Historia Norvegiæ*, (surviving only in part), written around AD 1170 by an anonymous Norwegian cleric, and the mid-thirteenth-century Norwegian work *Konungsskuggsjá* (*King's Mirror*), whose author is likewise unknown. The latter is written in the form of a dialogue between a father and his son and reflects familiarity with both the Norwegian royal court and the practical world. Its anonymous author was obviously also well versed in the theological and secular learning of his time and wove standard bookish lore into the practical advice the father offered his son. Neither the *Historia Norvegiæ* nor the *Konungsskuggsjá* mentions Vínland, but both suggest that Greenland was part of an Arctic land mass connected to both westernmost and easternmost Eurasia, the only continent then known besides Africa. In other respects, the two works share many of Adam of Bremen's notions and show a similar mixture of factual information and conventional medieval lore and superstitions about the Far North. For example, what better explanation for the many perils Arctic travellers were likely to encounter on land and at sea than that supernatural powers were to blame?

With the 1837 Copenhagen publication of Carl Christian Rafn and Finn Magnusen's *Antiquitates Americanae* the reading public got a major compendium of sources. Written in Icelandic with Latin and Danish translations, it brought together sources which the authors hoped would help with the understanding of medieval Norse activities in Greenland and North America. It also had an English summary that widened its potential readership considerably. As Chapter One as well as the 'Postscript' will note, however, indiscriminate reliance on the work has brought some enduring problems in discussing the Norse Greenlanders.

Professional archaeology was still in its infancy when Rafn and Magnusen mined the written sources available to them in Copenhagen and produced not only the *Antiquitates*, but the three-volume *Grønlands*

Historiske Mindesmærker (*Historical Monuments of Greenland*), a massive work published during the years 1838–45. Although many of the authors' commentaries inevitably contain ideas that have since been rendered moot by modern research, it is still useful today.

There are still some who insist, like the Norwegian adventurer and writer Thor Heyerdahl (1914–2002), that the Vatican Archives became a repository of much vital and accurate information about the medieval Norse in general and about the Greenlanders in particular. We just haven't found all the documents yet, the sanguine argument goes. Actually, historians following the Norse Greenlanders' trail picked over the Vatican documents with great zeal in the nineteenth and early twentieth centuries and promptly published what they found. Besides, the pope and Curia were as hopelessly confused about the north throughout the Middle Ages as everybody else in southern Europe. It is nevertheless appropriate to honour the scholars of Norse history who first deciphered key documents and texts in archives from Iceland down to Rome and made them available in print, sometimes with commentaries and sometimes without.

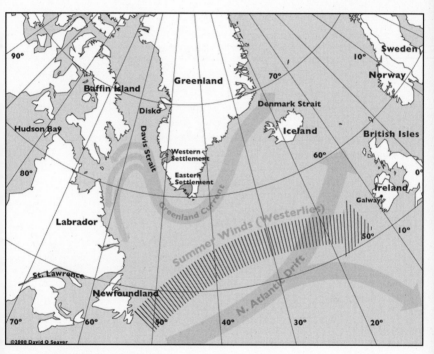

Fig. 1   Map of the North Atlantic.

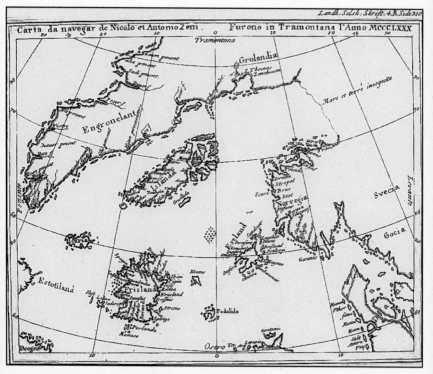

Fig. 2   Map by Nicolò Zeno the Younger, 1558. As shown here, the map was published in 1793 in Henrich von Eggers, "Priisskrift om Grønlands Østerbygds sande Beliggenhed ('Prize winning essay on the true location of Greenland's Eastern Settlement'). The Zeno map greatly influenced the thinking of cartographers and historians until the late 1800s, when the map was declared a fake and investigators had definitively ruled out a Norse settlement on Greenland's east coast.

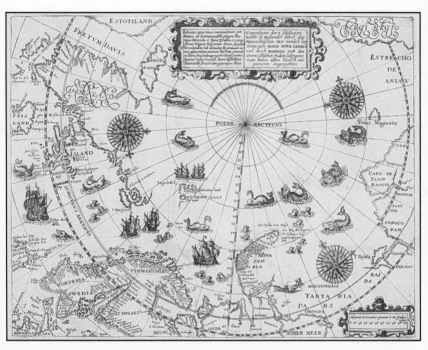

Fig. 3   Map of the north by the Dutch explorer Willem Barentsz. The map, which was drawn in 1598 and published posthumously, shows strong influence from the Zeno map in its depiction of Greenland. Barentsz had discovered Spitzbergen Island (Svalbard archipelago) in 1596 and believed it to be a part of Greenland's eastward extension.

INTRODUCTION

The Norse colonisation of Greenland, late in the tenth century, and their voyages to North America early in the eleventh, mark the farthest reach of the medieval Norse quest for land and livelihood. By about AD 1500, that distinction had returned eastwards to Iceland, and the Norse Greenlanders and their North American forays quickly receded into the mists of myth.

The fate of the Norse colony in Greenland, unknown to this day, is a contentious historical arena by any measure. Despite much recent knowledge gained from archaeological excavations and research in several related fields, discussions about the Norse Greenlanders are still afflicted with ideas rooted in nineteenth-century thinking about such topics as dietary requirements, the effects of isolation, the viability of non-industrial cultures and the influence of ecclesiastical and secular authorities. Chauvinism spices the debate, and additional seasoning comes from the demonstrable fact that, around the year 1000, the Norse Greenlanders became the first Europeans to reach parts of North America. This aspect of the Norse Greenland story was in itself a bone of contention until archaeologists determined that the ruins at L'Anse aux Meadows on Newfoundland's Northern Peninsula, which Helge Ingstad discovered in 1960, represent a Norse site dating from around AD 1000. Even with that issue settled, both the extent of Norse exploration in eastern North America and the problem of defining Canadian territories by their Norse designations and descriptions continue to be hotly debated.

Far from being the precious prerogative of fussy experts, a talent for wrangling seems to be embedded in most of us, and bickering over both academic and nonacademic approaches to historical conundrums may go on for generations. Genuine historical enigmas pose a challenge to even the most conscientious among us and are, by their very nature, prone to conflicting interpretations. More serious problems arise when attempts at riddle-solving blossom into fanciful creations because records are spotty and scarce or, better yet, nonexistent. Much is now known about the history of the Norse Greenlanders, however, and more is learned every year. Because the reality here is far more interesting than any made-up story, I want to share what I have gleaned from decades of research and many travels in Greenland.

My reading has left me so deeply indebted to colleagues in many fields that I cannot name them all, but the list of works cited in this book should serve as a guide. Even with the wealth of written material out there, one needs teachers and colleagues, however, especially in a field that involves not only history, but archaeology, linguistics, and the history of geography and cartography. My special thanks, therefore, to Peter Barber and his wonderful staff at the British Library Map Library, to map experts Francis Herbert, Sarah Tyacke and Andrew Cook (also in London), to Benedicte Gamborg Briså at the Norwegian National Library's map collection in Oslo, to Kari Ellen Gade at Indiana University, to Anna Agnarsdóttir at the University of Iceland, and to Jette Arneborg, Mogens Skaaning Høegsberg, Niels Lynnerup and Søren Thirslund in Denmark, Joel Berglund in Sweden, Kevin Edwards in Scotland, Christian Keller in Norway, Patrick Plumet in France, Georg Nyegaard in Greenland and Robert Ferguson, Karen McCullough, Robert McGhee, Peter Schledermann, Patricia Sutherland and Birgitta Wallace in Canada.

Last, but not least, my husband Paul Seaver, right here in California, combines all the best features of an historian and a patient mate. We also have a graphic designer son, David, who invariably stands ready to help with his skills, and a daughter, Hannah, who is ever willing to hear the latest hot news about the medieval Greenlanders and let me have her reactions.

It takes a large village indeed to make a book.

Kirsten A. Seaver
Palo Alto, California, USA

1

NO FORWARDING ADDRESS

PHYSICAL DESCRIPTION OF GREENLAND

Greenland, the world's biggest island, is definable and real, although it is a remote place to most people even now and obviously was even more so in the days before aviation. Reaching from latitude 59° 46'N at Cape Farewell in the south to 83° 39'N, Greenland covers almost 840,000 square miles and is surrounded by some of the world's most dangerous seas, which is why its island nature was not confirmed until a piecemeal circumnavigation had been completed early in the twentieth century. Ashore, the landscape is equally intimidating with its huge proportions, its immense distances and its massive spine of granite running north–south to a height of two and three kilometres, weighed down by a vast ice sheet between two and three kilometres thick. In conjunction with the Arctic climate that prevails over the entire island, this towering, ice-crowned ridge is in large part responsible for the sudden and extreme changes in weather for which Greenland is known.[1] Despite these awesome features, Greenland nurtures beautiful, resilient flowers (Fig. 4) and is a botanist's delight as the home of around five hundred wild species of vascular plants, including five types of exquisite small orchids. It is also a geologist's paradise.

Geologically speaking, Greenland is essentially a part of North America, separated from it in the north only by the narrow Smith Sound. To the east, its nearest neighbour is volcanic Iceland, which the medieval Norse

Fig. 4   Fireweed (*Chamaenerion latifolium*), ubiquitous in Greenland, is the country's hardy and beautiful national flower

began to settle in AD 870, completing the initial process in about sixty years. After that time, it became difficult for newcomers to claim good land, which was one reason why the feisty Norwegian-born Icelander Eirik 'the Red' Thorvaldsson, when setting out to found a colony in Greenland, was accompanied by a number of Icelandic families ready to clear new land.

THE PUSH WESTWARDS

It indicates tremendous energy and momentum that the comparatively rapid colonisation of Iceland and Greenland took place while the Norse were also tightening their grip on Ireland, England and Scotland. Norsemen from those islands were in fact among the earliest settlers in Iceland; others came directly from Scandinavia, primarily from areas in western Norway that were little able to sustain a growing population. That included Jæren in the southwest, where Eirik the Red Thorvaldsson appears to have grown up.[2]

Eirik spearheaded the Norse settlement of Greenland just before AD 990, and the colony endured for about five centuries. Discussions abound about what happened during that half millennium, because it is a complex topic that involves both modern archaeological reports and a miscellany of early written sources.

Ari the Learned's *Íslendingabók* (*Book of the Icelanders*), which begins by describing Iceland's early settlement around AD 870, includes a brief account of Greenland's colonisation, the oldest known reference to Eirik the Red's ambitious undertaking. The description was based on what Ari had learned from his own uncle, Thorkell Gellison, whom he had good reason to trust.

> The country called Greenland was discovered and colonised from Iceland. A man called Eirikr the Red, from Breiðafjörður, went there and took possession of land in the district which has since been called Eiriksfjörður. He gave the country a name and called it Greenland, and said that people would be more eager to go there if it had an attractive name. They found there human habitations, both in the eastern and western parts of the country, and fragments of skin boats and stone implements, from which it can be concluded that the people who had been there before were of the same kind as those who inhabit Vinland and whom the Greenlanders call Skrælings. He began colonising the country fourteen or fifteen winters before Christianity came to Iceland [985 or 986] according to what a man who had gone there with Eirikr the Red told Thorkell Gellison in Greenland. [3]

Like many other Icelandic sagas, our two most important sources – the 'Saga of Eirik the Red' and the 'Saga of the Greenlanders' – were based on oral traditions, and both were written down in the early thirteenth century.[4] That prompts the question of how reliable Norse oral history would have been after the passage of two centuries, especially when both sagas give evidence of influence by the intellectual currents of the anonymous authors' own time. Fortunately, it has become increasingly clear that the Norse were able to preserve oral genealogies and family traditions for many generations, a good example being a boastful runic inscription in the Orkney megalithic tomb of Maeshowe: 'These runes were carved by the best rune-master in the western ocean, with the ax that belonged to Gauk Trandilsson in the southern part of the country [Iceland].' The inscription dates from the winter of 1153–54, when a group of Norse raiders harrying in the Hebrides had sought shelter inside the howe, and the boast was the work of Thorhall Ásgrimsson, the great-great-great-grandson of the man responsible for Gauk Trandilsson's death as described in 'Njál's Saga'.[5]

Commentaries on the sparse source material we have to work with are as plentiful as they are easily outdated. Fortunately, the primary sources themselves do not alter, only the light by which each generation of scholars reads them. A sharper distinction between commentaries and sources would probably have minimised current problems in discussions about the Norse in Greenland and North America. Students of Norse Greenland may trace a number of woes to the 1837 Copenhagen publication of Carl Christian Rafn and Finn Magnusen's *Antiquitates Americanae*. Written in Icelandic with Latin and Danish translations, it was a compendium of sources the authors hoped would help with the understanding of medieval Norse activities in Greenland and North America, and it had an English summary that widened its potential readership considerably. It was deservedly welcomed on both sides of the Atlantic. Unfortunately, the volume's publication also encouraged scholars and non-scholars alike to speculate rather freely about the Norse in North America and Greenland, because the compilers asserted that an old, round tower in Newport, Rhode Island had been constructed as a medieval Norse church and thus demonstrated a successful and enduring Norse presence in that area throughout the Middle Ages.[6] This structure and other supposedly Norse creations have fed a cult history that is much too fat and happy to die of its own accord, and which the 'Postscript' discusses in conjunction with the *Vinland Map* and other dubious creations credited to the medieval Norse.

Problems also arise from the fact that modern archaeologists working in Greenland – usually under very difficult conditions – have had an extra cross to bear in the form of unskilled, early digs in Norse Greenland ruin sites. For example, when it transpired that there was an ancient Norse graveyard on the Herjolfsness site (in the southernmost reaches of the main Norse settlement), a Danish commercial assistant named Ove Kielsen excavated there for two and a half days in 1839 and found some wooden crosses, a skull with blond hair still attached, and a garment identified as a 'sailor's jacket' but later shown to be part of a medieval man's gown. After receiving a stipend of four pounds sterling as a reward for his work so far, Kielsen hired twenty-four men to work for five more days, during which time they dug up a large part of the churchyard to a depth of two or three feet. Their efforts, which constituted sheer vandalism by today's standards, turned up a number of modest objects, in varying states of preservation, which experts back in Copenhagen deemed worthless.[7]

One of the things learned since the mid-nineteenth century is that the medieval North Atlantic expansion, which resulted in the Norse Greenland colony, preserved a remarkable cultural affinity among all the Norse societies around the North Atlantic and the North Sea. At the same time, settlers in their various new island homes very soon came to regard themselves as denizens of their new homelands, not of Norway. This two-edged situation gives added significance to contemporaneous comments on Greenland found in the *Historia Norvegiæ*, and also to statements in the *Konungsskuggsjá* (*King's Mirror*).

Both books recognised that not the least of a mariner's perils was the chance of getting lost at sea. The *Historia Norvegiæ* relates that some Icelandic sailors encountered fog while returning home from Norway and drifted so far off course that they had no idea where they were. When the weather finally cleared, they reportedly observed land between Greenland and Biarmaland, the Norse name for the White Sea region and beyond. There, they vowed, they had seen marvellously large men, and on a nearby island there were maidens who reportedly became pregnant from drinking sea water. Having delivered these sops to standard medieval lore, the *Historia*'s author retreated into contemporaneous geographical ideas and explained that beyond those marvel-lands, and separated from them by icebergs, one would find Greenland, which Icelanders had settled. Greenland forms Europe's outer boundary to the west, the author explained, and it reaches all the way towards the African Islands where the Great Ocean flows in. Dredging his mind for further information, he added that far to the north of the Greenland Norse settlements live a race of short people whom hunters call Skrælings, and who make their weapons from walrus tusks and sharp stones because they lack iron.[8]

In the *King's Mirror*, after the father had cautioned his son that an aspiring merchant must be prepared for many vicissitudes, whether at sea or in heathen countries, he provided a description of Ireland taken straight from the writings of Gerald of Wales (about 1146–1223), praising the island's mild climate in which people need no clothes even in winter and averring that Ireland is so holy that neither snakes nor toads are found there. Those who venture farther north would need to take care, however, the father admonished, because the Greenland Sea is prone to hafgerðingar (probably tsunamis) and features many monsters, including the margygr with long hands and the large-breasted upper body of a woman, but with a man's long hair and beard. They had not been seen very frequently, the father believed, but 'people have stories to tell about them, so men must have seen or caught sight of them'. Rather more useful to traders would be the rostungr (walrus) found in Greenland waters and described as a species of seal, with two big tusks in its upper jaw yielding ivory, and with tough hide which, when cut into strips, provided strong ropes. Along with various kinds of animal skins, those products made Greenland a worthwhile destination for a trader willing to brave the perils of that northern sea, including the frightful ice off

Greenland's east and northeast coasts. The father nevertheless wanted his son to know that while the country provided good conditions for man and beast, few people lived there, and few went there to visit. Those who did so, wanted to satisfy their curiosity, to win fame, and to gain wealth by means of a trade from which one might expect a good profit in a place that 'lies so distant from other countries that men seldom visit it'.[9]

MODERN VOICES OF GLOOM AND DOOM

Home to barely 65,000 people, Greenland is sparsely populated even today, and the Norse of a thousand years ago would have amounted to mere specks in that huge landscape. Of the twenty-five open, square-rigged ships that set out on Eirik's colonising venture some time between AD 986 and 990, laden with emigrants and their belongings, only fourteen made it all the way to Greenland after a crossing that caused some to perish and forced others to return home. However, that was sufficient to start the main colony in the southwest (the Eastern Settlement) and a satellite colony (the Western Settlement) some 400 miles farther north – the latter name reflecting the settlers' awareness that the Greenland west coast veers noticeably west as it runs north. Recent scientific evidence has confirmed that both of the Greenland Norse settlements were populated around AD 1000.[10]

To a man and woman, those pioneers were accustomed to hard, physical work and to conditions in the Far North, where the struggle for existence was an even greater challenge than in the rest of medieval Europe, and they were determined to create a society where their inherited hunting, fishing and farming culture could continue to flourish. Expert at exploiting the natural resources of the Far North, they emigrated to Greenland precisely because of that country's rich resources, and they were obviously successful, given that five centuries passed before smoke no longer rose above the turf-covered roofs of their settlements.

Although the duration of the Norse tenure in Greenland equals the length of time that has passed since the European 'rediscovery' of America, their venture is almost without exception seen as having failed in some way. Despite their proven ability to survive in such a challenging environment for half a millennium, they have routinely been portrayed in posterity as tragic victims of external circumstances exacerbated by their own shortcomings, and there have been many explanations for why a doomed society supposedly developed from the sturdy seeds planted by

Eirik the Red. Suggestions include genetic deterioration, malnutrition, incompetent resource exploitation, fatal skirmishes with encroaching Inuit, failure to learn from the Inuit, pestilence brought from Europe, pirates descending from Europe, isolation from Europe, the breakdown of an already fragile social order, an eastward return to Iceland and Norway and last, but certainly not least, climate change.

In his 2005 bestseller *Collapse: How Societies Choose to Fail or Succeed*, the American author Jared Diamond makes Norse Greenland his poster child for societal failure and states unequivocally: 'Greenland Norse society collapsed completely: Its thousands of inhabitants starved to death, were killed in civil unrest or in war against an enemy, or emigrated, until nobody remained alive.' Their society was doomed from within and without, Diamond writes. He suggests that we may learn from studying that society's collapse because, in his view, many of our own problems are broadly similar to those which the Norse Greenlanders faced because of their 'unintended ecological suicide' and general lack of foresight, as well as due to poor adjustment to Greenlandic conditions. Norse Greenland society provides our most complex case of prehistoric collapse, Diamond believes, adding that it also represents the case for which we have the most information, given that it was 'a well-understood, literate European society'.[11]

Certainly, the Norse Greenlanders were European, but their literacy rate remains unmeasured and unmeasurable, and their society is not particularly well understood even now. Public misconceptions about Norse Greenland abound, including about the developments which Diamond considers likely to have caused the Norse Greenlanders' self-inflicted demise: 'environmental damage, climate change, loss of friendly contacts with Norway, rise of hostile contacts with the Inuit, and the political, economic, social and cultural setting of the Greenland Norse.'[12] There is clearly a call to examine both current knowledge about the political, economic, social, and cultural setting of Norse Greenland, and the fatal deficiencies supposedly besetting this European outpost and distant beacon of the medieval Roman Church. Two questions invite themselves: what was the Norse Greenlanders' fate in fact? And do the proposed contributing circumstances stand up to scrutiny?

Common sense suggests that erosion and changes in the climate would not in themselves have caused an entrenched population to vanish while there was still food on the land and in the sea. Medieval Icelanders had environmental problems similar to the Greenlanders' and suffered calamitous volcanic eruptions besides, but they survived and recovered from every disaster, including the Black Death, which finally reached

Iceland in 1402. There is no evidence at all that the Black Death ever invaded Greenland. Nor should one suppose that the Greenlanders, being of the same sturdy stock as the Icelanders, had less ability to cope with weather fluctuations by the late fifteenth century, or less will to live, than either their ancestors who had accompanied Eirik the Red or their contemporaries in Iceland.

Prompted by current discussions about global warming, the climate situation at the time of the Norse Greenlanders' colonial tenure nevertheless crops up frequently and terms like the 'Medieval Warm Period' and the 'Little Ice Age' are tossed about rather too freely. Although the 'Little Ice Age' was not an observable phenomenon in the far northwest until just before 1700, in writings about Norse Greenland the term has often been applied to a period beginning as early as about 1350, when there was a cooling trend interrupted by several periods of milder weather. Although much of the 'information' about that cooling trend derives from misinterpretations of supposedly fourteenth-century sailing directions to Greenland, which suffer heavily from seventeenth-century interpolations, they have strongly influenced interpretations of complex climate data from that vast region.

Recent climate research, which indicates that cold and/or erratic weather affected the Eastern Settlement during a period prior to the colony's desertion, has prompted renewed suggestions that a worsening climate contributed in a major way to the Norse Greenlanders' disappearance. Such cause-and-effect reasoning is meaningless when we know neither the exact time of the Eastern Settlement's closing down nor the relationship between the climate at any time and the medieval inhabitants' situation – or indeed how they responded to climate variability. What we do know is that around AD 1000, average temperatures in southwestern Greenland were about the same as around 2000, and that the millennium in between saw many climate fluctuations. The big climate changes that allow forestry and agriculture on an unprecedented scale have come after 2000, with Greenland's experiencing a warming with no known parallel in the preceding thousand years, not even at the tail end of the Medieval Warm Period when Eirik the Red and his pioneers cleared the first farms in their new colony. Palaeo-botanical studies of seeds and other plant remains from both the Eastern and Western Settlements show that while the Norse could cultivate hardy root crops and that they had managed to grow flax, they were unable to raise even the hardiest grain to maturity.[13]

Another persistent explanation for the end of the Norse Greenland colony is that severed contact with Norway around 1400 must inevitably have struck a mortal blow to the Norse Greenlanders' existence. However, the Eastern Settlement lasted for a century or a century and a half after the rupture of formal Norwegian connections, which suggests that the experience was quite bearable. The question of Norway's role in the Norse Greenlanders' lives is nevertheless a weighty one and will be taken up in various contexts in later chapters.

What is beyond dispute is that the Norse Greenlanders did vanish. Recent archaeological investigations indicate that the Western Settlement closed down around 1400 (not around 1350, as is usually claimed) and that, except for a few possible stragglers, the Norse inhabitants had left the Eastern Settlement by about 1500. Even the best available historical and archaeological information fails to illuminate either the circumstances or the timing of the decisions to close down these communities. Nobody witnessed the departure of the Norse Greenlanders, and nobody knows why they left and where they went.

2

EIRIK THE RED KNEW
WHERE TO GO

'Viking Millennium' celebrations in the year 2000 fortified the popular notion that violent Norse seafarers had streamed out of the Far North to plunder and vanquish hapless Europeans, until they finally met their match in American natives. It is an arresting image, but as a general picture of the medieval Norse it is about as relevant as a photograph of sunbathers used to illustrate global warming.

The terms 'Norse' and 'Viking' are often subject to the same lack of differentiation as the Nordic countries themselves. There was a Viking Age, spanning roughly from the end of the eighth century to about 1050–1100, and the Vikings were certainly Norse, but not all Norse people were Vikings. Our discussion here will primarily concern Norse societies with their roots in Norwegian culture, not the group of people from Norway, Sweden and Denmark who, because of their violent profession, came to be known as 'Vikings'. Moreover, given the different geographical and topographical circumstances dictating each country's domestic economy and relationship with neighbouring regions, the histories and cultures of Norway, Sweden and Denmark developed along separate lines from early on. Hence, the Norse eastward expeditions across the Baltic and the White Sea and deep into Russia along its huge rivers were chiefly undertaken by Swedish and Finnish people, while westward enterprise generally involved people from Norway, especially western Norway, and from Denmark.

Most Norse people did not make their living from pillage even when superior ships and first-rate seamanship enabled pirates from

the Far North to terrorise people both within and beyond their
Scandinavian homelands. Instead, they relied on farming, fishing, hunting
and trade, and some used their maritime advantages to find new land
for settlement. In a constant quest for profit, pirates and non-pirates
alike probed new locations and uprooted themselves from their old
ones. Their women and children came along on a long voyage only
when the intention was to make a new home; they did not engage
actively in Viking raids. By about AD 1000 Vikings as well as non-
Vikings from the west had established English, Irish and Scottish
colonies that included the Isle of Man, the Hebrides (Fig. 5), the
Orkneys and Shetland; they had also made themselves at home in the
Faeroes and created viable new societies in distant Iceland and
Greenland. In all of those places, archaeologists have found evidence
of families living off the land and the sea, not just off stolen goods
and extortion.

Most of those Norse emigrants will forever remain nameless, but
among the few who were immortalised by Icelandic sagas, Eirik 'the Red'
Thorvaldsson remains the stuff of legend to this day. By any yardstick,
spearheading the Norse colonisation of Greenland in the waning years
of the tenth century was daringly ambitious, and the colonists' vanishing

Fig. 5 A sheltered bay in the Isle of Lewis, Hebrides – a Norse home-away-
from-home

act half a millennium later merely enhances the impression of valiant confrontation with the unknown.

MEDIEVAL GEOGRAPHICAL KNOWLEDGE

As noted earlier, knowledge about Eirik's venture comes from the 'Saga of the Greenlanders', the 'Saga of Eirik the Red' and Ari's *Íslendingabók*, all of which have been mulled over by generations of historians and archaeologists.

Ari's terse, but factual synopsis is an improvement on the rather fanciful image of the Norse Greenlanders proffered by Adam of Bremen, who never mentioned Eirik the Red and his circle with a word, but the Icelandic historian and the Bremen cleric nevertheless had key cosmographical concepts in common with each other as well as with Eirik the Red and his fellow navigators. Although the information Adam had received from King Svein of Denmark was limited, it had at least enabled him to envision Greenland's approximate location relative to other places he and his contemporaries had heard of and to realise that on a spherical earth, Greenland lay west of Iceland. Given that time's lack of awareness of America and the Pacific Ocean, Adam's concept thus placed Greenland close to the Eurasian northeast coast, but still somewhat nearer to the known regions of the world than Adam's 'second Thule'.[1] The latter location clearly referred to the theoretical northern apex espoused by Ptolemy and other mathematicians in Antiquity. The designation is unlikely to have intruded upon Eirik's thinking about the northern seas he sailed, although he shared other geographical ideas with Adam and his contemporaries.

Adam's thinking was perfectly in line with medieval geographical theories, a good many of which had been inherited from Antiquity and none of which allowed for the American continent and the Pacific Ocean. Because eastern Asia was thought linked with eastern Africa, making the Indian Ocean an enclosed body of water, people believed that the Atlantic was all that lay between the eastern and western coasts of a massive, tri-continental land mass. Medieval cosmographers made a generous allowance for islands off either coast, however, and often gave island status to poorly known places, therefore Adam assigned Asian island status to Greenland and Iceland as well as to Vínland which the Norse had reportedly found beyond Greenland. A somewhat similar idea appeared almost two centuries later in the *Historia Norvegiæ*, whose author explained that Greenland reached all the way [i.e. along the East

Asian coast] towards the 'African Islands' – islands assumed to be reaching northwards from a conjoined East Africa and East Asia.[2]

Adam's geographical ideas can be understood only if one is aware that the medieval circular mappaemundi were graphic devices for showing the spherical world on a flat surface. It is therefore a mistake to assume that Adam and his contemporaries thought in terms of a world laid out on a disc – a notion that became fashionable in the nineteenth century. The idea still endures in some circles, but today's map scholars know that the lesson about the earth's sphericity was learned in Antiquity and never forgotten.[3] A medieval European mentally crossing the Atlantic westwards would have expected land on the opposite side sooner or later and regarded that distant shore as Eurasia's eastern extremity. As even the earliest literary works in Iceland and Norway suggest, well-informed people in the Far North, including Eirik the Red and his men, would have shared this world view. The Norse of a thousand years ago moved boldly ever farther into the Atlantic, confident that they did not risk 'falling off' an imaginary edge when they used Iceland as a stepping stone to Greenland and North America.

EIRIK THE RED GOES WEST

Eirik the Red and his father Thorvald left their native Norway for Iceland some time in the second half of the tenth century because they had killed a man and emigration seemed expedient. On their arrival in Iceland, they found all the good land spoken for, but when Eirik married Thjodhild Jörundsdaughter, the tough-minded daughter of a well-to-do Icelandic farmer, he obtained some land on his father-in-law's property in the western part of the island. A longhouse believed to have been the home Eirik built for himself and his family was recently excavated – its modest proportions make it easy to understand why he seized the opportunity to do better.

Before that happened, however, Eirik's life took a decided downturn. In Iceland, too, his career was marred by violence. According to the 'Saga of the Greenlanders', he killed two men (the 'Saga of Eirik the Red' notes that this happened after quarrels that began when one of those men killed a slave belonging to Eirik), and he was banished from his home in Haukadale. He then settled on an island in the Breidafjord and, while there, he lent his bench boards to a man who refused to return them when asked.[4] Not surprisingly, quarrels and fights ensued, and he was outlawed for three years for murder, probably around AD 983.[5] His sentence meant that anyone in Iceland was free to kill him on sight for as long as his outlawry lasted, therefore he had good reason to dedicate the period of his banishment to exploring Greenland.

Considering the scrapes Eirik got into, it is probably safe to assume that his temper matched his hair colour, but more important to judging his achievement were his solid family background and his experience as a mariner, in addition to personal attributes that made him an able planner and administrator and a forceful executive. Although those positive qualities are fully evident in the sagas, which assume both his accomplishments and other people's willingness to follow his lead, those attributes are almost universally ignored in the history books. They tend to give full play to his brawn instead and leave the impression that he must have been a rough and untutored fellow. Rough, perhaps – he had to be – but he was a dynamic, well-connected leader who would have been fully aware of the general knowledge of his own time and place.

Eirik would also have had a good idea of where he was headed and of what to expect when he decided to explore to the west of Iceland, because his two kinsmen Gunnbjörn Ulfsson and Snæbjörn Holmsteinsson had preceded him on voyages in that direction.[6] Like Eirik himself, Gunnbjörn Ulfsson was a fifth-generation descendant of the Norwegian chieftain Öxna-Thorir and thus a nephew of the Viking Nadd-Odd, who had reportedly blown off course to Iceland in the days before its colonisation.[7] In keeping with family tradition, Gunnbjörn was also storm-driven, in his case past Iceland, where he saw some skerries west in the sea and deduced that there must be land beyond them. Known to this day as the 'Gunnbjarnarskerries', their location has long been vaguely defined as somewhere near the Ammassalik region in southeastern Greenland, but the Canadian scientist Waldemar Lehn has demonstrated persuasively that Gunnbjörn had almost certainly spotted a manifestation of what the Norse called hillingar – a mirage of the Greenland coast projected towards Iceland and 'arising specifically from optical ducting under a sharp temperature inversion'.[8] The phenomenon is certainly not uncommon in those northern waters. (No less a person than the explorer Robert Peary reported from his 1906 Arctic journey that he had spotted a vast 'Crocker Land' at the edge of the Arctic Ocean, which the 1913 Crocker Land Expedition subsequently discovered to be an immense 'Fata Morgana' – an illusion just like King Arthur's fairy sister Morgan le Fay.) Being an experienced northern sailor, Gunnbjörn would no doubt have seen the mirages as harbingers of a real coast somewhere farther on. Eirik's mind evidently worked along similar lines, because he continued west, without worrying about missing the 'skerries', until he reached the huge mass of the world's biggest island.

NORSE NAVIGATION

Eirik had kept a steady course all the way from Snæfellsness (Snow Mountain Peninsula) in westernmost Iceland. The large glacier for which the peninsula is named was a trusted navigational marker among Norse seamen, and Eirik most likely knew that the peninsula also represented a good latitude for approaching Greenland. Norse mariners were experts at latitude sailing and relied on a wealth of accumulated knowledge about coasts and currents and the migration patterns of birds, fish and sea mammals. Knowledgeable about celestial features, they navigated by the North Star when the sky was dark enough to provide contrast, while during the summer months, when the pale sky in the Far North could make it difficult to discern even the North Star, they observed the sun's passage across the firmament. As others before them had done, they also told time as well as compass directions from the sun's position in the sky at familiar latitudes.

The art of telling time by the sun's position is closely related to the practice of dividing the horizon into compass points, and this linked knowledge is the basis for making either a sun dial for telling time or a simple bearing dial for navigation. Either device records on a disc the shadow cast by a perpendicular stick (gnomon) during the sun's gradual passage across the sky at the general latitude and season of the dial's intended use. The principle was already understood when Facundus Novius built his horologium in Rome between 13 and 9 BC, and it would be surprising indeed if Vikings and Norse traders had failed to notice the use of sun dials on their travels to Mediterranean countries as well as to England, where a sun dial is known to have been in use at Canterbury around the year 1000. It would be equally surprising if mariners from the Far North had failed to employ the gnomon's shadow-curve to locate or stay a latitudinal course at sea.

The English scholar Peter G. Foote was the first to suggest that the Old Norse word sólarsteinn (sun stone) applied to a navigational device using the sun's refraction in a piece of crystalline Iceland spar.[9] It was an ingenious idea, but the literary as well as the practical evidence points elsewhere. For one thing, Icelandic documents used the word sólarsteinn about both time-telling and navigational devices until the mid-fifteenth century, when mechanical clocks and magnetic compasses were coming into use in the north, and church inventories in the Hólar See and at Hrafnagil use 'sólarsteirn' (sic) about a cased sunstone for telling time while employing 'kluckur' to distinguish church bells from sun clocks.[10] Moreover, an incised gnomonic bearing dial, made of either wood or stone, would have been so easy to use and so cheap to produce that a medieval northern mariner would have had little incentive to invest in a magnetic compass even when these were in use farther south. Tellingly, the Venetian monk Fra Mauro wrote on his ca. 1450 world map that sailors in the Baltic navigate 'without chart or compass but only with lead and line', and Olaus Magnus, the last Catholic Archbishop of Sweden, described fishermen in the north of Norway, early in the sixteenth century, who relied on a homing device consisting of a simple sun compass, or bearing dial.[11]

When the Danish archaeologist C. L. Vebæk excavated an Eastern Settlement farm ruin at Uunartoq in 1948, he found the remaining half of a bearing dial, or a demonstration model for making one, in a cultural layer dating back to the Norse settlement period. Once a full-circle prototype had been made on the basis of the old half-dial, seasoned modern yachtsmen – including the English mariner Sir Robin Knox-Johnston – tested the device successfully during ocean navigation. More recently, a small dial suggesting similar navigational use turned up at Qorlortoq in the Eastern Settlement, and that discovery provides an additional reason to suppose that Eirik the Red and his companions used a simple sun compass. It would have helped them to find their way to the 'Gunnbjarnarskerries' and beyond and to return home, as well as to enable themselves and others to retrace their steps to Greenland.[12]

Locating Greenland was just one difficulty among several which those Norse pioneers were likely to encounter, however. Accessing the country was another. Among the obstacles confronting them was the formidable belt of drift ice that to this day intimidates travellers approaching Greenland's east coast, and Eirik wisely decided not to push his way inside the belt. It is in any event unlikely that he would have been tempted to go ashore on that dismal eastern shore where, some four years earlier, his wife's relative Snæbjörn galti (hog) Holmsteinsson had been killed by disgruntled shipmates. Snæbjörn's grim tale in fact became the first in a series of Norse stories illustrating the forbidding nature of the Greenland east coast, where shipwrecked sailors were likely to freeze or starve to death before anyone could come to their aid. The Icelander Thorgils Thordsson survived such a shipwreck, however, according to a harrowing (and somewhat suspect) tale told in the *Flóamannasaga*. Having left home for Greenland shortly before AD 1000, Thorgils was caught up in a storm and eventually found himself stranded with his shipmates on Greenland's east coast. Four dreadful winters later, the survivors supposedly managed to cobble together a skin boat and sail to the west coast of Greenland, where Eirik the Red would now have been living.[13]

On his own first voyage out to Greenland, Eirik made it safely past Cape Farewell and began to investigate the deep fjords reaching into the southwest coast between latitudes 60°N and approximately 61° 30'N, in the area soon to become known as the Eastern Settlement. In this region, located just far enough south of Iceland to enjoy some additional hours of winter daylight without losing the 'white' summer nights that northerners cherish, Eirik claimed land on the western side of what became the Eiriksfjord (now: Tunulliarfik). Modern archaeological evidence confirms the saga information that, after overwintering, Eirik explored northwards (Fig. 6) to the present Nuuk region and penetrated the inner fjord districts that were to become the Western Settlement. At the sheltered head of the long Ameralik fjord, which the Norse dubbed Lysufjörðr (Cod Liver Oil Fjord), Eirik made another land claim for himself and his family, most likely at Sandness, the best and most strategic farm site in the area. Not long afterward, Sandness also played a key part in the first Norse ventures

Fig. 6   This is the landscape Eirik the Red saw when he sailed north along Greenland's west coast

to North America, which were tightly controlled by Eirik the Red and his circle.

In both of the Greenland regions Eirik investigated over a thousand years ago, the heads of the fjords still feature lush, green areas contrasting starkly with the glaciers and massive granite ridges inland as well as with the scoured granite fronting the outer coasts. The seas which Eirik and his companions saw teemed with fish, seals and whales; inland lakes were also full of fish; the hinterland in both regions featured reindeer and smaller game; and a variety of birds promised eggs, meat, feathers and down. The natural resources of the two potential settlement areas nevertheless differed in some respects. Those differences clearly also factored into Eirik's early plans for his colony.

The Western Settlement, located some four hundred miles north of the Eastern Settlement, endured harsher winters and had less pasture land than the main colony farther south, but it was considerably better positioned for an early start to the High Arctic hunts that would soon be an essential part of the Norse Greenlanders' resource exploitation. On those Arctic forays, the Norse settlers were also to experience their earliest encounters with Arctic natives, first with people of the Dorset culture and subsequently with Thule Eskimos, the ancestors of the modern Inuit. Farther south, where the Norse settled, neither Eirik's reconnaissance party nor the early colonists encountered any natives at all. They found only scattered reminders of an earlier human occupation, as Ari noted in his brief account. In Iceland, where the Norse had apparently been preceded in the island by only a few Irish monks, settlement had been equally uncomplicated by hostile encounters.[14]

A DARING REAL ESTATE VENTURE

When Eirik's three years of banishment were up and he returned to Iceland, he was in every way convinced that the new land he had explored should be settled. There would be no conflict with natives, and the country's natural conditions were well suited to Norse pastoral farming with its combination of animal husbandry, fishing and the hunting of land and marine mammals. However, he also knew that a bountiful larder for people was not enough, although the Norse had not been discouraged from settling Iceland despite the country's name assigned by the disgruntled Norwegian explorer Flóki Vilgerdsson after a hard winter there. Eirik took no chances. His fellow Norse would need sufficient fodder for the cattle, sheep and goats they relied on for leather and wool, milk and milk products and the occasional meat dish, and for their sturdy little horses, which were needed for their muscle and also eaten. To entice fellow Icelanders to join him in his new land, he named it Greenland, 'because people would be much more tempted to go there if it had an attractive name'.[15] Eirik's instincts served him well.

The saga literature gives the names of several of the first land claimants in the Eastern Settlement, but it does not name those who led their people farther north, nor do the written sources disclose who, besides Eirik, had taken part in exploring Greenland prior to its colonisation. We are told only that some of Eirik's friends had seen him safely on his way out to the open sea, presumably to protect him from being killed as an outlaw. There are nevertheless strong clues to the names of three friends who must have accompanied him all the way on that first voyage and secured prime farm sites for themselves, just as Eirik did. Their identity is suggested by the outstanding advantages of the farms' sites with which all four men came to be associated.

Sagas as well as archaeological reports reveal that, besides Eirik the Red's chieftain seat Brattahlid (Steep Hill), the properties named Gardar, Hvalsey and Herjolfsness were the Eastern Settlement's most significant farms and trading sites throughout the Norse Greenland colony's existence. Recently, approaching each of these farm sites from the sea, starting at Herjolfsness and going north, I realised how usefully they are spaced from each other and how perfectly each location combines good land with fine harbours and easy access by water.[16] I believe that on Eirik's first voyage, he had enjoyed the company not only of Einar, the settler at Gardar (to whose son he later gave his daughter Freydis in marriage), but of his cousin Thorkell-the-Far-Travelled who settled at Hvalsey, and of Herjolf Bárdsson, the settler at Herjolfsness.

The southernmost harbour, Herjolfsness (Fig. 14), would have been the first Norse haven a medieval voyager reached after rounding Cape Farewell or coming through Prince Christian Sound. Its entrance is easily recognisable from the outer shore, where rocky arms open wide to welcome weary travellers to the sheltered waters and sandy shore inside. Combined with the story of Herjolf's son Bjarni (see below), told in the 'Saga of the Greenlanders', that distinctive portal to the splendid harbour beyond is evidence that the first owner of Herjolfsness had been along on Eirik's initial expedition to Greenland, and that the same is therefore likely to apply to the settlers at Gardar and Hvalsey.

When Eirik and his companions returned to Iceland to persuade others to join them in that new land in the west, and before they set out for Greenland a second and final time, they would have been able to leave directions behind in Iceland for anyone who wanted to go west after them. Wanting to go west was, according to the 'Saga of the Greenlanders,' exactly the situation in which Herjolf Bárdsson's merchant son Bjarni found himself when he returned from Norway to Iceland the summer after Eirik and his followers had colonised Greenland.

Bjarni expected to spend the winter with his father as was his habit, but that was not to be, because Herjolf had emigrated with Eirik. Wasting no time, Bjarni set out for Greenland, but stiff northerly winds drove his ship far off course to the southwest, where fog prevented him from judging his whereabouts until the sun reappeared and he was able to get his bearings. He told his crew that the forested coast they saw could not be Greenland, so he sailed north along the Canadian coast until he reached a stretch of glaciers and barren rocks. That landscape did not sound much like what he had been told about Greenland, either, but after four more days of sailing, now clearly bearing eastwards, his ship was within sight of a land that matched more closely the description he had of his destination, and at dusk that day he arrived at Herjolfsness, his father's new farm.[17] Herjolf was no doubt pleased to see his son, but he probably was not surprised that Bjarni had managed to find him.

Bjarni will feature again later in the context of Norse sailings to America. He was 'a man of great promise,' according to the 'Saga of the Greenlanders', and his father Herjolf was described as 'a man of considerable stature' – a standing from which Bjarni presumably benefited when he went to Norway some years after reaching Greenland and was received by Earl Eirik Hákonsson, who at that time ruled Norway.[18] In the present context, however, the saga indications that Bjarni knew both the latitude and the visual landmarks to aim for when he first set sail for Greenland take precedence over his pedigree, because his knowledge could only have come from information Herjolf himself had provided to people back in Iceland before he emigrated to Greenland for good. Moreover, the saga account demonstrates that when Bjarni found himself in an unfamiliar setting after drifting off beyond Greenland, he used the sun to get his proper bearings, for which he would have needed only the simple sun compass described above.

DIVIDING UP A NEW LAND

In the Eastern Settlement, Herjolf's fellow emigrants Ketil and Hrafn gave their names to Ketilsfjord and Hrafnsfjord respectively, while a man named Sölvi staked a claim to Sölvadale and Thorbjörn Glora took land in

Siglufjord. Helgi Thorbrandsson liked what he saw in Alptafjord, and Eirik's good friend Einar had good reason to be content with his choice in Einarsfjord, the next large fjord southeast of Eiriksfjord. There, on the largest plain in the entire Eastern Settlement, Einar laid out his farm, Gardar, which less than a century and a half later was also to become the seat of the Greenland bishop. An arm of the Einarsfjord took its name from the settler Hafgrim, who did very well for himself by also claiming the fertile inland region the Norse called Vatnahverfi because of its many lakes. The chieftain Arnlaug chose Arnlaugsfjord for his people.

Eirik the Red's cousin Thorkell farserkr (the Far-Travelled) had already helped himself to land between Eiriksfjord and Einarsfjord and to all the territory around the Hvalsey fjord. His farm and the surrounding region were named for the island Hvalsey (Whale Island), on which Thorkell pastured some of his animals. When Eirik came to call one day while there was no boat available on Hvalsey farm, Thorkell reportedly swam the mile or so over to the big island, killed an old neutered ram and swam home with the animal slung over his back. If this story has a kernel of truth, Thorkell may have braved the ice cold water to swim out to an island nearer the shore, which would have been larger then than after a millennium of rising water levels. In passing along the tale, the *Landnámabók* laconically noted that Thorkell was 'unusually strong', but the written sources are silent about how Eirik liked the meal laid on by his eccentric host. After Thorkell died, he was buried in his own home field and was said to haunt his descendants,[19] but his ghost can't have done much harm, because his farm retained its importance among the Norse Greenlanders. To this day, it is widely known for the iconic fourteenth-century church whose roofless ruin still dominates its verdant surroundings and embellishes many a modern tourist brochure.

EIRIK THE RED SETTLES IN

Eirik was the leading chieftain for the Western as well as the Eastern Settlement, and both settlements were soon benefiting from his meticulous provision for the domestic and export aspects of their economy. The site he chose for his own new homestead is a good example of his foresight and gift for planning. Brattahlid is the northernmost of the four major Norse Greenland farms and thus the nearest to the Western Settlement, and it had many other advantages. Brattahlid was close enough to the opposite shore in the inner Eiriksfjord to benefit from the deep-water harbour where ships still dock today, while the sloping bank of Eirik's own shore would have made it easy to pull up shallow-draught Norse vessels in front of a large field suitable for trade and other public gatherings. His family's dwelling was up on the hillside and fronted the fjord (Fig. 7), so anyone stepping outside could see almost to the head of the fjord as well as a long way down towards its opening, which meant that no ship could approach unobserved. Abundant food resources from land and sea were close at hand; driftwood still collects at the river-mouth eddy a little farther into the fjord; and Eirik's old home fields still get generous doses of sun in the summer months.

Eirik had brought along his wife Thjodhild and their sons Leif, Thorvald and Thorstein, whose ages at the time of settlement are unknown. A supposedly irascible girl child, Freydis Eiriksdaughter, is also accounted for in the saga literature, but it has often been suggested that she was born to a woman other than Thjodhild.[20] This would not have been unusual, especially considering that Eirik kept slaves in Iceland. Eirik evidently acknowledged Freydis as his daughter, however, and she would in any case have been a useful addition to a new land where women were badly needed for procreation as well as for outdoor and indoor labour. She eventually married a man named Thorvard, who was 'rather feeble', but whom she married for his wealth, according to the 'Saga of the Greenlanders'. She lived with him at Gardar.[21]

Freydis Eiriksdaughter's husband was presumably the son of her father's settler friend Einar, so even if Thorvard had the makings of a hen-pecked husband and compared unfavourably with his wife's three half-brothers, his wealth and social position would have made him a suitable son-in-law for the chieftain at Brattahlid. It is unlikely that Freydis herself had been consulted about her marriage, for in any medieval Norse society a free woman's male relatives were in charge of marrying her off, and they were expected to do it as advantageously to the whole family as possible.[22] Quite apart from the shortage of suitable women of marrying age in such a young community, Eirik's status as the new colony's undisputed leader put him in an excellent position to bargain over his daughter.

It would have been to the advantage of both the Gardar and Brattahlid families to strengthen their already close ties with a marriage bargain. The Greenland land-takers had arrived in large family groups with servants and slaves, determined to create a viable society in which kinship would remain a vital social and economic force, also when other forms of social organisation had been established. Family ties were of central significance to all the Norse societies on the North Atlantic rim, and the more power and wealth an extended family commanded, the more of the same sort its members were likely to see in the future.

ESTABLISHING HOMES IN THE WILDERNESS

Regardless of social and economic status, life would have been very hard for everyone in the beginning, when approximately five hundred souls are thought to have been readying themselves for their first winter in a new land.[23] Eirik had spent three winters in Greenland during his initial exploration of the country, therefore he knew that he and his fellow pioneers must waste no time in creating shelter for themselves and their animals before the onset of short days and winter's chill. The others must have shared his sense of urgency, for archaeologists have found evidence that at least some of the early settlers cleared land by burning off the ubiquitous Greenland scrub.[24] It wasted fuel, but it saved valuable time and labour for the backbreaking tasks of gathering winter fodder and constructing shelter. Those impenetrable thickets grow to the height of a man, and personal experience with them tempers my criticism of this form of land clearing. Moreover, the Norse Greenlanders were never as desperately short of fuel as some writers have claimed that they were. Quite large birch trunks dating from the Norse period have been found in sheltered regions in the Eastern Settlement; recent studies of Norse Greenland farms suggest that the settlers had brought with them the habit of using turf for fuel; and archaeologists have been struck both by the amount of wood the Greenland Norse used in their houses and by the fact that they wasted wood chips from activities such as shipbuilding and house construction.[25]

The immigrants had brought a style of architecture with them from Iceland that was well suited to an environment abounding in rocks and turf, but with no native large timber to supplement scattered accumulations of driftwood. The Greenland settlers and their descendants used rocks for their house foundations and sometimes in the walls, which otherwise depended on turf 'bricks' cut from the ground and left to dry before being stacked into walls five or six feet thick. Inside, a series of upright poles shored up a sloping roof made of turf and resting on a foundation of wooden beams and interwoven branches. There were no windows and chimneys, only a smoke-hole in the roof with an adjustable stone cover as protection against rain and snow.

The front door would have been made of wood and, when available, wood was also used in wall panels, inside doors, loom frames, bed frames and high seat posts, or to cover banked-up soil for the pallets and benches people used for both sleeping and sitting. Festive occasions served as an excuse to decorate the inside walls with woven and embroidered hangings for those who could afford them, while fires and oil lamps added everyday indoor comforts just as back in Iceland. Open fireplaces were usually, but not invariably, in the centre of the floor, providing welcome heat and light as well as a place to prepare food. The floors themselves most often consisted of packed-down soil and gravel, on which there might be a cover of twigs and heather for added warmth during the height of winter at a latitude where darkness falls a little after three in the afternoon and ends around nine next morning. Indoor storage areas housed foodstuffs that must be easily available, such as water, milk, milk products and pickled foods, all of which were kept in barrels. In time, many farms added a separate storage building raised well off the ground in order to protect fish and meat from the elements as well as from wild animals, and sometimes made of rocks so large that one marvels at the strength of the people who handled them.

As soon as practicable, Norse Greenland farmers would also have wanted a bath house as well as barns for winter fodder and separate shelter for some of the livestock, but it is unlikely that these amenities were built during the first rush. Fortunately, Norse sheep were hardy creatures and could survive outside in their woolly coats provided they found enough to eat, but they might die in droves in the cold season if they lay down for the night on ground where snow had melted during the day, because the snow was likely to freeze to their wool at night and make it impossible for them to get up later. Nowadays, after a large number of Greenland sheep died from being frozen stuck in the 1960s, the animals enjoy winter shelter in large barns. In summer, sheep still graze among the ruins of Eirik's former chieftain's seat, which is now a part of the small, modern sheep farming village of Qassiarsuk.

BRATTAHLID THEN AND NOW

There have been several excavations at Brattahlid after it was established that the remains there, and not the mammoth ruins down at Gardar, belonged to Eirik the Red's farm (Fig. 7). Fresh from his pioneering work at Herjolfsness, the Danish archaeologist Poul Nørlund led the first professional excavations at Gardar in 1928 and tackled Brattahlid in 1932. Among his discoveries on Eirik's old farm were the remains of a church built around 1300, which gave additional evidence of the farm's wealth

Fig. 7   Ruins at Eirik the Red's farm Brattahlid ('Steep Hill') in southwest Greenland. The reconstructed 'Thjodhild's church' with its little bell tower visible in the left background

and enduring importance. Later excavations beneath that structure have revealed an early dwelling about thirteen metres long and eight metres wide, which may have been the longhouse Eirik built during the early settlement period.[26] In the past couple of years, further excavations have used a quite different approach from the earlier ones, so additional information about the site's Norse history will very likely be presented in the future.

In 1961, a team of archaeologists found the remains of a small church on a knoll just south of Eirik's old farm houses. Datable to about AD 1000, the ruin was dubbed 'Thjodhild's church' because its location fit the statement in the 'Saga of Eirik the Red' that Thjodhild had caused a church to be built near the farm, but not near enough to offend Eirik's heathen sensibilities. (On that delicate issue between the spouses, the 'Saga of Eirik the Red' reports that Eirik was greatly annoyed because Thjodhild refused to live with him after she was converted.) The ruins indicated that the tiny church building had consisted of three thick turf walls enclosing a small wooden structure, with an all-wood west wall where the door had been, and with floor slabs made of the local red sandstone with white dots. The structure had been surrounded by a small, circular graveyard, evidently used from the end of the tenth century until the end of the twelfth. It contained the remains of 144 persons, among them fifteen small children and a male with a knife still stuck in his ribs. A mass grave just a bit south of the church held the jumbled bones of fourteen males of various ages, their skulls facing west as in the other burials. During a careful examination of these bones, the Danish forensic anthropologist Niels Lynnerup found marks suggesting that these fourteen people had died in battle, although there was no telling where or why the battle had taken place.[27]

The horseshoe-shaped outline of the church is still visible today, and the view east across the iceberg-studded fjord is essentially the one which the first tiny congregation would have enjoyed a thousand years ago. Until recently, there was also an unobstructed view of how the church and the other buildings on Eirik's farm would have fitted into the landscape, but that situation is in the process of changing as a consequence of the site's importance to tourism (Fig. 8). On my first visit to Brattahlid, in 1987, a discreet memorial on a rock face was already in place next to the farm's

Fig. 8   This modern plaque marks arrival at Brattahlid, the site which Eirik the Red chose for his chieftain's seat around AD 985

core, but now a large and prominent statue of Leif Eiriksson also gazes down on anyone walking up the lush hillside towards the farm. The statue was a gift to Greenland from a group of people in Seattle on the occasion of the Viking Millennium celebrations in 2000. Two Brattahlid building projects were also undertaken for that event, both structures fortunately placed so that they do not cover any of the known medieval ruins. On the farm site proper, a reconstruction of Thjodhild's church, with a bell tower, was added near the remains of the original site, while a reconstructed early longhouse stands somewhat closer to the farm's centre.

On the outside, the plain little church is probably similar to the original building, but its beautiful interior represents current handicrafts, not anything that Thjodhild and her co-religionists would have experienced. The little sanctuary nevertheless exudes peace and tranquillity of a sort one may hope that the Norse worshippers a thousand years ago also felt, giving them a respite from violence, worries and hard work. The essentially generic longhouse reconstruction gives a sufficiently convincing impression of medieval Norse domestic arrangements that a visitor requires only a little imagination to conjure up the smells of sweaty bodies and wet wool, of oil lamps burning blubber and cod liver oil, of boiled seal and fish, or of meat being smoked above a turf fire. Pungent, homey odours that would have brought a coveted feeling of safety and shelter to medieval occupants.

Brattahlid was eventually divided up into at least three separate farms,[28] but there is no telling whether this happened through inheritance or sale, because there is no record of Eirik's descendants past his own four children and Leif's son Thorkell, who is briefly mentioned in the 'Saga of the sworn brothers'. Archaeologists are far from done with either Brattahlid or other known Norse ruin sites in the Eastern Settlement, however, nor with investigating the Western Settlement, where the most exciting and extensive recent Greenland Norse excavation involved the so-called Farm Beneath the Sand. The results are still being analysed, but it is already clear that the farm's archaeological layer cake began with a settlement period house, presumably built by one of Eirik the Red's unnamed contemporaries.[29]

Leif inherited both Brattahlid and Eirik's position as the most powerful chieftain in both settlements, but even before his father died, he had become famous for his own accomplishments. In ventures that justify the expression 'heredity tells', he gained a lasting reputation as an explorer of substantial courage and administrative ability.

3

FORGING A NEW HOMELAND

The Greenland settlers had no time to lose before adjusting to the immense scale of their new country and to the climate conditions arising from their island's long reach towards the High Arctic. Instead of experiencing the comparatively mild maritime climate familiar to coastal farmers in Iceland and western Norway, the Norse Greenlanders found their outer coasts bracing, while the heads of their deeply indented fjords reached so far inland that the climate there was continental, with relatively warm summers for which people paid with harsh winters. The sheltered areas where the Norse built their farms are still as green and bright with flowers in summer as they were a thousand years ago, when Eirik gave Greenland the name he thought it deserved, and in late September the hillsides are aflame with dwarf birch, but the island was and is even more notable for the perpetual winter of its mountainous interior, where innumerable peaks (nunataks) cut through the Greenland Ice Cap and where the weather gods live.

Studies of Greenland's climate history over the past couple of millennia show that there were large variations during the whole period of Norse tenure, and that both 'cold' and 'warm' climate periods may have interludes of warm or cold years. To be sure, even fairly small temperature swings may have quite an impact in northern latitudes, but the colonists must have been able to accommodate themselves to these climate fluctuations to survive for half a millennium. Indeed, the modern Icelandic historian Gísli Gunnarsson warns against a simplistic approach to the environmental and economic consequences of erratic weather.[1]

The Norse settlers would soon have become familiar with the foehn winds produced when warm air hits Greenland's central ridge and moves down its leeward side with such speed that temperatures may quickly rise more than twenty centigrades as warm air displaces cold air near the surface. Although the Norse had no instruments with which to record the process, they would certainly have been aware of its effects. Their choices of farmsteads indicate that they had also tacitly acknowledged another phenomenon which scientists have measured later, namely that every hundred metre's drop in altitude in Greenland raises the air temperature by one centigrade. If the temperature over the Ice Cap at 2500 metres is minus fifteen centigrades, it will measure a balmy plus ten centigrades when that air hits sea level. Among people familiar with conditions in Iceland and Norway, it would not have required rocket science to sort out the best farm locations.[2] Eirik the Red and his fellow settlers knew how to evaluate their chosen land.

A NEW SOCIETY TAKES SHAPE

The 'Saga of the Foster Brothers' observes that in the early eleventh century, the free farmers' Annual Assembly (similar to the Icelandic Althing) was no longer held at Brattahlid but somewhat farther south, at the large farm of Gardar in Einarsfjord. That does not mean that Brattahlid had lost its status, however, only that an increased number of inhabitants very likely necessitated a larger gathering place for the centrepiece of their society's legal and judiciary concerns. A report by the priest Ívar Bárdsson, the Bergen bishop's temporary representative at Gardar in the mid-fourteenth century, noted that the Lawman always lived at Brattahlid, but one cannot be certain what that title is supposed to mean, because by Ívar's time, the old office of the Law Speaker had been replaced by a royally appointed Lawman in both Norway and Iceland.[3]

The most important person at the Annual Assembly was the Law Speaker, charged with memorising the community's laws and reciting them as needed. His was essentially an elective office, but one that naturally benefited from hereditary wealth and power. The Assembly was also vital to maintaining other social and cultural conventions the colonists had brought with them from Iceland and western Norway, where hard-scrabble landscapes had likewise promoted communities of scattered, separate farms instead of villages and towns. Around midsummer each year, independent farmers came from all over to the Annual Assembly to enact laws, to solve legal disputes and to trade. Besides the barter of surplus goods for luxuries as well as for necessities, trade at the Assembly likely involved many a marriage bargain and agreements concerning fosterage of children. Whenever Icelandic sagas mention so-and-so's foster father or foster mother, they refer to the custom of involving other adults besides the parents in supervising and teaching a child, either in the child's own family or in the foster parent's home. The system promoted extended loyalties and allowed for the teaching of skills that ranged from runes and healing to marksmanship and decorative arts.

PUTTING FOOD ON THE TABLE

With their social tools in place and with appropriate adjustments to Greenlandic resources, the colonists could settle down to a life of eking out pastoral farming with fishing and hunting, as had been the practice for centuries in all but the most fertile districts of Norway. Their chief agricultural efforts went into cultivating their haying fields for maximum yield, and into gathering hay, dried leaves and other animal fodder for the winter. While there is no evidence that they were able to raise any kind of grain to maturity, deeper soil pockets in sheltered areas would have served crops intended for human consumption. Not only linseeds, but seeds of common weeds like knot grass and chickweed have turned up in Norse Greenland samples of human faeces. Large stands of angelica found near farm ruins suggest that this umbrelliform herb was nurtured for its taste and general usefulness, and farmers also seem to have encouraged native stands of lyme grass. Iceland moss (alias Irish moss) was used for both nutritional and medical purposes, and there was no shortage of the reddish seaweed dulse, which the Norse dried in barrels in order to obtain a treat that tastes salty-sweet and smells like the inside of an old fish barrel.[4]

On the whole, the Norse Greenlanders' diet and cuisine probably would not suit today's western tastes, but it was varied and wholesome and kept people in good health to the colony's very end. The colonists ate roots, berries and herbs of many kinds, seaweeds and shellfish, dairy products, and meat from both terrestrial and marine mammals. Last, but certainly not least, people and animals alike would have depended on fish.[5] A recent Danish study of twenty-seven human bone samples, representing Norse Greenlanders throughout the better part of their colonial tenure, showed that there had been an increasing reliance on marine foods from early on.[6] This is surely what one would expect of people who commonly ate seal and other marine mammals and who had plenty of fish in their lakes, fjords and ocean. That included three kinds of cod, of which the most desirable, then as now, was the Atlantic cod, Gadus morhua.

The writer Mark Kurlansky has observed that the range of medieval Norse exploration and colonisation in the North Atlantic exactly equals the range of the Atlantic cod.[7] This is again what one would expect, because the medieval Norse depended on their ability to catch and preserve fish to survive extensive ocean voyages and the rigours of long northern winters. It merely requires a cold, bright and windy climate, coupled with experience and skilled hands, to turn lean-fleshed cod into stockfish, an exceptionally durable and easily stored dried food. The right climate conditions for curing the fish would have been just as available to the Norse in Greenland as to their Icelandic neighbours and the people of Northern Norway, and the settlers would have brought the necessary skills with them. Stockfish requires no salt, an expensive commodity in medieval Europe, which in turn means that no extra investment was needed. The resulting high-protein product was ideal for consumption during long voyages when drinking water would be at a premium and cooking a high-risk endeavour. No cooking is necessary to make stockfish digestible – both at sea and ashore the wind-dried fish would have been torn or pounded into thin strips and spread with butter or blubber for added calories.[8]

The logical place for large-scale fishing and fish-drying would have been away from the main Norse settlements, in the region formerly called the Middle Settlement but now considered the northernmost extension of the Eastern Settlement. (The area's badly eroded ruins have so far been poorly explored by archaeologists, but one hopes this may someday change.) The richest Greenland cod fishing banks could be found right outside the coasts of both Norse settlements, where the cod would be particularly plentiful from May through July, but where it might also arrive as early as March.[9] The only fly in the Norse ointment would have been the drift ice still blocking the entrances to the Eastern Settlement fjords during the months of May and June, because that would have prevented people in the inner fjords from reaching the cod fishing banks on the outer coast early enough in the season to get a good start on drying the fish during optimal conditions. A fishing settlement on the outer coast would have made good sense.

Medieval Norse cod fishing was always done with hook and line, not with a net. The hooks were large and, whether of metal or bone, painstakingly fashioned by hand. Thus they represented property too valuable to lose through carelessness, and a hook of any size left lying on the ground would also have been a danger not only to animals, but to people who often went barefoot. Several years ago, the American palaeozoologist Thomas McGovern, a deservedly recognised expert on Norse middens, was so struck by the shortage in Norse Greenland middens of fish hooks and sinkers, as well as by a comparative lack of codfish crania and backbones, that he argued that the Norse had made strangely little use of the fish swimming right along their shores. This claim has since been disproved by sophisticated recent archaeological investigations in the Western Settlement, which revealed plenty of fish-bone fragments from a number of species, including from large cod. Although the heads of only capelin and arctic char were found, that was not surprising, given Norse traditions in fishing and curing cod, in which heads and spines were preferably removed before the cod were hung across wooden poles to dry. Fish entrails apart from the valuable livers were often used as fertiliser, while other fish scraps – dried and crushed heads and spines included – would have been food supplements for both people and animals.[10] A large codfish head is still considered a delicacy in both Iceland and Norway. My grandfather would travel sixty miles by train if my mother called to say she had got one for him, and he would meticulously take the head apart to enjoy the unique delight of each cavity. It would have been no different five hundred or a thousand years ago, except that in the Middle Ages a broken-apart cranium would be tossed on a midden, where it would disintegrate faster than if complete.

No reputable archaeologist has claimed that the Greenland Norse had a taboo against eating fish. Throughout history, in any part of the world, people have survived by using what their environment provided. If the Norse Greenlanders had decided on a 'taboo' against eating fish, their most widely available food, they would have perished so quickly that there would not have been five hundred years of history to argue about. Overall, modern research on the Norse Greenlanders' nutrition shows convincingly that the colonists enjoyed an exceptionally varied and wholesome diet and that they sometimes went to considerable trouble to add to it. For example, while recent studies of beluga territory have demonstrated that these blunt-nosed, white whales have never occurred along Greenland's southwest coast where the Norse lived, McGovern and his colleagues have identified beluga remains at Norse Greenland sites, which they see as evidence that the Norse had brought butchered beluga home from quite some distance away.[11]

THE ROLE OF DOMESTIC ANIMALS

Common sense has long prevailed in the matter of dairying among the Norse Greenlanders, who are known to have valued their cows, sheep and goats. Despite the lack of butter or cheese remains found in Norse Greenland ruin sites, well before archaeologists had discovered barrels with milk residue in Eastern Settlement ruins the processing of dairy products in Norse Greenland was taken for granted by scholars. Even the most desk-bound Nordic historians of the nineteenth and twentieth centuries (who, incidentally, ate fish several days a week) knew that butter, cheese and other milk products were valued in their own society and therefore assumed that the same held true for the Norse Greenlanders who had shared their culture.

The appeal of cheese and butter needs no explanation. Visitors to modern Iceland who have enjoyed skýr (a creamy product derived from milk treated with rennet) will probably understand why the medieval Norse also enjoyed it. Whey – a byproduct of soured milk – would perhaps not have much appeal today, but to the medieval Norse, this thin, acid, bluish liquid was an invaluable and nourishing staple, so rich in milk sugars that in modern Norway it is used to make sweet brown cheese. The Norse mixed whey with water to make a thirst-quenching drink and used it like vinegar to pickle and preserve food.

ADAPTING TO GREENLAND

Men and women usually had well-defined occupations in traditional medieval societies, and so it was in Norse Greenland. Dairying, cooking and food preservation would have been among the women's many indoor and outdoor responsibilities. From the very beginning of the Norse colonisation of Greenland, exploiting marine and terrestrial food resources of all kinds would have made for a harsh existence for women as well as for men, therefore it is no surprise that Niels Lynnerup's forensic studies of Greenland Norse skeletal material showed that people of both sexes had been well muscled from hard labour.

Lynnerup also found bones that had healed after fractures due to accidents or that gave evidence of violence. Many Norse Greenlanders had apparently suffered from arthritis as well as from other common ailments, such as persistent middle ear infections. Significantly, there were no signs of malnutrition and genetic deterioration, but in an earlier study, Lynnerup had nevertheless found indications of shorter stature over time.

Dental studies of Greenland Norse skulls have likewise suggested a slight decrease in the size and development of teeth. However, these changes are not necessarily signs of degeneration, in Lynnerup's opinion. Quite the contrary, they may demonstrate the Norse colonists' efficient adaptation to their Greenland environment. Lynnerup was therefore surprised at the lack of a parallel cultural adaptation suggested by Thomas McGovern. Other scholars have also observed the discrepancy between these forensic studies and maladaptation theories, including the fact that the dental studies found no significant differences in evidence of stress when comparing early and late-period samples.[12]

An oft-repeated claim that the Norse Greenlanders' society had suffered from maladaptation in several areas – the presumed lack of fish exploitation among them – has for many years found easy acceptance among a number of readers and authors. One influential scientist allowed that the Norse Greenland economy was 'characterised by skillful coordination of communal labour and seasonal abundance of terrestrial and marine resources', but he also believed that it operated on too tight a margin and was so inflexibly managed that '[t]he Norse extinction … may be seen as a failure of human managers to select effective responses to climatic stress'. Other defects, in his view, were that the Norse Greenlanders 'did not produce the sort of whaling, fishing and sealing villages that characterise modern Greenland' and that they had not copied Eskimo dress and hunting methods in order to survive.[13]

Recently, we have seen such views amplified.[14] 'Why didn't the Norse learn to cope with the Little Ice Age's cold weather by watching how the Inuit were meeting the challenges? … Unlike the Norse, the Inuit represented the climax of thousands of years of cultural developments by Arctic peoples learning to master Arctic conditions.' Supposedly, all of these trials could have been avoided if the Norse Greenlanders had set aside their 'European focus' and stubborn insistence on a subsistence pastoralism based on 'honoured cows' and 'despised goats', eked out by hunting wild animals for meat. It made matters even worse, we are told, that the cows did not like the dried seaweed collected for winter fodder, so that farm hands had to live in the muck in the barns and force-feed the animals in the winter.[15]

Because not one of these claims is backed by evidence, and because the present chapter is concerned with how the Norse Greenlanders lived, not with how they died, some comments are necessary here. On Norse farms in the Middle Ages, it was not unusual for farm hands to share buildings with the animals, but the notion that they had to live in the muck in the cow barns, force-feeding the cows to get them through the winter, runs counter not only to what is known about medieval Norse societies everywhere, but to the behaviour of hungry cows. During the German occupation of Norway, farmers had to feed their cows cellulose, cabbage stalks and anything else at hand, and while the milk tasted memorably bad, at least the animals ate what they were given and survived. Farmers normally do everything they can to salvage their livestock, and no sane farmer anywhere, at any time, 'despises' any of the animals on which he and his household depend for food, clothing and a possible surplus for trade. The Norse Greenlanders would have valued the robust sheep and goats that gave so much in return for so little care.

It gives some perspective on the Norse Greenlanders' daily existence if we remind ourselves that their lives in Greenland were in fact no more harsh than those of their contemporaries in large parts of Norway and, if we are realistic about how most Europeans lived in the Middle Ages, including in England. Farmers, fishermen, servants and slaves led unimaginably harsh lives. Even the most privileged landowners and townspeople faced illnesses for which there were few remedies, and they all suffered from winter's cold. Furs were especially valued as linings for clothes, including for night clothes, and were cleaned in the spring with chalk or other grease-absorbing substances.[16] That tells us much about the comfort levels people elsewhere expected indoors, as well as about their state of hygiene, and it suggests that we ought not to regard the Norse Greenlanders as pitifully backward.

COWS VERSUS SHEEP AND GOATS

The availability of good land for grazing and haying would have played a significant part whenever a Norse Greenland farmer weighed his options. If provided with shelter and winter fodder of a higher quality than that required by sheep or goats, cows produce more human food relative to grazing acreage than do sheep, but that extra care also demands much more human labour. The modern Icelandic historian Axel Kristínsson notes that Iceland's pastoralist farmers have always had to consider whether the labour invested in keeping cows could outweigh the disadvantages of a property smaller than the large area needed for sheep farming. So long as there is plenty of what Kristínsson calls 'search-and-destroy pasture', sheep and goats can manage with far more spartan conditions than cows are able to handle, thus freeing up time for the farmer who does not have to fertilise his haying fields or gather in the hay and quantities of other winter fodder.[17]

There was and is plenty of 'search-and-destroy' acreage in Greenland, and Norse livestock were not picky eaters. Sheep and goats in particular are voracious animals and will happily eat tree seedlings before they have a chance to grow large enough to produce the foliage which Norse farmers used to gather and dry for winter fodder, along with heather and seaweed collected for the same purpose. The salt found in seaweed attracts both bovines and caprines – it is mesmerising to watch Icelandic sheep devouring fresh seaweed down by the shore when they have only to walk a few steps up a sloping shore to reach green grass. Modern investigations of seaweed-eating sheep in the Orkney island of North Ronaldsey show that the animals there developed a unique gut flora, and radioisotope readings from the animals' bones and wool were equally distinctive.[18] One may safely assume that Norse Greenland sheep were equally adaptable.

CULTURAL DISTINCTIVENESS

The Norse Greenlanders encountered both people from the palaeo-Eskimo Dorset culture, who were already present in Northern Greenland when the Norse arrived, and the somewhat later-arriving Neo-Eskimo Thule people. Both of these Arctic peoples had concerns for their families and communities similar to those faced by the Norse, and they dealt with them by hunting methods, living arrangements and social customs developed during their long familiarity with the High Arctic, just as the medieval Norse all around the North Atlantic rim depended on their own ancestors' experience. Neither the Dorset and Thule people nor the Norse needed to copy each other's very different lifestyles, because both groups had the skills and customs they needed to hunt, fish and otherwise gather food, to raise their children and to function as communities and last, but not least, to keep warm.

There are no indications that sporadic contact between the Norse and either Dorset or Thule people led to meaningful cultural change on either side, and nothing that archaeologists have so far discovered about the Norse Greenlanders suggests that their existence was threatened just because they maintained their cultural distinction and lived in the manner to which they were accustomed. Remains of their houses, their tools, their bones and the food they ate show that to the very end of their colony, they had shelter and clothing that had stood the test of time and that were suited to their daily indoor and outdoor tasks. They hunted, fished, farmed and traded much as people did in Iceland and Norway, and they fit so well into their unique environment that they also survived hunting in the High Arctic.

Needlessly discarding fundamental aspects of one's own culture hardly qualifies as adaptation. The idea that the Norse Greenlanders should have 'adapted' by copying Eskimo hunting methods, clothing and social customs makes little sense overall, and it becomes grotesque if we try to imagine a Norse woman tending to her cooking dressed only in a natit (essentially a G-string worn indoors by adults in traditional Inuit societies), or going about her milking and dairying clad in heavy furs. While neither she nor her family would have been strangers to wearing fur, for the most part they would have kept warm and comfortable in garments made from the homespun wool cloth called vadmál – a product of female skill and ceaseless labour on which both Icelanders and Greenlanders relied for their domestic needs as well as for export. At the National Museum in Copenhagen, remarkably well-preserved medieval garments from Greenland bear eloquent witness to the skill and inventiveness a Norse Greenland woman was prepared to lavish on stylish garments for herself, her husband and her children. Much of her time indoors would have been spent standing by her upright loom, and practically wherever she was, she would have filled 'idle' time with spinning. Really profound changes in how a Greenland Norse woman spent her time would have had to include the disappearance of the domestic animals providing most of the raw materials for her traditional labours. 'Adjusting' to Eskimo ways would have involved corresponding dislocations in male occupations.

FUEL

The Greenland Norse have also been faulted for wanton consumption of fuel, including by boiling water with which to sterilise the vessels used in dairying.[19] Fortunately, they knew well enough how to make the most of their natural resources and their own efforts. A housewife would heat stones in the fire and drop them into a pot to keep the contents simmering, and to clean the wooden vessels she used for milk and milk products, she would have used cold water – probably along with sand for scrubbing – because she would have known that hot water darkens the wood and makes milk proteins harden and stick to the vessel. Clean vessels and utensils would then have been set outside for the sun to dry and sterilise them according to ancient practice.

As mentioned in Chapter Two, the Norse suffered no shortage of wood for fuel. They also used the widely available turf, and the number of soapstone oil lamps found in Norse Greenland farm ruins indicate that, just like elsewhere in Europe at the time, oil and blubber were used for light and heat. There would have been ample need for both in the long Greenland winters, when both men and women kept busy indoors. Much of their time would have been taken up with handicrafts of various kinds, but the frequent appearance in farm ruins of gaming pieces, children's toys and lovingly decorated everyday articles bears witness to a lighter side of life as well.

SLAVES AND HIRED HANDS

On the larger farms, hired hands would have helped keep the household running, and in the earlier part of the colony's existence, there would quite likely also have been slaves of both sexes. The Norse contributed generously to the slave trade that flourished in various parts of Europe in the period 800–1200, especially when Viking raids on Irish and other sites in the British Isles intensified in the second half of the ninth century, and business was still brisk at the end of the tenth century when Eirik the Red and his followers settled Greenland. The casual mention of slaves in accounts of Iceland's settlement suggests that captive labour was integral to the backbreaking work of clearing new land, and Eirik had clearly kept slaves in Iceland, because the 'Saga of Eirik the Red' recounts the troubles that arose when his slaves had caused a landslide to fall on a neighbouring farm. However, when the Irish slave trade petered out in the early twelfth century, along with the 'Viking Age' itself, the effect on Iceland and Greenland would have been negligible. Hired labour, rather than slaves, appears to have become the norm there by then, for economic and social reasons that did not include Christian love and heightened sensitivity to the plight of fellow humans.[20] The end of slavery among the Norse was an entirely pragmatic development.

For both women and low-ranking males, the line between freedom and slavery in their daily lives was not always clearly drawn. Medieval Europeans everywhere experienced violence and slavery, separately or linked, as part of their daily lives, and there is no reason why the Norse in their North Atlantic outposts would have been any different. Slaves and low-paid wage earners were usually given jobs which their owners or employers preferred to avoid, and even a well-born Norse woman, a free person by every legal definition, was sexually unfree because the question of whom she married was decided by men. Men's wishes also determined where she was to live, however far afield that might take her.

Among Norse-related material from a medieval Dorset site in northernmost Baffin Island, the Canadian archaeologist Patricia Sutherland discovered strands of yarn expertly spun from the fur of Arctic hare – evidence that the work had taken place locally. Unless bondage in Norse Greenland had lasted longer than in Iceland, the Norse woman who sat spinning so far from home in the late thirteenth or early fourteenth century would have been technically 'free', but she would have had to stay at her High Arctic camp site until the hunters who had brought her decided to go home.[21]

SOCIAL STRUCTURE

Like the Icelanders, the Greenlanders had set out to govern themselves without royal interference from Norway, in a hierarchical society run by free men. Chieftains were more equal than other men, of course, and wives, concubines and slaves would in most cases have counted for little. However, their system of self-government provided stability and probably also a high degree of participation by the inhabitants, not the abject submission by many to the power of a few argued by writers convinced that Norse Greenland society was destined to implode, or describing Greenland Norse society as 'communal, violent, hierarchical, conservative, and Eurocentric … to an extreme degree' – a 'tightly controlled society, in which the few chiefs of the richest farms could prevent anyone else from doing something that seemed to threaten their interests – including anyone experimenting with innovation that did not promise to help the chiefs'.[22]

The only part of this picture that corresponds in any way to reality is the reference to the hierarchical nature of the Norse Greenlander's society. Inflexible it was not, nor did it contain elements of the feudalism known elsewhere in Europe. In the medieval Norse culture which the settlers had brought with them to Greenland, the assumption was always that a chief enjoyed power only for as long as he had people willing to follow him rather than someone else, and there would have been limits to even the most powerful chieftain's ability to maintain rigid authority in a community of scattered farms in a hard-scrabble setting. Under such circumstances no farmer, rich or poor, would have survived for long without plenty of self-reliance and enterprise. At the same time, cooperation was the key to both individual and community survival.

Researchers in both Norse Greenland settlements have found considerable evidence of effective redistribution of inland and coastal food resources within the colony's domestic economy, and documents testify that the colonists exported goods to maintain their foreign trade. Such a degree of sophistication, in an economy that included the high-risk occupations of hunting and fishing, required coordination by the chieftains as well as the willing cooperation of the rest of the population. Any chieftain concerned with maintaining his authority over his followers and collecting tribute from them, would have welcomed both individual enterprise and collective effort, knowing very well that mere coercion would not send anyone to the High Arctic to confront walrus and polar bears or make people spend months fishing along the outer coast.

VOYAGES TO THE HIGH ARCTIC

Disko Bay (Figs. 9, 10) was the centre for the northern hunting grounds which the Norse called Norðrseta and which was also exploited by Arctic natives past and present, but the name appears also to have included both the Lancaster Sound area in northeastern Canada and the West Greenland coast at least as far as to about 73°N. Some Norse may conceivably have sailed to almost 83°N in the Smith Sound-Kane Basin region, judging from discoveries of Norse artefacts by the archaeologists Peter Schledermann and Karen McCullough during their work in Ellesmere Island. A small, but incontestable, piece of evidence for the Norse Greenlanders' High Arctic voyages is the small rune stone found in connection with three cairns on the island of Kingittorssuaq, directly opposite the entrance to Lancaster Sound (the eastern end of the Northwest Passage). The stone, now in Copenhagen, still carries the finely chiselled message from three young men believed to have carved their runes some time in the mid-thirteenth century, so early in the year that they must either have overwintered or else have headed north early from the Western Settlement to begin the spring hunt.[23] Arctic hunts provided the Norse Greenlanders with their most valuable export goods. Walrus tusks were prominent among these products but, as Chapter Seven will discuss, there is no basis for the claim made by Danish and Norwegian writers in recent years that walrus ivory was so crucial to the Greenland colony's survival that a fourteenth-century drop in African ivory prices spelled the beginning of the end for the Greenlanders. The price of African ivory did not drop until after AD 1500, and the Greenlanders had in any case never depended on walrus ivory for their survival.[24] Food for their everyday needs was as available to them as to everyone else in the coastal North Atlantic; grain and other imported food stuffs were luxury items. Bog iron and fresh

Fig. 9   Towering icebergs dominate the inner Disko Bay, where the Norse went to fish and hunt and where the modern Greenlanders have a major halibut fishery

lumber for ship construction were the only vital resources the Norse Greenlanders could not find in their own country.

MISSING RESOURCES

Archaeological evidence as well as chance mention in the written sources tell us that the Norse Greenlanders knew how to build ships and boats. However, as recent research on medieval Norse ship construction has shown, neither salt-soaked driftwood nor Greenland's spindly, native trees and shrubs would have met Norse shipbuilding needs, which called for fresh heartwood planks.[25] The received wisdom has therefore been that they imported lumber all the way from Norway, just as the Icelanders did, but there is in fact no historical or archaeological evidence for such imports to Greenland.

Birch and mountain ash were native to post-Ice Age Greenland, and tall specimens still grow in sheltered areas along with willow, dwarf willow and dwarf birch, just as when the Norse arrived and found those trees and

Fig. 10   Icebergs are continually calving off the receding glacier near Ilulissat, inner Disko Bay. This photograph, taken in early July 2006, may not bring 'summer hunting' to mind, but the region was and is a summer larder

shrubs as familiar and useful features in Greenland's sub-Arctic landscape. Some 450–800,000 years ago, southern Greenland was covered with a forest of pine and spruce, and a modern visitor to the Eastern Settlement will see healthy stands of pines in sheltered areas, but these lofty evergreens were recently reintroduced through human agency.[26] If the Norse Greenlanders wanted ship's timber, they must look elsewhere.

The iron worker's craft was equally central to shipbuilding and general self-sufficiency. The number of smithies found on Norse Greenland farm ruins testify to ample skills in making finished metal objects that ranged from knives and tools to ornaments and ships' rivets. The archaeologists Claus Andreasen and Jette Arneborg have noted that iron occurs surprisingly often in Norse Greenland finds, with the worn-down blades on most of the knives looking no different from those used elsewhere in Scandinavia. The *King's Mirror* stated that a merchant headed for Greenland would be well advised to have iron in his cargo, which has often been taken as evidence that Norway must have been the source of the various iron articles found in Norse Greenland farm ruins, but the Danish scientist Niels Nielsen queried this interpretation. He found evidence in

Norse Greenland smithies of slag from reworked crude iron blooms and concluded that it made no sense for the Greenland farmers to import crude blooms, rather than ready-to-forge iron, all the way from Norway. He therefore reasoned that the Norse Greenlanders must have smelted their own bog ore in hearth pits.[27] The problems with that scenario are that no hearth pits used for smelting bog iron have turned up on any Norse Greenland farm, and that local bogs contain no iron ore – that is, small quantities of iron oxide mixed with organic and other matter.[28]

All the same, there is no doubt that the Greenland Norse mastered the medieval Norwegian and Icelandic method of roasting bog iron with charcoal made from fresh, green wood to produce crude iron blooms. We know that they brought this skill with them to North America at the beginning of the eleventh century, because archaeologists have found a Norse hearth pit furnace at the L'Anse aux Meadows site in northern Newfoundland.[29]

The impetus for the Norse Greenlanders' North American exploration was not Bjarni Herjolfsson's adventure as described in the 'Saga of the Greenlanders', but a clear and immediate need for lumber and iron.

4

LEIF EIRIKSSON EXPLORES ANOTHER NEW LAND

While no aspect of the Norse Greenlanders' life, culture and achievement inspires sweet agreement, few topics in their history are as combustible as the question of what they accomplished by sailing to North America. Examining their reasons for going there is not likely to extinguish any fires, especially given the differing accounts of the enterprise provided in the two Vínland sagas, but it is worth considering what encouraged that further westward movement from Greenland and weighing those expectations against what we know of their achievement.

NO GAME OF CHANCE

Throughout the period of their Davis Strait crossings, the size and continental nature of North America were as unknown to the Norse Greenlanders as the Englishman John Davis (1550–1605) and the name America, first used on the 1507 Waldseemüller world map known as 'America's baptismal certificate'. They had not been slow to perceive the existence of more land to the west of their own country, however. We may be certain that the first planned Norse expeditions to North America were as deliberate as Eirik the Red's exploration of Greenland. Like his father, Leif knew from the outset that there was something there worth exploring.

The epic of the ever-lengthening Norse reach into the North Atlantic is studded with examples of new land discovered through a combination of accident and inevitability, and there is little reason to suppose that the Norse knowledge of coasts beyond Greenland followed a different pattern. When Helge Ingstad began his search for Norse landing sites in North America, he explored along both sides of the Davis Strait in a small craft and found that where the Davis Strait narrows to about two hundred sea miles near Holsteinborg, one need not sail very far out to sea to spot the mountains on Baffin Island. High mountains near Holsteinborg would also allow a glimpse of the far shore, Ingstad noted. 'In short, it is more than probable that at quite an early period the Norsemen had knowledge of the coasts of Baffin Land, and these pointed the way to other parts of North America.'[1]

Written evidence for voyages far north along the Greenland shore of the Davis Strait begins with the late twelfth-century work *Historia Norvegiæ*. Consequently, the received wisdom has been that the Norse colonists waited for some generations before engaging in far northern hunts.[2] The historical and archaeological record does not support that view, however. Moreover, it is clear that Eirik the Red already had northern hunts in mind when he founded his Greenland colony, and the prize game would have been walrus. Walrus are large animals that must haul up out of the water to rest, therefore they follow the drift ice in the summer season as it recedes northwards to the narrowing of the Davis Strait, where the ice becomes trapped. Norse hunters pursuing their prey that far north would have had to steer west to remain in open water, and some would have gone far enough to see the distant glaciers of Baffin Island across the strait. Experienced seafarers that they were, they would soon have linked that other coast with Bjarni Herjolfsson's tale or similar stories and reasoned that they might find forests along that western shore by heading far enough south.

If Bjarni's tale ('Saga of the Greenlanders') about the forests he had seen from afar actually represented news, his information would certainly have been welcome in a land so lacking in timber as Eirik the Red's new colony, but it is also possible that, for artistic reasons, the saga narrator conflated several reports by other Norse sailors who had also observed land farther west. This part of the saga's narrative is further confounded by the conflicting report of the 'Saga of Eirik the Red', which credits Eirik's son Leif both with spotting that alien coast and going ashore, while Leif's experiences supposedly took place during a stormy homeward voyage from Norway, where he had consorted with Olaf Tryggvason (king of Norway 995–1000) and had been converted by him. That segment of the saga was added by an Icelandic monk, Gunnlaug, who was primarily intent on polishing Olaf Tryggvason's image as a missionary monarch, therefore this detail of the Vínland story is now heavily discounted.[3]

The 'Saga of the Greenlanders' relates that after Bjarni's safe arrival in Greenland, he told about his sightings of new coasts. Although he reportedly gave up trading once he had settled on his father's Greenland farm, some time later he sailed to Norway again, this time to visit Earl Eirik Hákonsson, who had become the country's regent after the death of King Olaf Tryggvason in 1000, holding that position until 1012. The earl received Bjarni well, according to the saga, but when he and others in Norway heard Bjarni's story about the unfamiliar coasts he had seen, they chided him for not having investigated that new land. Others in Greenland had the requisite curiosity, however.

The following summer, Bjarni returned home from Earl Eirik's court and found the Eastern Settlement abuzz with plans for an expedition to explore the new coasts in the west. There can be no doubt that the explorers hoped to profit from New World resources because, in accordance with Norse custom, the place names which Leif assigned on the American side (see below) reflected an assessment of each particular region's economic potential.

THE MEN IN CHARGE

The two Vínland sagas represent the subsequent events somewhat differently, but both sagas make it clear that Eirik the Red and his family provided the initiative as well as the leadership for all of those early expeditions, which is just what one would look for in a social and economic hierarchy dominated by the chieftains, among whom Eirik ranked foremost. The captains on the voyages commemorated by the Vínland sagas were his sons and other members of his immediate circle, such as the visiting Icelandic merchant Thorfinn Karlsefni (Makings-of-a-Man) Thordsson and some of his Icelandic kinsmen and friends. Karlsefni's part in these ventures is central to the story told in the 'Saga of Eirik the Red', which treats Leif Eiriksson's explorations as a part of his zigzagging voyage from Norway to Greenland, whereas the 'Saga of the Greenlanders' describes separate American voyages by all four of Eirik's children, his daughter Freydis included. Karlsefni's enterprise is also featured in the latter saga, because he had become 'family' by marrying Gudrid Thorbjörnsdaughter, the widow of Leif's brother Thorstein. The saga also stresses that Leif's voyage retraced Bjarni's reported sightings in reverse, first heading north along Greenland to the strait's narrowing and then crossing over.

Nobody knows when Eirik the Red died, but the two Vínland sagas create the impression that his death occurred while the earliest voyages of exploration were taking place. When Eirik died, Leif would have had the ultimate say concerning further voyages. Eirik's death would also have involved sharing out Eirik's property among Leif and his siblings. Brattahlid would have gone to Leif along with the chieftaincy, but Eirik had property in the Western Settlement as well, and that property would, from the start, have been a strategic staging site for deliberate expeditions whose sole focus was on exploring the economic potential of North America.

While Leif's brother Thorstein was alive, he owned half a farm in Lysufjord, says the 'Saga of Eirik the Red'. This is most likely a reference to Thorstein's share of his paternal inheritance which, when Thorstein died, would have passed to his widow Gudrid Thorbjörnsdaughter, Karlsefni's wife-to-be. In describing the Karlsefni-led voyage, the 'Saga of Eirik the Red' notes that the expedition first went up to the Western Settlement before proceeding to the Bjarn Isles (Bear Islands) – either Disko Island or other islands farther north. Chances are good that Karlsefni and his crew, reportedly consisting of sixty-five men, stopped at the Western Settlement in order to take on water and other provisions, presumably at Sandness.

REACHING THE OTHER SIDE

When Eirik the Red explored Greenland, he had not seen anything to tempt settlers until he ventured far into the country's deep western fjords and found green hillsides with orange-berried mountain ash and quivering birches. Sailing into those long, unfamiliar inlets with their many twists and branches was an act of faith on his part, but it also reflected a sure sense that the farther into a fjord or bay he went, the more benign the landscape was likely to be. The Vínland sagas suggest that the Norse appreciation of sheltered conditions also led them to investigate bays, fjords and other inlets when they reached the other side of the strait, and that they exercised the same kind of caution Eirik had shown during his first winter in an unknown land by overwintering on an island, because there was no telling who else might be sharing the land and seas around him. As it turned out, circumspection was particularly well advised along the alien shores to which Leif and his fellow explorers assigned the names historians still use today when discussing Norse travels in North America a millennium ago.

The rock slabs and glaciers of Baffin Island on the stretch they named Helluland (Slab Land), offered little which the travellers could not have found back in Greenland, but the 'Saga of the Greenlanders' notes that Leif nevertheless sent in a shore party so that nobody could accuse him of dereliction of duty. In the 'Saga of Eirik the Red' Karlsefni is credited with naming this region Helluland because of its huge rock slabs. His shore party clearly did some hunting as well, because they described the place as full of foxes and are unlikely to have refrained from bagging as many as possible of this valuable fur animal.[4]

Once Leif's expedition reached Napartok Bay at 58°N, the present northern limit for forests on the American northeast coast, their designation for the land they saw was Markland (Forest Land), signalling that they had come far enough south to locate the trees they had hoped to find. The forest belt in northeastern America has an undulating northern perimeter and continues both west and south for a very long way, with a varying mix of tree species, therefore it is impossible to define either the perceived boundary between Helluland and Markland or where Markland flowed into Vínland (Wine Land). The latter name indicates that in a landscape that obviously still featured trees, the Norse had found a remarkable new feature, vínber (wine berries), thus the region deserved a name of its own. But where was Vínland?

Even before Helge Ingstad's 1960 discovery of a Norse ruin site datable to around 1000, at L'Anse aux Meadows on Newfoundland's green and grassy Northern Peninsula, the discussion about the true location of Vínland included the claim that Vínland should be translated as 'grassy field'. According to this reasoning, the name's prefix had had a short vowel, not a long one, and therefore corresponded to the suffix '-vin' as, for example, in Bergen's old name of Bjørgvin. The problem with this argument is that this particular usage of 'vin', both as a suffix and a prefix, was outmoded well before the colonisation of Iceland and Greenland took place. It is absent in place names of Norse origin not only in Iceland and Greenland, but also in the Scottish Isles and the Faeroes.[5] If Vínland had still signified 'land of green meadows' when Eirik the Red hoped to attract settlers to Greenland, he might just as well have signalled the presence of good pasturage by calling his new land Vinland (short vowel) and not Greenland. It is doubtful, moreover, that with sufficient pastures back home in Greenland, the Norse would have become overly impressed by meadows on the American side.

The Norse had been trading with and on the European continent for several centuries when they set out to explore North America, therefore they knew very well the ingredient required for making wine (vín). Vikings who wintered in France and on the Iberian Peninsula were probably not slow learners in matters of food and drink, and stay-at-home Norwegians would have enjoyed imports of wine and raisins as well as of fresh grapes from no farther away than Germany.

The island of Newfoundland is grapeless now and was grapeless a thousand years ago, therefore Vínland cannot be equated with Newfoundland, but parts of the island were doubtless included in the name given to the southernmost American region the Norse investigated. The Canadian archaeologist Birgitta Wallace, currently in charge of the L'Anse aux Meadows site, calls the location the 'gateway' to Vínland and reasons that the Norse must have explored at least parts of Nova Scotia, where both wild grapes and the American butternut tree (Juglans cinerea) grew and still grow, because fruits and wood (worked with metal tools) of butternut have been found in the Norse culture layer at L'Anse aux Meadows. Like her predecessor Anne Stine Ingstad, Wallace notes that the thinness of that culture layer suggests use of the site for a decade or two at most, during which time the place seems to have functioned as a trans-shipment station for American goods intended for Greenland-based trade. Excavations of the ruins point to the presence of three or four chieftains in charge of large crews, who used the place for ship repairs, overwintering, exploration and miscellaneous resource exploitation.[6] The houses at L'Anse aux Meadows are now widely believed to represent Leif Eiriksson's strategically selected wintering camp, used and expanded for a while by subsequent skippers and crews, much as implied by the sagas.

LIFE AT L'ANSE AUX MEADOWS

As it turned out, the sagas were also on firm ground in mentioning female Norse participants in these early European ventures in America, most notably Gudrid Thorbjörnsdaughter, who went along as Karlsefni's wife and gave birth to their son Snorri while there. Archaeological investigations at L'Anse aux Meadows, under the leadership of Anne Stine Ingstad, were still incomplete in 1964 when decisive evidence not only of the site's Norse origin, but of female occupants, turned up in the form of a small soapstone spindle whorl.[7]

Scientific evidence concerning the general composition of the groups using the place also confirms other aspects of the Vínland sagas. Although the two sagas diverge both on the number of voyages undertaken in the course of those first expeditions and on the names of the leaders involved, both sagas suggest that a sizeable contingent of Icelanders was involved in those ventures. Tests of ten jasper fire-starter fragments found in and around the Norse buildings at L'Anse aux Meadows tie in nicely with the Icelandic saga writers' focus on their own fellow countrymen. 'Fire stones' were personal equipment and usually wore out from their frequent use, thus a fragment had likely accompanied its owner fairly recently to the place where the piece was found. When the 'fingerprints' of the L'Anse aux Meadows jasper fragments were compared to one another and to samples from Norway, Iceland, Greenland, Newfoundland, New Brunswick, Nova Scotia and Maine, as well as from down the eastern coast of the United States to the Great Lakes drainage, both Greenlandic and Icelandic jaspers were found among the ten samples. Significantly, Greenlandic jasper from the outer coast of the Western Settlement region was found only in and around 'Hall F', which evidently ranked highest among the buildings at the L'Anse aux Meadows site, while Icelandic jasper predominated in and around all of the dwellings, suggesting that Icelanders stayed in every house while a relative few shared 'Hall F' with the Greenlanders in charge of the main operation.[8]

It is nevertheless a mistake to think that all the details in the two sagas have equal factual value in the form they have reached us. The orally transmitted Vínland stories were first committed to parchment more than two centuries after the events took place, and those who transcribed the information would scarcely have been human if they had been impervious to ideas current in their own time. A good example is the description in the 'Saga of Eirik the Red' of the 'self-sown wheat' found in Vínland. This phrase is an embellishment of the 'unsown crops' mentioned by Adam of Bremen, who may well have heard about the wild rice growing in the St Lawrence region both then and now.[9] The literary mutation is easily explained. By the thirteenth century, the Roman Church had been established in Iceland for over two centuries, and wine and wheat were the two ingredients essential to the Eucharist, as Pope Gregory IX had made quite clear to the Norwegian archbishop Sigurd in 1237. Beer was not an acceptable substitute for wine, the pope wrote sternly; the celebration of the Eucharist required panis de frumento et vini de uvis (bread made of wheat and wine made from grapes).[10] Both wine and wheat had to be imported into Iceland, so that distant western shore, where both ingredients supposedly were available for the taking, must be a blessed land indeed! It scarcely needs saying that nobody ever attempted to alleviate Icelandic needs with American sacramental imports.

DISCOVERING VÍNLAND GRAPES

It is quite possible that Leif Eiriksson had been baptised by the time he introduced his exploration party to the delights of Vínland, and that others among his crew were either nominal or convinced Christians, but a good many of them would still have been heathen and unlikely to worry about the doctrine of transubstantiation. In any event, the 'Saga of the Greenlanders' does not specify the religious affiliation of Tyrkir the Southerner, the foreigner credited with discovering the grapes in Vínland.[11] Tyrkir had reportedly been with Eirik's family for a long time as Leif's foster father, possibly as a slave, and Leif had been devoted to him as a child. The saga describes Tyrkir as having 'a prominent forehead and shifty eyes, and not much more of a face besides; he was short and puny-looking but very clever with his hands'. (Such capsule characterisations, intended to make an audience visualise both the outer and inner person concerned in a story, are common in the Norse sagas.) Leif obviously valued his chinless foster father despite those 'shifty eyes' and other unprepossessing features, because he had taken him along on his voyage to the new land and was very upset when Tyrkir went missing one day while out with an exploration party. Leif went out with a search party, and they soon encountered Tyrkir, walking towards them in such a state of excitement that he lapsed into a long tirade in German before switching to Old Norse to report that he had found vines and grapes.

The Norse party enthusiastically filled their tow boat with grapes and cut vines and timber besides. By the time they left for Greenland the following spring, they had an excellent cargo and were so pleased with their venture that Leif 'named the country after its natural qualities and called it Vínland'.

FOLLOW-UP VOYAGES

When the good news had been reported back home, Leif's brother Thorvald became the next to go across to Vínland and the houses Leif had built. The new group of explorers settled in there for the winter, 'catching fish for their food'. Came spring, they explored the country further by ship and very much liked what they saw. Not the least of the new land's attractions was the fact that the only discernible sign of a native population was a 'wooden stack-cover' – a structure whose agricultural identity has not been determined to this day. The following summer, however, Thorvald and his men ran into nine members of an indigenous Beothuk tribe who were hiding under some skin-covered boats.[12] The Norse killed eight of the natives, but the ninth got away and presumably made straight for the 'humps' signifying a settlement farther up the fjord, because a swarm of skin boats soon approached the intruders. During the ensuing battle, Thorvald Eiriksson suffered a mortal wound, and his men buried him in accordance with his wishes before they rejoined the other members of their expedition. Next, says the 'Saga of the Greenlanders', they gathered grapes and vines, spent another winter at Leif's houses and in the spring returned to Brattahlid, where Leif was now in charge after Eirik's death.

Although both of the Vínland sagas note that the third brother, Thorstein Eiriksson, had married Gudrid Thorbjörnsdaughter, only the 'Saga of the Greenlanders' reports that Thorstein, accompanied by his wife, made an abortive attempt to reach Vínland and bring back Thorvald's body. Both sagas agree that Thorstein soon died up in the Western Settlement, and the 'Saga of the Greenlanders' notes that his young widow, an intelligent woman 'of striking appearance', then returned down to the Eastern Settlement to stay with her brother-in-law Leif. While there, she soon found favour with the visiting Icelandic merchant Thorfinn Karlsefni, 'a man of considerable wealth'. He had arrived at Brattahlid prepared for trade and was invited to spend the winter with Leif, so he had ample opportunity to appreciate Gudrid's sterling qualities. They were married that same winter.

There was still much talk about Vínland, and at the urging of his bride and many others, Karlsefni decided to make the crossing himself and to consider the possibility of a permanent settlement over there. Sixty men and five women, Gudrid included, went along, bringing some livestock, and they arrived safely at Leif's houses. Both people and animals found plenty to eat, and they passed a busy, but uneventful winter. Change came the following summer, when a large number of natives suddenly appeared and became so frightened by the visitors' bellowing bull that they tried to enter the Norse houses, from which they were immediately barred. When the situation eventually cooled down, it transpired that the natives were hoping to barter furs and pelts for Norse goods, preferably weapons. In the 'Saga of the Greenlanders' version of Karlsefni's first interaction with North American natives, he forbade his men to sell arms, however, and ordered the women to bring out milk instead.

The 'Saga of Eirik the Red' for its part describes pre-Karlsefni crossings only perfunctorily in a reference to Vínland 'where, it was said, there was excellent land to be had'. Having recently married Gudrid, Karlsefni decided to mount an expedition across the strait, and he left with two ships carrying full crews consisting primarily of Icelanders, as well as with a third ship with mostly Greenlanders on board, including Thorvald Eiriksson, Eirik's son-in-law Thorvard and Thorvard's wife, Freydis Eiriksdaughter. After making their way via the Western Settlement to the other side, the explorers spent a tough first winter in the new land, camping in a place they called Straumfjord (Current Fjord), which has proved as contentious a location as Vínland itself. Nowhere in this saga is there any mention of the houses Leif had built, because Leif's role in this version had merely been to spot the new coasts first and subject them to only a brief inspection ashore before heading home to Greenland.

One likely reason Karlsefni and his company did not immediately build shelters for themselves in Straumfjord is that they had failed to anticipate the severity of the weather during the cold season. The place had been so welcoming when they arrived that 'they paid no attention to anything except exploring it'. There was ample food for them and their animals until the cold season struck and both man and beast ran short of food. The group 'had made no provisions' – that is, no fish had been caught and cured, and no hay and leaves had been gathered and dried. The party made it through to spring, however, when they could resume their fishing and hunting. No natives were to be seen, and all should have been well, but disagreement broke out among the Norse about where they should go next.

ENCOUNTERING VÍNLAND NATIVES

Ten of the Greenlanders sailed north, supposedly in search of Vínland, and came to a bad end. Karlsefni wanted to go south, where he reckoned the country was likely to improve. The remaining men decided to go with him and felt rewarded when they reached an estuary which they named Hóp. Here, they found wild wheat growing everywhere on the low ground and grapevines on the higher ground, and there were fish and game aplenty as well as grazing for the livestock they had brought with them. They had been enjoying this lovely spot for two weeks when a number of skin boats suddenly appeared, carrying men who made much noise by waving sticks. The Norse went down to meet them, and the newcomers came ashore to get a close look at the intruders in their land, stared their fill and got back in their boats and rowed away. Karlsefni and his people subsequently built a settlement on a slope by the lakeside and spent a pleasant winter there, with no snow and with the livestock able to fend for themselves.

An earthly Paradise Hóp was not. One morning in the spring, such a large number of skin boats approached from the south that 'it looked as if the estuary were strewn with charcoal', and sticks were being waved from every boat as on the first occasion. The Norsemen 'raised their shields and the two parties began to trade'. As in the 'Saga of the Greenlanders' story, weapons were high on the natives' wish list, but they reportedly also wanted to buy red cloth, which Karlsefni was happy to trade for grey pelts until every scrap of cloth was gone. Just at that moment, the bull belonging to the Norse came charging out of the wood with furious bellows, and the terrified natives ran to their boats and rowed away. Three weeks went by with no further sight of them, but when they returned, they came in such numbers and howled so furiously that Karlsefni realised they were primed for battle. And a fierce battle it was, leaving four natives and two of the Norsemen dead and Freydis Eiriksdaughter flushed with the knowledge that she had managed to frighten the enemy just by baring her breasts and slapping them with a sword.

Deciding that there was no future for their little Norse band in a place with so many hostile natives, Karlsefni and his companions packed up and returned to Straumfjord, killing five sleeping natives on their way. By this point in the narrative, the 'Saga of Eirik the Red' has differed from the version in the 'Saga of the Greenlanders' in so many ways that it comes as no surprise when the saga writer interjects yet another possible variant of what 'some people' told about these events in Vínland. The 'Saga of Eirik the Red' embroiders its version further by having Thorvald Eiriksson killed by a Uniped's arrow and with a tale about the mythical Hvítramannaland (White Man's Country), before the whole party returns to Greenland. There, they spent the winter with Eirik the Red, who was still alive and well in this saga, at least.

The 'Saga of Eirik the Red' also notes that when Karlsefni and Gudrid returned to Greenland, they had with them their three-year-old son, Snorri, born during their first autumn in Straumfjord. After wintering at Brattahlid, the little family went back to Iceland to live on Karlsefni's farm, where a second son, Thorbjörn, joined them. Both of Karlsefni's sons became the progenitors of Icelandic bishops, and 'there this saga ends'.

The 'Saga of the Greenlanders' likewise records the arrival of little Snorri, the first European child born in America, at about the time of the first Norse trading encounter with American natives. That trading event had ended peacefully, and when a much greater number of natives arrived early the following winter with furs to trade, it looked as if this second occasion would also end safely. However, when one of the natives attempted to steal weapons from one of Karlsefni's men, he was killed for his efforts, and the natives then fled head over heels, leaving their clothing and fur bundles behind. Karlsefni reasoned that they would soon return to exact revenge, and he planned accordingly. Not long after, the battle did take place, and many natives lost their lives before the rest of them disappeared into the forest. Although there was no further sight of them during the rest of that winter, when spring came, Karlsefni declared that he wanted to return to Greenland. After gathering together 'much valuable produce, vines and grapes and pelts', they all sailed away and spent the next winter at Brattahlid.

In this saga's telling of Karlsefni's battle with the natives, there was no Wagnerian appearance by Freydis Eiriksdaughter, because she was not one of the five women on Karlsefni's expedition. Instead, shortly after Karlsefni had returned to Greenland with his little family, Freydis reportedly got permission from Leif to borrow his houses in Vínland and organised an expedition of her own, with two ships. Her husband Thorvard was kindly permitted to tag along, and five women were supposedly also in the party, as revealed in a short description of how Freydis took an axe and personally beheaded all five women because the men in her party had refused to do so. It is a Byzantine tale of deception, greed and cruelty from start to finish, and more than one scholar has wondered whether it was not inserted merely to contrast Freydis's black and heathen soul with the saintliness of Gudrid Thorbjörnsdaughter, who ended her days as an anchoress and whose early descendants included three Icelandic bishops.

Notwithstanding these divergent accounts of the early voyages to Vínland and hopelessly vague descriptions of the locations mentioned in those Norse odysseys, the two sagas speak with one voice in stressing both the central part played by the Brattahlid family and the successful Norse focus on the new land's resources, lumber and furs prominent among them. The 'Saga of Eirik the Red' describes the native Americans as eager to barter for cloth, which certainly differs from the lucrative trade in milk in the 'Saga of the Greenlanders', but both cloth and dairy products were reliable Norse export commodities, so there is no mistaking both writers' assumption that this far-flung western voyage was a commercial venture.[13]

The two sagas mention no further use of Leif's houses beyond that already described. This circumstance fits well with the archaeological evidence for Norse tenure of a comparatively short duration at the L'Anse aux Meadows site, the only place which so far has unassailable evidence of Norse houses in America.

THE AFTERMATH

Stray Norse objects found at other American sites suggest that later voyages from Greenland were oriented towards more northerly resources and that they were seasonal, involving small crews who brought from home only what they needed for the tasks ahead and evidently saw little need to construct permanent housing. The 'Norse longhouse' foundations which the Canadian archaeologist Thomas Lee thought he had found in the Ungava Bay region have been the subject of much discussion, but they have been persuasively identified as remains of Dorset structures.[14]

The lack of stories about further crossings from Greenland to Vínland led to a widespread post-medieval belief that the Norse had become so disillusioned by their experience with North American natives that they never returned to any part of that newfound land. Modern archaeology has provided ample evidence for later American voyages by the Norse Greenlanders, but there is a perfectly good reason why there is no literary record of continued crossings, although knowledge of further forays must necessarily have reached the medieval Icelanders through continued contact between Iceland and Greenland during the more than two centuries that separate the Vínland voyages and the penning of the sagas. The reason is that the two Vínland sagas merely commemorated events that had involved a good many Icelanders, including some very prominent ones, and that what the Greenlanders did on their own later was of little concern to Icelandic writers intent on preserving historical details of interest to Icelanders. Each time other Icelandic sources mentioned later westward crossings from Greenland, Iceland had somehow been involved.

For example, when several Icelandic annals noted that Bishop Eirik Gnupsson 'of Greenland' went in search of Vínland, it was because Bishop Eirik originally came from Iceland. Three annal entries for 1347 recording that an anchorless small ship had drifted off while on its way back to Greenland from a voyage to Markland, were occasioned by the fact that the ship had ended up in Iceland.[15] Interestingly, the annal writers who included this episode did not bother to explain that Markland was the forested western region on which the Greenlanders still depended for lumber, and they never mentioned Vínland. Presumably, they and their fellow Icelanders were aware that the forests of Markland were of far more interest to the Norse Greenlanders than either grass or grapes.

The wild grapes in Vínland were useful garnishes in the subsequent literature, however, and so was the glamour of a climate that offered year-round pastures. Nevertheless, Icelanders and Greenlanders alike were realistic and shrewd traders who knew that middlemen interfered with profits and that European merchants, who already dealt in grapes, raisins and similar goods obtained from reasonably predictable sources, would not have waited anxiously for shipments from Vínland by way of Greenland and Norway. Small wonder, therefore, that upon weighing the luxury produce of Vínland against notoriously troublesome relations with the natives in that region, the Greenland Norse decided that there was no profit in future voyages taking them several hundred miles farther south than necessary for their needs. Their export economy required thick, glossy, northern furs and the spoils of maritime hunts, all of which were obtainable at Helluland latitudes. For their domestic needs, materials for shipbuilding took precedence, and for those they needed only to access the trees and bog iron in Markland, which they had found long before they reached Vínland.

Wood analyses of ships' parts from Norse ruins at both Greenland settlements gave six indications of larch, and Poul Nørlund also found larch used in a coffin at the Herjolfsness churchyard, in an area where the graves mostly dated from the fourteenth century onwards.[16] Larch did not grow in either Greenland, Iceland or Norway at that time; it is native only to North America and parts of Siberia. It is common in the Labrador region of Markland, to which we know the Norse were still sailing in 1347.

Other discoveries also indicate protracted Norse contact with North America. In a late-occupancy stratum at 'The Farm Beneath the Sand', a Western Settlement site finally abandoned around 1400, archaeologists found bison hairs and fur fibres from brown or black bear, most likely obtained through the extensive trade network on the American side because neither animal could have come from Greenland. Also found at 'The Farm Beneath the Sand' was a length of expertly spun yarn with fur from Arctic hare and goat hairs, done in the same technique as the long Baffin Island strand examined by Pat Sutherland, which has been radio-carbon-dated to the late thirteenth or early fourteenth century along with pine pieces with holes from iron nails found at the same Baffin Island site.[17]

The so-called 'Maine penny', a Norwegian coin from 1065–80 found at a twelfth-century Amerindian site on the Maine coast, is likely a modern 'plant.'[18] Rather more convincing evidence that voyages from Greenland to the Canadian shores had continued is an arrowhead excavated in the Christian churchyard at Sandness in the Western Settlement, thus necessarily postdating the early Vínland voyages, which took place before Greenland was a Christian country. The weapon was made from chert (a flint-like quartz) of a kind often associated with Ramah Bay on the outer Labrador coast, but also with the Ungava Bay region, and in the style commonly used by the North American natives in southern Labrador and Newfoundland between 1000 and 1500.[19] Dorset Eskimo sites along the coasts of Hudson Bay and the Hudson Strait have yielded small fragments of smelted metal that probably also indicate Norse contact with both Dorset and Thule people.[20] The Thule people arrived early enough in the

Hudson Bay area to overlap with the Dorset inhabitants who lasted there until around 1500, and it was on a thirteenth- or fourteenth-century Thule site, on the south coast of Baffin Island, that the Canadian archaeologist Deborah Sabo found a small carving of driftwood which immediately gave rise to a discussion about medieval travellers in the region. While agreeing that the figurine represents a European, opinions have differed sharply on the nationality as well as the profession of the person who inspired the carving, but the sex was always assumed to be male. However, given the recent evidence for further Norse forays into this region and for Norse women accompanying crews crossing the Davis Strait, there is good reason to believe that the figurine represents a human female, possibly pregnant under loosely fitted clothing that has been split to facilitate walking.[21] One may well wonder what her life had been like.

Several crude iron blooms of a medieval type were found on Baffin Island, in sites associated with Martin Frobisher's 1576–78 search for the Northwest Passage and for gold. Radiocarbon dates obtained on a couple of these blooms fall within the Norse tenure in Greenland, and an analysis of charcoal fragments in the blooms indicates spruce or larch, birch and alder – the wood species which the Norse would have been likely to use if smelting bog iron in the southern Ungava Bay region or elsewhere in the forested parts of Labrador.[22] The southwestern corner of Ungava Bay would have been the closest place to home where the Norse Greenlanders could obtain iron as well as green wood for charcoal, as the Norse smelting methods required. There was also lumber for ship construction.

Although the trees farther south would be considerably bigger, the Norse did not need huge trees for their heartwood planks and may well have preferred less massive specimens. Other factors are also likely to have made the Ungava Bay region more attractive than areas farther down the Labrador coast, despite the notoriously treacherous nature of the waters of Ungava Bay and the Hudson Strait. The Norse would have been well advised to access areas occupied by Arctic natives, whose hostility does not appear to have been an acute problem, rather than to risk being grossly outnumbered by hostile Amerindians. A small group of Norse men would have been very vulnerable to attack – the Markland voyage of 1347, for example, reportedly involved only seventeen or eighteen men.

The cultural identity of the Greenland Norse was so closely tied to stock farming that they are unlikely to have left home in large numbers to take up permanent residence in the Ungava Bay region as hunters or lumberjacks, but a round-trip voyage during the open-water season in the Davis Strait, from late summer well into the autumn, would have been manageable for people used to sailing long distances in open ships, and there would have been enough time ashore to accomplish their tasks even if they did not overwinter. Evidence of Norse seasonal activities would be hard to find after six or more centuries, however, especially along a littoral as immense and as wild as the one in question here, and even more difficult to trace would be Norse interaction with the people whom the sagas call Skrælings.

5

WHO WERE THE SKRÆLINGS?

Recapitulating Icelandic saga literature in the *Antiquitates Americanae*, Rafn and Magnusen consistently referred to the Vínland natives as 'Skrælings', the designation first used in the 1120s by Ari 'the Learned' Thorgilsson, who assumed that fragments of skin boats, stone implements and other signs of an earlier human presence which the Norse had found when they arrived in Greenland, had been left by 'Skrælings' just like those in Vínland. The name has been made to serve for both Amerindians and Eskimo peoples ever since Ari's time.

Since 1977, 'Inuit' rather than 'Eskimo' has been the preferred term for the descendants of the Thule people who currently populate Eastern Arctic Canada and Greenland. There is still plenty of room for confusion, however, because scholars not infrequently refer to pre-1500 Dorset and Thule peoples collectively as Eskimos, another word whose origin has not been settled, but which is intended to distinguish both Arctic peoples from the indigenous North Americans whom the first post-1500 European explorers called 'Indians'. The European fishermen and whalers who descended on northeastern America after 1500 added to the terminological confusion because, until around 1700, 'Eskimo' was also used about Amerindians living in the region directly adjoining Thule territory.[1]

Ari did not question or explain his use of the expression 'Skræling', which suggests that he was familiar with the word's origin and meaning and expected the same knowledge from his fellow countrymen. Other early Icelandic writers were evidently also comfortable with the expression, because 'Skræling' is used in the same no-nonsense fashion in other medieval works describing Norse interaction with the people they encountered in North America: the 'Eyrbyggja Saga', the 'Saga of Eirik the Red' and the 'Saga of the Greenlanders'. All three sagas were first committed to parchment in the thirteenth century by men who, like Ari, were educated Christians, and who would have had even better opportunity than Ari to hear stories about Norse encounters with Arctic peoples.

Modern archaeology has shown that the Arctic natives immediately preceding the Norse in the southern part of Greenland must have been visiting hunters from the Late Dorset culture, the only Arctic people anywhere in Greenland when the Norse settlers arrived. The most recent wave of Dorset Eskimos had migrated from Canada into Greenland's Thule region in the eighth century and stood their ground in the north until about 1300, therefore it is quite possible that the Norse had encountered some of their number during Arctic hunts even before they sailed to North America. Later in the eleventh century, they would also have come across Thule people, the last neo-Eskimo culture that crossed to Greenland from the Canadian side, eventually becoming the ancestors of the modern Inuit. The Thule first settled in northern Greenland and then spread slowly down the west coast during the fourteenth century, until they reached the Norse settlement regions.[2] Like the Dorset people, with whom they overlapped in the northwest, and the Algonkians whom the Norse encountered in North America, the Thule people also acquired the designation 'Skrælings'.

Were the Norse unable to differentiate among three separate indigenous cultures whose members not only looked and dressed differently from each other, but who also differed in their tools, weapons and means of transportation? Far from it. The purpose of the Old Norse designation Skræling (plural: Skræling[j]ar) was to distinguish between the Norse themselves and the aboriginal peoples they encountered in both Greenland and North America. The medieval Norse habitually gave new people and places labels that highlighted a prominent characteristic, examples being the names Leif Eiriksson assigned to North American regions and the designation blámenn (blue men) used about black people the Norse had encountered in North Africa. Scholars on the whole agree that Skræling was a pejorative, because the way Norse medieval literature uses Skræling(j)ar reveals that the chief characteristic shared by the native peoples the Norse met on their westernmost voyages was their puny stature, a quality the medieval Norse disdained and equated with feebleness.

THE SPHERICAL WORLD PICTURE

Modern discussions do not focus primarily on how the term Skræling(j)ar was applied, but on how the word originated. Working within their own specialities, modern archaeologists, historians and philologists concerned with the Norse Greenland colony have challenged outdated assumptions with considerable success, but often without examining the ideas that informed their nineteenth-century predecessors. By far the biggest obstacle to finding an explanation for the origin and meaning of 'Skræling' has been the failure to suspect the nineteenth-century idea that medieval people – the Norse included – thought of the world as laid out flat on a disc, not as a sphere.[3]

The idea of the flat-earth-belief rested in large part on an invented account in the 1828 *History of the Life and Voyages of Christopher Columbus* by Washington Irving (1783–1859), who was adept at conflating history and fiction. Although the thinking of some nineteenth-century scholars was influenced by medieval maps contained within a circle (usually with Jerusalem at its centre), Enlightenment anticlericalism was the main glue cementing the flat earth idea among the middle classes in Europe in the early part of the nineteenth century, while in the US anticatholics accused the Roman Church of erroneous teaching in the Middle Ages. A substantial number of textbooks and encyclopedias had corrected the story by the 1980s, but in 1983 Daniel Boorstin (1914–2004), the former Librarian of Congress, revived it with his widely read book *The Discoverers*.[4] Cooler heads prevailed at last when the first volume of *The History of Cartography*, edited by the eminent cartographic scholars J. B. Harley and David Woodward, became available in 1987.

Thirty years later, this welcome general development has yet to influence modern scholarly perceptions of the two Nordic scholars who set the pattern for the 'Skræling' discussion, and who shared the nineteenth-century flat earth assumption. The Norwegian historian Gustav Storm (1845–1903) and the Danish cartographic scholar Axel Anton Bjørnbo (1874–1911) were prominent in their day, and both are still cited in the scholarly literature because of their meticulous work on the medieval Norse and their exploits in the northwestern Atlantic, but scrutiny has so far avoided their flat-earth-belief views. The unfortunate fact is that both the 'Skræling' discussion and the two men's interpretations of medieval geographical sources about the north were skewed by those views from the start. Storm, for example, gave it as his opinion that Adam of Bremen, too, believed in a flat earth.[5]

Both Storm and Bjørnbo acknowledged the importance of old maps and were deeply interested in the cartographic representations of Greenland, drawn around 1424–30 by the Dane Claudius Clavus (see also Chapter Ten). Just a presumed copy of an earlier Clavus map – the 'Nancy Map' – survives; a later map was presumed on the basis of two descriptive 'Vienna texts' from which Bjørnbo drew a reconstructed map.[6] This work faithfully reproduces the reference points and other allusions provided in the texts, but it is fatally flawed by Bjørnbo's failure to understand that medieval people, Clavus included, saw the world in the round, because it blinded him to the significance of the map legends, including the Careli infideles (Karelian heathens) whom Clavus had placed in northern Greenland.

In its long and turbulent history, Karelia has been partly Finnish (and Swedish-Finnish) and partly Russian, and its people were notoriously slow to accept Christendom. It appears that Clavus was aware of at least some of this and of the threat which the Karelians (Old Norse: kirjálar[7]) represented to the northern part of Norway, and he had evidently also heard that northern natives posed a threat to the Norse Greenlanders. He conflated the various rumours on his map, as did the 'Vienna texts', which state that the Greenland peninsula 'reaches down from the north, an inaccessible land, or unknown, because of the ice. Even so, as I have seen, the heathen Karelians continually descend on Greenland in huge numbers, no doubt coming from the other side of the North Pole.'[8] Pretending that he had been to Greenland (which he certainly had not) and had observed the Karelians menacing the Greenland Norse, Claudius Clavus combined the concept of a spherical world with a northern tradition, at least two centuries old, that envisioned Greenland connected by land to both sides of the Eurasian continent. Because he also shared his contemporaries' notion that the continent's northeastern portion did not extend much beyond the Kara Sea, he envisaged those Karelian infidels as having travelled a relatively short distance eastward from their homeland before spilling down into Greenland. On that eastward route, they would not even have had to contend with several other northern peoples, with whom the Danish map maker populated the wide land bridge that reached westwards from Wildlappelandi north of Norway to Greenland's eastern shore.

MONSTROUS RACES OF THE FAR NORTH

The Vienna texts mixed northern lore with conventional notions about the world and the monstrous races supposedly found at the outer edges of the world's habitable parts. They described the 'wild Lapps' as savage people completely covered with hair and owing tribute to the Norwegian king, while to the west of them lived 'the small Pygmies, one ell long, whom I have seen after they were captured on the Ocean in a skin boat, which now is hanging in the cathedral in Trondheim. There is also a long craft made of hide, which also was once captured with such people in it.' On the Nancy map, those Pigmei maritimi (coast Pygmies) appear just to the right of centre on the land arch stretching towards Greenland, while Unipedes maritimi (coast Unipeds) live farther west along that same shore. Unipeds (described by Pliny as 'the Umbrella-foot tribe, because in the hotter weather they lie on their backs on the ground and protect themselves with the shadow of their feet') were such a staple of western medieval lore that Old Norse saga writers had a word for them too, namely Einfoetingar. A specimen was spotted by the Karlsefni party, says the 'Saga of Eirik the Red'.[9]

Neither Lapps nor Unipeds interested Storm and Bjørnbo, however. They were looking for Skrælings. Bjørnbo agreed with Storm that both the Karelians and the Pygmies were Greenland Eskimos, although he disagreed with his colleague's supposition that 'careli' was the Eskimo pronunciation of Skræling, which Storm argued would have been pronounced 'Karálit' in Inuktitut – close enough, as far as he was concerned.[10] But Claudius Clavus must surely have known that the Nordic name for Eskimos was Skrælings, Bjørnbo wrote, pointing out that a firm distinction had been made between Karelians and Skrælings in the *Historia Norvegiæ*, which placed the Kiriali among the peoples living beyond Norway towards the east and described the Skrælings as short people whom the Norse had encountered north of their Greenland settlements and who, for lack of iron, used weapons made of walrus tusks and sharp stones. Bjørnbo fully subscribed to the notion that the Greenland Norse had had a catastrophically adversarial relationship with Arctic natives, therefore he believed that the people Claudius Clavus had referred to as 'Pygmies' were simply a handful of Eskimos who had been caught at sea and brought to Norway, whereas the Karelians on the Nancy map and in the 'Vienna texts' constituted dangerous flocks of Eskimos in Greenland.[11]

Once Storm and Bjørnbo had concluded that Clavus had had Eskimos in mind with both 'Karelians' and 'Pygmies' and that both peoples thus were Skrælings, the debate about the origin of Skræling essentially became a linguistic one, and not a finely honed one at that. For example, noting that the meaning of Skræling is uncertain, a modern English scholar suggested that the word may be related to modern Norwegian skræla, meaning 'scream'. Another recent contribution refuted any linguistic relationship between Skrælings and the word Kalallit (which the Greenland Inuit used in describing themselves) or between Kalallit and Karelians; the author preferred a possible link between Kalallit and the Icelandic word klaedast (skin), signifying people dressed in skins.[12]

Such 'sound-alikes' are unlikely to convince linguistic experts at the best of times, however, and in this case they have not proved useful to discovering either the etymology of Skræling or the reason why the Norse applied this name to three different races of people whose most outstanding physical characteristic was short stature, and who lived where, to the medieval mind, the West met the East.

People familiar with Old Norse as well as with modern Norwegian have proposed a possible etymological link between 'Skræling' and the modern Norwegian word skral, used about people or objects in inferior condition.[13] Although that explanation runs against commonly accepted rules for vowel changes and consonant doubling in Old Norse, it is a good fit if one goes back to Ari's matter-of-fact first use of a word he had first heard spoken when his uncle Thorkell told about the natives the Norse had encountered in Vínland. It also links up with the Pygmies to whom Claudius Clavus assigned a place on the land bridge to Greenland. Although the Skrælings were unlike any other races known from long-distance Norse trading and Viking voyages – to the 'blue men' of North Africa, the Slavs and Balts of Novgorod and the Abbasid Muslims of Baghdad – they already had their assigned place in European lore, and prominent people among the Norse would have known their name: Pygmies.

No explanation would have been needed in either Greenland and Iceland, because Skræling(j)ar was a direct Old Norse translation of Pygmæi (Pygmies), used specifically about one of the monstrous races assigned to the extreme edges of the world, first by the authors of Antiquity and then perpetuated in the medieval Christian canon. Skræling(j)ar were the small people who constituted the least threatening and most evolved of the monster races, and who lived on the far northeastern fringes of the habitable world as imagined by knowledgeable Europeans – Eirik the Red, Thorfinn Karlsefni and other leading figures in the two Vínland sagas among them.

Knowledge of general lore was neither limited to people with formal learning nor the monopoly of professed Christians. While Eirik's wife was credited with having a small church built at their Greenland farm, Eirik the Red was reportedly a heathen when he emigrated to Greenland and essentially remained so until his death, but he and his circle would nevertheless have shared in the ideas circulating among their converted friends elsewhere.

THE WEST HAD FINALLY MET THE EAST

Given the geographical and anthropological ideas circulating early in the eleventh century, the Norse had every reason to believe that in their Vínland ventures, they had sailed far enough west to reach a part of the Far East accounted for in principle, but still unexplored by other Europeans. And when they finally met the inhabitants of that alien shore, they clearly found them looking and acting like human beings, but they were none the less regarded as inferior compared with the high standard the Norse believed set by themselves. Moreover, the indigenous people both looked and lived much as the legendary Pygmies were said to look and live. Originally relegated to the outer edges of the Mediterranean region in which the Homeric poem the *Iliad* (about 800 BC) took place, since the time of the Roman historian Pliny the Elder (AD 23–79) the Pygmies had been seen as elusive hunter-gatherers occupying cave or dirt mound dwellings in cold, mountainous lands far to the alien northeast.[14] Moreover, they were described as small, dark-haired and olive-skinned, therefore Eirik the Red and his circle could reasonably believe that they had met the legendary Pygmies. Ari, who wrote his report in the Norse vernacular, used the translation Skræling(j)ar fully understanding its meaning, and the anonymous author of the 'Saga of Eirik the Red' showed himself equally well versed in medieval myths when he had Thorvald Eiriksson killed by a Uniped's arrow, while the natives threatening Karlsefni and his men at Hóp were described as men who 'were small and evil-looking, and their hair was coarse; they had large eyes and broad cheekbones'.

Other evidence that Skrælings and Pygmies were one and the same to the medieval mind occurs in surviving fragments of the English work *Inventio fortunata* (circa 1360) and its implied connection with the Norwegian priest Ívar Bárdsson, who returned to Bergen in 1364 and reported on twenty-three years spent in Greenland. The name of the *Inventio*'s author is not known (but we do know that it was not Nicholas of Lynn, as has so often been postulated); we owe the surviving passages of the *Inventio* to the traveller Jacobus Cnoyen of 's-Hertogenbosch, who was present in Bergen in 1364, and to a 1577 letter to the English polymath John Dee from the Dutch cartographer Gerard Mercator, who had read Cnoyen's account, and whose letter Dee then translated and annotated. Mercator observed that only twelve miles separated Norway from the 'Province of Darkness' belonging to the Great Khan (northeast Asia). 'North Norway stretches as far as the mountain range which encompasses the North Pole... Near here, towards the north, those Little People live of whom there is also mention in the *Gestae Arthuri*', and from that remote region eight people reportedly came to Norway in 1364, including a priest with an astrolabe. The priest told the Norwegian king that an English Minorite and good astronomer from Oxford had arrived in 'these Northern Islands [Greenland]' in the year 1360.

The Minorite gave an astrolabe to the Greenland bishop's officialis (at that time Ívar Bárdsson) in return for a Bible, before continuing north on the voyage of exploration which he later described in his work *Inventio fortunata*, which had evidently been available to Cnoyen. Reportedly blocked by the mountain range surrounding the North Pole, the friar had resumed his voyage, now clearly heading westward across the Davis Strait. He found no habitation 'except on the east side where in that narrow land (isthmus)…there were 23 people not above 4 feet tall'.[15]

To any medieval European, that 'east side' represented the ultimate transatlantic 'west' – even after Martin Frobisher's 1576–78 voyages to Baffin Island, the Canadian Arctic above Frobisher Strait was still thought of as northeast Asia. The 'Little People' the friar saw were most likely Thule Eskimos on the southeast Baffin coast, where there is a relatively large concentration of medieval Thule house ruins, and where the tiny, fourteenth-century Thule carving of a Norse person was found (Chapter Four). Mercator noted in his letter that he assumed that these natives were Pygmies – '*Pygmæi credo dicti*'.[16] When the English friar and Ívar exchanged gifts in Greenland, their discourse would very likely have touched on the natives in those northern regions, and because their conversations would have taken place in Latin, any reference to *Skræling(j)ar* on Ívar's part would have had to employ the word Pygmæi.

The equation of 'Pygmies' with 'Skrælings' was not to last. The splendid 1550 manuscript map by the Dieppe priest Pierre Descelier shows Pygmies in the eastern Canadian interior and 'screlinges' along the south coast of a Greenland visually linked to Eurasia. Mercator was quick to follow suit in his 1569 world map, and for a long time thereafter, Pygmies and Skrælings were two separate peoples in the cartography of the North American-Greenlandic Arctic.[17]

NORSE INTERACTION WITH ARCTIC NATIVES

Ívar gave his oral report in Bergen in 1364, but the earliest extant version of his 'Description of Greenland' is a seventeenth-century copy of the presumed early sixteenth-century transcription made for Archbishop Valkendorf of Norway (Chapter Eleven). It is in Danish, and there is no mention of Pygmies, only of 'heathens' and 'Skrælings', in the report's description of an expedition to the Western Settlement with the ostensible aim of saving the Norse colonists there from heathen Arctic natives threatening them.[18] It is not surprising that when later historians read Ívar's description, it suggested to them that the Thule people represented the ultimate threat to the Norse Greenlanders' existence. That perception was further exacerbated by seventeenth-century works such as Björn Jónsson's *Greenland Annals*. Earlier written sources do not create that impression, however, and the archaeological record to this day shows no sign of any such Doomsday violence against the Norse.[19] Nothing remotely classifiable as a Norse genocide by Arctic natives took place in either the Western or Eastern Settlement.

Occasional skirmishes between Norse and Thule people were probably inevitable, given that both parties habitually carried arms of one sort or another, but by the same token both would have been able to give as good as they got. There is no reason to think that relations between the two peoples were lethally hostile. Norse–Thule encounters would primarily have taken place during Arctic hunts and perhaps while hunting reindeer inland, and in such a huge landscape it would have required unusual circumstances to precipitate a fight distracting both groups of hunters from their business. Moreover, when the Thule people moved far enough south to approach the Norse settlements, they built their winter houses along the outer coasts and made no discernible attempt to push out the Norse, who remained on their farms in the inner fjord areas.[20]

A letter in which the Gardar officialis Eindride Andreasson and the priest Páll Hallvardsson attested that the 1408 autumn wedding at Hvalsey had conformed to church doctrine, revealed that many people had been present at the wedding and that social intercourse and customs were the same as elsewhere in Scandinavia at that time (Chapter Eight). Had there been widespread fear of Thule or other people, the Norse Greenlanders would surely have hesitated to travel long distances to meet their friends at church.[21]

Discoveries of Thule artefacts in Norse ruins, and of Norse items in both Thule and Dorset medieval ruins, indicate that all three peoples had dealings with each other and that they appreciated novel artefacts, which in turn makes some sort of trade very likely. Interactions with the Skrælings described in the Vínland sagas strongly suggest that the natives there took an interest in Norse iron weaponry, and the many samples of Norse forged iron found at Dorset and Thule ruin sites tell us that Arctic natives valued iron from sources besides the meteoric iron they also used. Unlike the Norse, they did not smelt metals (which they cold-hammered), but even small pieces of iron – from a ship's rivet, for example – could be carefully shaped into points for arrows or spears.

Peter Schledermann and his team in 1978 and 1979 found a fascinating collection of Norse items when they excavated medieval Thule ruins on an island off Ellesmere Island. Among their discoveries were a copper blade, pieces of wool cloth of Norse manufacture, chain mail, an iron boat rivet, iron points, an iron knife, pieces of barrels and a Norse carpenter's plane without its iron blade.[22] There is no telling whether these and other Norse-related objects found in the Ellesmere region had been acquired at the same time, or whether they were simply pilfered from one or more Norse ships that had foundered in the High Arctic, but Schledermann assumes that at least some of the artefacts may have been trade items with curiosity value at the time of acquisition, but which were left behind when the hunters moved on because they were not worth taking along.

There is good reason to suppose that there was both indirect and direct trade contact between the Norse and the Arctic natives they encountered in shared hunting areas. So far, the most compelling piece of evidence for direct trade is the piece of a Norse bronze scale which Patricia Sutherland found on a Thule tenting site on the west coast of Ellesmere Island.[23] There is no telling if it had been used for weighing iron, for example, but if the Dorset and Thule people were chiefly interested in obtaining metal, what could they offer the Norse in return? Items that combined novelty with usefulness certainly come to mind with Poul Nørlund's discovery, in a grave inside the Herjolfsness church, of a person buried with his head resting on an oval box with baleen sides and wooden bottom – a ubiquitous artefact in medieval Thule sites from Alaska to Greenland. However, any direct trade up north between the Norse and Arctic natives might well have involved walrus tusks in return for whatever the Norse were able to provide. It could also have included polar bear skins and other desirable export items, or even meat and blubber if the Norse food supplies were running short. Judging from bison hairs and brown bear fibres found at the Western Settlement 'Farm Beneath the Sand', exotic furs were also valued among the Norse for their own use and not just for export. It would in any case have been worth travelling some distance in order to obtain these and other goods through the extensive medieval trade network that operated from the east coast of the Canadian Arctic down into the New England region and for which the Dorset people would have been middlemen from northern Labrador northwards.[24] The Norse were capable of hunting many kinds of animals themselves, but they are unlikely to have gone far enough south in North America to hunt either bison or brown bears at any time during their Greenland colony's existence. Such hunts would have been the province of one or another Amerindian group.

Patricia Sutherland, currently studying Dorset–Norse interaction in connection with her Helluland project, notes that a small soapstone bowl with decided Dorset characteristics, found among Norse remains at the L'Anse aux Meadows site, constitutes the earliest known indication of contact between the Dorset and the Norse. It is also the most southerly evidence of such contact. More significant accumulations of Norse artefacts at Dorset sites occur northwards from Hudson Bay and Hudson Strait up to northernmost Baffin Island. Sutherland has also focused on a number of Dorset carvings with European-like features, such as a long nose, a beard or a long and narrow face.[25] Most are just as meticulously executed as the other small carvings for which the Dorset are famed, but they are so strikingly unlike the Dorset representations of either their own people or of mythical creatures that, whether singly or as part of the multiple-heads carvings for which the Dorset are also known, the observer's eye is immediately caught by the faces immortalised during a period when the Norse Greenlanders were the only Europeans around. The inspiration for Dorset craftsmen to produce Norse likenesses would have had to come from contact close enough for detailed observation and not at the point of a spear.

Recent radiocarbon dates for Late Dorset and Thule presence in the High Arctic during the period of Norse tenure in Greenland suggest that the two Eskimo cultures overlapped until shortly after 1400, which would have provided ample opportunity for the Norse to interact with both peoples. In Dorset settings in South Baffin, Sutherland has found samples of Norse yarn and Norse-worked wood similar to items she had already studied from northernmost Baffin Island and the 'Farm Beneath the Sand', and she considers it a strong possibility that direct trade without intermediaries (rather than long-distance trade or trade involving mutual wary observation but no direct contact) took place from time to time in key congregating spots in Arctic Canada. She cautions, however, that we cannot know the full extent of the story when fewer than one per cent of an estimated two thousand Late Dorset occupation features in the High Arctic have been studied.[26]

We are also a long way from knowing the full story about contacts between the Norse and the Thule people, but excavations of medieval Thule ruins from Hudson Bay north along the Canadian east coast as far as to Ellesmere (as well as in western Greenland) show evidence both of goods exchanged and of Thule artists producing miniature carvings that clearly represent Norse men and women. Thule artists never carved facial features on their human figures, nor did they include arms, but their figurines found in Greenland nevertheless give a sure sense of how they saw the Norse who shared their island with them. The Norse are shown dressed in the working clothes of fishermen-farmers, usually featuring a hood with a shoulder piece, and the impression is again of personal observation under non-threatening circumstances – which is not to say that squabbles never happened.[27]

No evidence has surfaced that the Skrælings in Vínland preserved their impression of their Norse visitors through carvings. Nor have genuine Norse artefacts surfaced down along the North American mainland. If the Vínland sagas are anything to go by, however, the aborigines in that region were just as eager for trade as the natives farther north, and it is anyone's guess how matters might have fared if fear and misunderstanding on both sides had not led to open hostilities that boded badly for the Norse, who were seriously outnumbered by the Amerindians. The numerical balance would have been different in their dealings with Dorset and Thule people, who lived in small groups rather than in villages. Moreover, repeated encounters with Arctic neighbours over several hundred years must surely have produced a measure of intercultural acceptance, if not of real understanding or of a wish to emulate one another's way of life. Archaeologists and anthropologists have so far found no indication that either of the two Eskimo cultures attempted to copy Norse farming or other culture-specific activities, nor is there any reason why they should have done so.

The fact that the Norse persisted in referring to Arctic natives as Skrælings, even when they had come to see the Dorset and the Thule as real humans who functioned effectively both socially and economically, should probably be considered a sign that they continued to regard themselves and their way of life as superior. They had their farms and their churches, their good times and bad, and they suffered no worse from the vagaries of Mother Nature than did Arctic nomads who battled ice and snow most of the year and had no domestic animals to rely on. Furthermore, even when the Thule people had reached as far south as the Norse settlements, they kept to the outer coasts as if they, too, considered separation the natural order of things.

6

RELATIONS WITH CHURCH AND CROWN

The growth of the Roman Church in Greenland, from a handful of Christians among the first generation of settlers to an episcopal establishment at Gardar See that reached its zenith in the thirteenth and early fourteenth centuries, is closely linked with trade and its connections to the ecclesiastical and secular authorities in Norway. The bishops and archbishops in Norway were actively engaged in trade during this period because they received their incomes in naturalia, and the bishops of Bergen eventually became responsible for collecting taxes from Greenlanders and Icelanders for the Church as well as for the Crown. Although shipping between Greenland and Norway was infrequent enough that it probably served both private enterprise and Church business, such records as still exist of Greenland imports were kept by the Church, and that circumstance has given rise to the perception that the Church in particular and contact with Norway in general were the beams upon which the Norse Greenlanders' economic and spiritual well-being rested, but there is no evidence that this perception is justified.

For reasons which Chapter Eight will note, scepticism is also in order concerning the persistent claim that the Greenlanders, like the Icelanders, submitted fully to the Norwegian king's rule after 1264 and became liable for royal taxes in addition to already established church tithes. The manoeuvres involved in ordering – but not necessarily receiving – both secular and ecclesiastical levies are key issues in assessing the vigour of the Greenland settlements, but grasping their impact requires stepping back from nineteenth-century notions about the influence of ecclesiastical and secular authorities on the Norse Greenlanders. Above all, one needs to bear in mind that the Norse Greenlanders left no record of how they viewed their relations with the outside world.

GEOGRAPHICAL INDEPENDENCE

The Greenland colony began as a Norwegian outpost with a solid North European affiliation and with a strong sense of self-reliance among the settlers, who valued their independence from Norwegian kings too distant to constitute the threat they eventually became to the Icelandic republic. Greenland's location, at the very edge of the European sphere, further accentuated a need for self-reliance that was necessarily at odds with efforts at outside control.

An interesting parallel to this situation occurred during the Second World War, when the German occupation of Denmark severed connections between Denmark and its Greenland colony on 9 April 1940. Deprived of Danish imports, the Greenlanders paid for goods bought in the US and Canada with the proceeds of continued mining at Ivigtut of the essential mineral cryolite, and the system of government also changed. A 1925 law which said that, under extreme circumstances, Greenland's two resident governors could take direct control, was put into action. Whereas Greenland had been a protected and very isolated society until 1940, during their period of self-government and independent relations with their neighbours to the west, the inhabitants developed a sturdy sense of self-reliance. When the war was over, a 1946 Danish commission report counselled against any radical reform to the Greenland system, but a grand commission founded to explore changes in the colony's governance reported in 1950 that Greenland was to be a modern welfare society sponsored by Denmark. When home rule was granted in 1979, Greenland became a distinct nation within the Kingdom of Denmark, although still subject to the Danish constitution and to the Danish Parliament's decisions regarding foreign affairs, defence and foreign exchange. Change was inevitable once the constraints of dependency had slackened, and further changes are presently under negotiation, with overwhelming support for further independence voiced in the November 2008 elections.

Equally remote from Europe, and dependent on medieval modes of transportation besides, the Norse Greenlanders never relied on their trade and general communication with the North Atlantic and North Sea communities for their daily physical and spiritual well-being. That was fortunate, because both personal and institutional communications with Norway became increasingly attenuated and finally ceased altogether. Significantly, the first outside institution to break its ties with medieval Greenland was also the last one to have been invited in, namely the Church of Rome.

CHRISTIANITY REACHES THE NORTHWEST ATLANTIC

The path to the Norse Greenlanders' official conversion was both slow and intermittent, but that does not mean that Christianity was unknown to the first settlers. It would in fact have been impossible for Eirik and his companions to ignore the ongoing efforts by rulers in their northern world to edge out the heathen Norse religion and replace it with Christianity.

The Vínland sagas agree that Eirik the Red was a heathen when he led his band of colonisers to Greenland, and the 'Saga of Eirik the Red' also describes his stubborn resistance to his wife Thjodhild's attempts at a formal conversion. As noted earlier, Thjodhild was sufficiently receptive to Christianity to have a small church built at their Greenland farm, and the 'Saga of the Greenlanders' mentions that a Christian from the Hebrides was aboard the settler Herjolf's ship when it sailed from Iceland, where Christianity was just taking hold anew after a period of dormancy. Several of the earliest Norse settlers in Iceland had been Christians, notable among them Aud the Deepminded, the widow of King Olaf the White of Dublin. She was reportedly a devout Christian when she emigrated to Iceland with her entire household.[1] The majority of her fellow settlers were nevertheless heathen, and Christianity appears to have had a tenuous hold for the first century or so until about 981, when a North Icelander who had been converted in Saxony brought home a German priest, Friedrich, to act as a missionary bishop. Before Friedrich left in connection with a violent incident five years later, he had performed a number of baptisms and inspired the construction of at least one church.[2] The next two missionaries who came out to Iceland, in 996, were sent there during King Olaf Tryggvason's reign (995–1000).

A dubious later incorporation with the 'Saga of Eirik the Red' (Chapter Four) claimed that Leif Eiriksson stayed with King Olaf during a visit to Norway, was baptised by him and was subsequently charged with bringing Christianity to the Greenlanders. The king may well have insisted that Leif be baptised, but history does not support an oft-made claim that a devout Leif carried the Christian message to both Greenland and Vínland.

When the monk Gunnleif wrote his story about Olaf Tryggvason, he was no doubt extrapolating from the Icelanders' own experience with King Olaf, who held a number of Icelandic chieftains' sons hostage while he sent two highborn converted Icelanders out to Iceland with the message that the inhabitants would face severe retributions from Norway unless they chose Christianity as their official religion. This the Icelanders did, in 999 or 1000 (depending on how one reads the contemporary calendar), and in so doing they prevented civil war between the Christian and heathen factions in their country.

In faraway Greenland, a similar threat from King Olaf would have had little impact, but the Greenland chieftains would nevertheless have been aware of King Olaf's mandate to their Icelandic cousins and of the fact that Olaf was not the first Norwegian missionary king. Hákon 'the Good' Æthelsteinsfóstri (c. 920–961) had made sincere, but ineffective, efforts to bring his fellow countrymen around while Eirik was presumably still living in Norway. Olaf Tryggvason was killed before he could carry through his own hard-fisted conversion efforts, but King Olaf 'the Saint' Haraldsson (995–1030) succeeded, in large part because he soon came to be seen as having died a martyr's death and his remains deemed capable of miracles. The one thing those three missionary kings had in common was that they had all been converted to Christianity in England and had brought English priests and bishops with them to Norway.[3]

IMPORTED FROM THE BRITISH ISLES

The association with England was a natural one in the North Atlantic and North Sea context. The forerunners of the flexible, clinker-built Viking ships already existed around the year 300, and at least two centuries before Vikings in their square-rigged sailing ships descended on Lindisfarne and other hapless British locations, Norsemen in large, oceangoing rowing vessels had apparently made peaceful trading voyages to the Continent and, quite likely, to the British Isles, adding to their store of exotic goods.[4] The more impressionable among the visitors would also have got their first whiff of Christianity, which had become well established since Saint Augustine of Canterbury arrived in 597 to push back the heathen faith of the Saxon conquerors in an uphill battle to which Irish monks added the needed push.[5] With Church organisation came cathedrals and monasteries of whose existence and wealth the Norse had clearly taken note, for when Viking raids began in earnest, such establishments ranked high on the marauders' list of targets.

Some Vikings had let themselves be baptised or at least prime signed while abroad and, despite Adam of Bremen's conviction that the archbishopric of Hamburg-Bremen had been the instrument that vanquished heathendom in the Far North, England in particular seeded the spread of Christianity to Norway, Iceland and Greenland. Adam was at least partly right, however, in his grudging admission that 'Christianity of late has also winged its way' to those people who 'are green from the salt water ... and live in the same manner as the Icelanders'.[6]

Olaf Tryggvason and Olaf Haraldsson imposed English-inspired, organised Christianity on Iceland, and when the new religion gradually reached Greenland it reflected 'an Anglo-Norwegian tradition with a Celtic basis', as evidenced by Norse Greenland church architecture.[7] The Celtic influence is especially visible in the circular dikes surrounding a number of Greenland churches with graveyards. Outside Greenland, circular or ovoid graveyard dikes are found in Iceland, the Faeroes and in Celtic regions in Ireland and the British Isles.[8] There are several possible sources of Celtic influence on the Greenlanders, starting with the fact that so many of the early settlers came from Iceland. A recent study of mitochondrial DNA in the modern Icelandic population found much of this maternal genetic material pointing not just to Norway, but to parts of the British Isles where the Norse had settled, and where they had captured slaves both before and after the Icelandic settlement began. A Celtic element thus seemed to form a salient part of the Icelandic gene pool studied, but the investigators cautioned that it was too soon to say with assurance where the early settlement females originated. There are also literary and archaeological indications, however, that many early settlers in Iceland had spent a generation or two in Ireland, Scotland or the Scottish Isles, therefore Icelanders with a Celtic genetic inheritance would not be unexpected, nor should one disallow an equally eclectic population mix in Greenland.[9]

ORGANISED CHRISTIANITY

The driving force behind both Olaf Tryggvason's and Olaf Haraldsson's determination to impose Christianity upon their Norwegian subjects was their wish to create a religious, economic and political apparatus useful to the Crown, but this did not come easily in Norway, and it was harder still to achieve in Iceland and Greenland. Differences were bound to develop between the motherland and outposts that had absorbed cultural elements not found in long-established Norwegian traditions, and also between Iceland and Greenland there were notable differences in how they responded to Norwegian efforts to impose centralised control. A key piece in the royal plans was the construction of local churches, which eventually could be placed under episcopal control, but this approach did not suit the Icelanders and Greenlanders. They built private churches on their farms when Christian worship replaced heathen ceremonies, and they retained control of those churches.

During the first century or so of the Greenland colony's existence, there is no record of ordained priests going out there to serve as missionary bishops with the power to ordain more priests. The Icelander Eirik Gnúpsson, who went to Greenland in 1112 with the title of bishop, may therefore have been the first ordained priest arriving for professional purposes, but he had no specific ranking in the Church hierarchy and is altogether an enigmatic figure. His place in Norse Greenland history is nevertheless assured because six different annals report that he went to 'search for' Vínland in 1121, after which time nothing was heard of him again.[10]

For several reasons, Bishop Eirik's Vínland enterprise has been the source of fierce debate both before and after the unveiling of Yale's *Vinland Map*. First of all, there is the expression 'search for'. The annal entries use the verb leita, which means 'go in search of' or 'go and find'. It is just as ambiguous in Old Norse as it is in modern English, because it does not indicate how much the searcher already knows about where to focus his search. Secondly, there is Bishop Eirik's stated goal of reaching Vínland, a location which by that time was tinted with myth, given the Greenlander's decision to concentrate on American regions farther north. Had the bishop merely heard the place favourably mentioned while still in Iceland or during his years in Greenland, or did he and his crew actually know where they were going? Thirdly, what was the reason for his expedition, which obviously must have involved others besides himself? And last, but certainly not least – did Bishop Eirik simply hope to make a profit from his voyage, or did he wish to offer his professional services to one or more small groups of Norse on the other side?

We will never know the answer to any of those questions. What is certain is that Bishop Eirik did not return to Greenland, and that when there had been no news of his whereabouts for three years – the traditional Norse waiting period when long-distance travels were involved – the Norse Greenlanders took matters into their own hands.

They had long been aware of Christianity's potential as a power tool. It was no coincidence that, despite Eirik the Red's dyspeptic view of the new religion, the first church in Greenland was built at Brattahlid and not on some other farmer's property, and that a larger church soon succeeded Thjodhild's church on Brattahlid land. Eirik understood power, and so did his successors. Although the 'Saga of the sworn brothers' (whose action takes place in the early eleventh century) says that the Althing or Annual Assembly was by then held at Gardar in Einarsfjord, not at Brattahlid, the mid-fourteenth-century account by the Norwegian priest Ívar Bárdsson claims that at that time, the 'lawman' still lived at Brattahlid.[11]

The lawspeaker/lawman called and presided over the Althing. Around 1123, the powerful farmer Sokki Thorsson was both the chieftain at Brattahlid and the lawspeaker, and he summoned the general assembly that voted to have Greenland made a proper episcopal diocese. The arrangement would more than fill the gap after the missing Bishop Eirik, because Sokki and his peers stood to gain financially from having a bishop and regular clergy in their country. Tithing to church owner-chieftains had been mandatory in Iceland for about twenty years by this time, and if the Greenlanders emulated the Icelanders, church owners might be entitled to as much as half of the tithes – one-fourth for the upkeep of the church building and one-fourth to the priest, who very often was the farmer himself or a member of his household. The bishop and the poor would supposedly share the remaining half.[12]

As told in 'The Tale of the Greenlanders', Sokki persuaded his fellow farmers to agree that they would share the cost of a bishop and that his son Einar should sail to Norway and petition King Sigurd 'Jerusalem-Farer'. In order to grease the Norwegian authorities and convince them of the Greenlanders' ability to support a bishop, Einar reportedly brought along plenty of walrus tusks and hides as well as a live polar bear, which King Sigurd evidently found acceptable.[13]

GREENLAND BECOMES A DIOCESE

Einar Sokkason secured his bishop in 1124, a Norwegian clerk named Arnold, who was consecrated in the Danish province of Lund. (The Norwegians did not get their own archdiocese until 1152, when the English-born papal legate Cardinal Brekespeare consecrated Archbishop Jón of Nidaros.) Bishop Arnold and Einar then left for Iceland, where they spent the winter of 1125–26, giving Icelandic annalists occasion to observe that three bishops had been present at the Icelandic Althing that year. The newly minted bishop and the son of the chieftain at Brattahlid no doubt also enjoyed the society of leading lay Icelanders. Once Arnold arrived in Greenland in 1126, he stayed until he was succeeded in

Greenland by Bishop Jón knútr around 1150 and returned to Norway. He was not idle for long; he became the bishop of Hamar in 1152.[14]

With Bishop Arnold's arrival, Gardar became the bishop's seat, but this should not be interpreted as a transfer of actual ownership of the whole farm. Rather, the owner of Gardar may have found the prestige of hosting the new bishop sufficient reward for turning over a portion of his farm to him as a kind of micro-Vatican City – an interpretation the archaeological picture also suggests. Some fifty ruins from the Norse period are scattered on the Gardar plain, but all are not necessarily contemporaneous with each other, nor has it been established which structures postdate the arrival of the bishop and what the function of each one may have been. Among the most visible Gardar ruins now are the remains of the buildings directly associated with the episcopal see (Fig. 11), including the bishop's personal dwelling, a large storage barn, a stable with space for some hundred animals and several smaller service buildings. There are also the remains of an extensive irrigation system fed by dammed-up lakes in the hills above, and the natural spring that supplied the bishops' well is still in use today.

The centre of the episcopal establishment was the cruciform cathedral dedicated to St Nicholas, the patron saint of seafarers. Its foundations are

Fig. 11   An August sky looms above massive stones left from the medieval bishop's establishment at Gardar in southwest Greenland

still visible today, but the remains one sees with the naked eye now are not of the church in which Arnold would have performed his services. The current archaeological reading of the church site appears to be that the cruciform church we see outlined today represented a thirteenth-century expansion of a Romanesque church constructed in the twelfth century. The Danish archaeologist Mogens Skaaning Høegsberg, author of a lucid and comprehensive account of these knotty problems, suggests that his recent reinvestigation of the church ruins also leaves room for the possibility that a later diminution of the cruciform church may have taken place, either to deal with dilapidations or to have the cathedral follow the latest architectural fashion abroad.[15]

Nobody knows the name of the Gardar farm's owner either in 1126 or later, but he likely had a direct or lateral connection to the first settler, Einar, who had come out with Eirik the Red and whose son later married Freydis Eiriksdaughter. The farm must have continued to prosper, because it remained one of the four main trading centres in the Eastern Settlement, obviously aided by accumulations of tithe goods but, as evidenced by a large festal hall of the same late date as the ones at Herjolfsness and Hvalsey, also continuing well past the last resident bishop's death in 1377 or 1378.

Bishop Arnold had the good, stiff bristles of a new broom and a keen sense of personal authority, which he augmented by staying on good terms with such local power mongers as Einar Sokkason and his father at Brattahlid, and presumably with the farmer at Gardar. The bishop also had a keen appreciation of money and played a major part in the central controversy in 'The Tale of the Greenlanders', in which some men hunting on the east coast found a cache of valuables in a deserted place near a ship and its dead Norwegian owners. Bishop Arnold encouraged the hunters to turn over much of this treasure to the church at Gardar so that masses could be said for the dead men's souls, and the rest of the loot was distributed among the finders, as was customary. When enraged Norwegian heirs sailed to Greenland to demand their money, the bishop stood firm and counted on Einar Sokkason and his father to support him. Einar and several others lost their lives in the protracted quarrel, but Bishop Arnold weathered the crisis so well that it did not even prevent his later advancement in Norway, where the tale had been told by the foiled heirs and their men.

About Arnold's successor, Jón knútr, we know little more than that his nickname meant knot or fist. Some thirty years after his arrival in Greenland he was succeeded by a second Bishop Jón, this one with the sobriquet smyrrill or sparrow-hawk, who had obtained the position after the Norwegian archbishop's first choice, the Icelandic priest Ingimund Thorgeirsson, had declined the honour. Ingimund nevertheless ended up in Greenland whether he liked it or not. Around 1189–90, he was Iceland-bound from Bergen aboard the ship *Stangarfóli*, when it was wrecked on Greenland's desolate east coast. The wreck was discovered in 1200 by Norse hunters, who also found the skeletons of six men and the undecomposed body of Ingimund Thorgeirsson. Next to Ingimund lay wax tablets with runic inscriptions that revealed the story of his death from starvation. The service over Ingimund's remains may well have been performed by Jón smyrrill himself, who had arrived in Greenland in 1189 after stopping in Iceland to meet Bishop Brand of Hólar and the aging Bishop Thorlak of Skálholt. He may also have picked up some suggestions about how to treat his flock-to-be, because Thorlak had become the first Icelandic bishop to demand that the churches and their income should belong to the Church, rather than to the chieftains. The issue was not settled for at least another 120 years in Iceland, however, and there is little reason to suppose that it was ever settled in Greenland, however inspired the new Greenland bishop may have felt by his Icelandic colleague.[16]

When Jón smyrrill arrived at his see, an episcopal farm and a cathedral of sorts already awaited him, but he had his own ideas about what was due to the Gardar See and to himself, and he may well have been behind the expansion of the St Nicholas Cathedral. Although no match for the ambitious ecclesiastical edifices going up elsewhere in Europe at that time, its cruciform structure made from the local red sandstone and with moulded soapstone trim differed dramatically in both size and shape from the surrounding stone-and-turf houses. The new cathedral also featured windows of opaque, greenish glass and had a separate bell tower, and a path of huge sandstone slabs led all the way from the sacristy to the main door of the episcopal dwelling, suggesting the importance given to formal processions. During excavations at Gardar in 1926, the skeleton of a strongly built man, buried with a bishop's gold ring and a fine crozier made of ash wood and carved walrus ivory, were found beneath the floor of the north chapel. The assumption at the time was that the remains were of Jón smyrrill, but a carbon-14 dating undertaken many years later gave an approximate date of around 1272 (1223–90), a time span that could accommodate several bishops. What is undisputed is that Jón smyrill spent the year 1203 in Iceland visiting his friend Bishop Páll Jónsson of Skálholt and then went on to Norway and Rome, and that he probably spent a few more years back in Greenland before he died in 1209.[17]

We may assume that this second Bishop Jón made an impact on the Norse Greenlanders' Christian practices, but the old ways were far from dead at Gardar, as Poul Nørlund discovered more than eighty years ago. Right outside their cathedral wall, in soil brought in to provide sufficient fill for a graveyard, the Norse had carefully buried more than twenty walrus mandibles with the teeth extracted. The jaws were still undisturbed when Nørlund found them, and they impressed him as having served some ritualistic or religious purpose. A much later discovery of an ox skull arrangement on an early Norse farm in North Iceland similarly indicates an attempt to placate a different god than the one served by the Gardar bishop. In addition, two careful arrangements of walrus mandibles – also with the teeth extracted – have been found on Willows Island, off the south coast of Baffin Island. On neither side of the Davis Strait have the Dorset or Thule people been known to make ritual assemblages of walrus mandibles, but there is no doubt about who had arranged the skulls at Gardar, nor about the heathen impetus behind the enterprise. Perhaps the Willows Island arrangements should also be attributed to Norse Greenland hunters hoping to please Lady Luck.[18]

During the expansion of the Roman Church in Greenland, an Augustinian monastery was founded in Tasermiut fjord and a Benedictine convent in Uunartoq fjord, each with a church attached. Benedictine nunneries were founded in the twelfth century in Iceland and Norway, and there is no reason why Greenland should have been different in this regard, nor is there any reason why the Greenland nunnery and monastery would not also have served as retirement homes and hospitals. When Nørlund and Roussell examined the church thought to be part of the monastery, they suggested a date of about 1200 for its construction. The nunnery's church, graveyard and large farm were excavated by C. L. Vebæk, who estimated the church to have been a relatively recent one from around 1300, but with signs of at least one earlier church on the site.[19] Beyond those observations, it needs noting that through no fault of the archaeologists and the technology available to them at the time, information on both ruin sites is as spotty as our knowledge about communal life there is nonexistent.

GREENLAND PRIESTS

By the time Jón smyrrill died, a number of churches and small chapels existed in the two Greenland settlements, but there is no way of knowing how many priests there were to serve them. Among the thirteen Eastern

Settlement church sites located by 1989, there were several small churches with round or oval churchyards from the early period, which Vebæk believed 'undoubtedly belonged to the very farms near which they were situated'. Because they are not named in Ívar Bárdsson's report or in other lists of Greenland churches, they were probably not parish churches, but chapels without a regular priest attached. Priests may in any case have been in short supply in several parts of the entire Norwegian archdiocese, because the pope admonished Archbishop Thorir in 1206 that if a dying infant was anointed with spit on the forehead and chest and between the shoulders, just because a priest and holy water were not available, it still did not constitute a proper baptism.[20] Under such difficult conditions, a priest might have charge of several churches and chapels – a practice well known elsewhere in Europe at the time.

Homilies from twelfth-century Iceland show clearly that the clergy there kept in touch with mainstream European Catholicism. Jón smyrill's friend Bishop Páll had gone to school in England, for example, and Bishop Thorlak had studied in Paris and at Lincoln for six years. The Mass and other services were conducted in Latin, although sermons in the Icelandic vernacular were not unknown.[21] Nothing is known about the church services in Greenland, nor about the educational background of Greenland bishops and priests. Greenland may not always have attracted those with the brightest prospects in Norway, however. It also needs to be said that in neither Norway nor its Atlantic outposts did gentle scholarship and Christian instruction exert undue influence on the congregations. Instead, papal letters from the opening years of the thirteenth century suggest that being a Norse priest or bishop was a risky business. In 1202, for example, Bishop Bjarni of Orkney's tongue was cut out on orders from Earl Harald of Orkney, and in 1206 a troubled Innocent III wrote to the Norwegian archbishop about priests in the Nidaros archdiocese who engaged in lay business, went to war, spilled blood and removed their ecclesiastical habit. In Iceland, bloody controversies, begun in 1203 between powerful northern farmers and the bishop of Hólar, culminated in 1237 with the bishop's seeking refuge with the famous saga-writer Snorri Sturluson, while the bishop's supporters were driven out of Hólar Cathedral and killed by his enemies. Two chieftains took over the bishop's farm, fields and tithes and forced the remaining priests to conduct services.[22]

During such a violent age, it would be surprising if the clergy and laity in Greenland were unfailing exemplars of sober deportment. Nor can the increasing intervals between resident bishops have helped matters. Three years passed between Jón smyrill's death and Bishop Helgi's arrival at Gardar around 1212, after the customary stopover in Iceland on the outbound voyage. We know nothing about Helgi's tenure in Greenland, but after his death in 1220 there was an interval of fourteen years before his successor, a man named Nicholas, was consecrated in 1234 and finally arrived at his see in 1239, only to die in 1242.[23] During these extended gaps between episcopal appointments, priests would have found it difficult to maintain their authority over the powerful laymen on whose farms the churches were located, especially after a decline in church construction suggests diminishing lay enthusiasm and respect for the Church hierarchy. Some of the bigger Eastern Settlement churches were built in the late twelfth or early thirteenth century, and no church appears to have been built later than about 1300, when the famous Hvalsey church was erected. The youngest of the three churches found in the Western Settlement dates to about 1300.[24]

A documented shortage of qualified people in Norway was one possible reason for the growing difficulty of finding Gardar bishops – and probably also priests – ready to serve far from home.[25] Growing Norwegian indifference to the Atlantic colonies, exacerbated by King Hákon Hákonsson's and Skuli Bárdsson's struggle for supremacy in Norway, is another likely explanation for a shortage of Greenland churchmen; the chaos created by the feud between Hákon and Skuli certainly influenced church appointments in Iceland. When the bishops of Hólar and Skálholt both died in 1237, the Icelanders quickly made their replacement choice, but their candidates were scuttled by the Norwegian archbishop in favour of his personal choices. Once the two new bishops had been consecrated and sent on their way, they were on their own, however, for when the Hólar bishop complained that he was treated with disrespect because nobody could tell from his hands and head that he was a bishop, the archbishop tartly responded that his own duty was to consecrate the bishops in his province, not to equip them with ring and mitre.[26]

Greenland was probably lower still in Archbishop Sigurd's priorities. Such an attitude would have forced the Greenlanders to make even greater efforts than the Icelanders to influence the Norwegian authorities, should they have wanted to do so, which it is not clear that they did. Power struggles between Norse Greenlandic chieftains and the Gardar bishop, or among the chieftains themselves, could be carried on quite satisfactorily without an eye to Norwegian interference.

ROYAL PRESSURE FROM NORWAY

Much of what we know about those turbulent days comes from Snorri Sturluson's nephew Sturla Thordsson (1214–84), whose long saga about

King Hákon IV of Norway – 'Hákonar saga Hákonarsonar'– was written during 1264–65, just a couple of years after the Icelanders had yielded to Hákon's relentless pressure to make them pay tribute to Norway (see also Chapter Eight). In a textbook example of how closely intertwined the powers of Crown and Church had become, King Hákon sent a cousin of Sturla's to Iceland with the newly (1247) appointed Bishop Heinrek of Hólar and ordered both men to pave the way for submission to the king's rule. Iceland submitted in 1263 to the covenant of union (Gamli sáttmáli) in which the Icelanders were promised peace and noninterference in domestic matters in return for paying taxes and swearing allegiance to the Crown. In addition, six supply-ships were to come from Norway every year unless circumstances prevented them from sailing, which often happened and not necessarily because of the weather.[27]

It has been widely assumed that the Greenlanders submitted to a similar arrangement, but the Danish historian Finn Gad has demonstrated that this assumption is shakily founded on an extrapolation from the Icelandic agreement and on a ludicrous 1568 letter (discussed in Chapter Eleven) from King Frederik II of Denmark and Norway to his supposed royal subjects still living in Greenland, in which he regretted the discontinuation of an 'old agreement' that two ships with supplies were to leave Norway for Greenland each year.[28]

The only other 'evidence' for the Norse Greenlanders' submission to the Norwegian king rests on two oblique statements in 'Hákonar saga Hákonarsonar' and is equally flimsy. According to Sturla, whose information for the saga was entirely second hand, the new Gardar bishop (Olaf) went to Greenland in the summer of 1247 with orders to persuade the Greenlanders to yield to kingly rule, and in 1262, three men returned to Norway after four years in Greenland and reported that the Greenlanders had agreed to pay compensation for murder to the Norwegian king. Sturla named the three men as Odd from Sjoltar, Pál Magnusson and Knarrar-Leif – the latter's a cognomen indicating that he had his own merchant ship.[29] These three men are mentioned nowhere else in the saga or in other sources, however. There is no explanation for who they were, how they had spent their four years in Greenland and how they had learned about a supposed community decision to pay murder compensation to the Norwegian king. One is left with a strong suspicion that the men had simply found it useful to produce a flattering tribute to the Crown.

There is not enough information about Bishop Olaf to tell us if his Gardar appointment was as transparently political as that of Bishop Heinrek's in Iceland, or whether Olaf had been chosen for other reasons and then been charged with carrying King Hákon's demands to the Norse Greenlanders. Olaf's career nevertheless provides a good reason to be sceptical about Norse Greenland's acceptance of Norwegian royal authority and oversight, especially given other developments around that time. Outwardly, the Church retained its vigour in Greenland well into the fourteenth century, with the construction of new churches peaking around the year 1300, as noted, but organisational cracks were appearing in both Norway and Greenland even before Olaf's tenure at Gardar had ended.

Bishop Olaf, who was consecrated in 1246, went to Greenland the next year and seems to have stayed in place until 1262, when he reportedly was shipwrecked in Iceland. It is not clear whether he went straight from Iceland to Norway, or whether he briefly returned to Greenland before going on to Norway. We do know that he was in Norway in the spring of 1267, attending the consecration in Nidaros of a new archbishop, which leads to the conjecture that he stayed on in Nidaros for some years hoping for a more attractive bishopric to come his way. That did not happen; he returned in 1271 to his Greenland flock, who had managed without him for several years, and who probably had responded no better than their Norwegian and Icelandic cousins to news of relentlessly increasing church taxes and tithes. He died in Greenland in 1280.[30]

THE SEA WAS STILL THE HIGHWAY

No sources enable us to guess how Olaf discharged his episcopal duties while he resided at Gardar, but it is clear that he had no compunctions about being absent and was not afraid of long and dangerous trips by sea. His several voyages also serve as a caution against the nineteenth-century trap of thinking that unless a voyage was noted down somewhere, it never took place. Greenland was no maritime King's Cross, but many more ships plied the sea lanes between Norway and Iceland, and between Iceland and Greenland, than those that earned a written mention because the crew had sailed on a prominent errand, for instance, had been shipwrecked or had got themselves in trouble otherwise. It is also useful to keep in mind that private trading voyages directly between Greenland and Norway, with no stopover in Iceland, would have been of little general interest to Icelandic annalists, and that merchants were unlikely to profit from a direct exchange of Greenland commodities for the same Icelandic staples the Greenlanders already enjoyed at home.

If Bishop Olaf spent a couple of years in Greenland again after being shipwrecked in Iceland in 1262, there may or may not be a connection between him and a ship coming from Greenland that was wrecked at Hitarness in western Iceland in 1266. That ship belonged to the Greenland bishop, according to the somewhat unreliable *Greenland Annals*, whose seventeenth-century compiler, Björn Jónsson from Skarðsá, also noted that a Greenland priest named Arnold had been aboard, having just been made chaplain to King Magnus Hákonsson. This Arnold had received a letter from another Greenland priest, Halldor, with a report that some people had been farther north in Greenland than any before them and had seen signs of Skrælings, but had not encountered the Skrælings themselves. Another expedition, sent by Greenland clerics, had supposedly gone even farther north to have a better look around, although without going ashore, before returning to Gardar.[31]

Three questions present themselves: Did Halldor intend for his priestly colleague Arnold to bring this report to King Magnus because the northern expeditions had been instigated by the Crown? Is there any link between this story and the tale in 'Hákonar saga Hákonarsonar' about the three Norwegians who returned home from Greenland in the autumn of 1264 after an absence of four years? Finally, assuming that the reports of these two expeditions have a factual basis, did Bishop Olaf have a hand in them?

Quite likely, the Greenlanders thought that they owed the Norwegian king nothing for as long as they were in their own country, and the Gardar bishop would not have been in a good position to go against the farmers who provided his living. Nevertheless, the saga's statement that the Greenlanders agreed to pay the Norwegian king compensation for murder committed in their own country, has been interpreted as evidence that the Greenlanders submitted completely to King Hákon, in which case it is conceivable that before Bishop Olaf knew about King Hákon's death in 1363, he went to Norway seeking praise for helping to bend the Greenlanders to the Crown's will. As noted above, however, Olaf's lengthy stay in Nidaros suggests that the real purpose of his Norwegian trip was to put himself forward for a bishopric nearer his home, therefore he would at least have been aware of the need for royal consent to the appointment of bishops and archbishops.[32]

SMALL ROYAL IMPACT ON GREENLAND

Effective kingly rule in Greenland would have required a locally resident royal ombudsman, but only two surviving sources mention a royal ombudsman for Greenland. Both date from the last quarter of the fourteenth century, and neither tells us anything useful about this official's place in the Greenlanders' daily lives. On 20 July 1374, King Hákon VI confiscated some property in Bergen which his Greenland ombudsman had bought despite the king's right of first option, and the ombudsman was then ordered to present himself to the lawman in Bergen within two weeks. This short lead-time shows that this official was actually in Bergen, where he must also have been when he bought the disputed property, so it is questionable if he had spent any time in Greenland at all. In the second instance, a document dated 20 May 1389 and connected with a trial in Bergen, the Greenland ombudsman's name is never mentioned. During the trial, some Icelanders who claimed to have drifted off to Greenland in the early 1380s and to have been forced to trade there against their will, piously noted that the royal ombudsman there had acted in accordance with his duties (Chapter Eight). There is no other proof of that ombudsman's existence than the mariners' say-so.[33] And neither these nor other written sources provide any evidence that a royal covenant similar to the Icelandic one was made with Greenland.

With communications so attenuated that an exchange of messages might take four years, it is doubtful that either the secular or the ecclesiastical authorities in Norway could exercise meaningful control over the Greenlanders. Moreover, royal power diminished steadily in Norway until the middle of the fifteenth century and had already peaked in 1263 when Hákon died. His heir, Magnus Hákonsson 'Law Mender' (†1280), had to cede the Western Isles and the Isle of Man to Scotland when he had been in power for only three years, and it is difficult to see how he could have imposed his will on the faraway Greenlanders.[34] Sufficient oversight by the Norwegian archbishop was equally unlikely and would certainly not have been enhanced by Greenland bishops who absented themselves from their see for years at a time.

TITHES AND TAXES INCREASE

Soon after bishop Olaf's return to Gardar, the Church Council of Lyon decreed that all Christians must pay Six-Year Crusading Tithes in addition to their other tithes. Letters that passed between Rome and Nidaros make it clear that this presented difficulties for the Norwegian archbishop and his bishops. The archbishop complained – with some justification – that Norwegian coinage had little value abroad and that coins were not used at all in some parts of the realm, but Pope John XXI countered that the tithes could be paid in naturalia and converted into gold or silver for shipment down to Rome. Moreover, he permitted the archbishop to appoint 'reliable men' to collect the new Crusading Tithes from Gardar, because the long and perilous voyage to Greenland would prevent the archbishop from going there in person. Two years later, the archbishop reported that while there were indeed great difficulties involved in reaching Gardar, two 'reliable men' had just been dispatched with the power to collect the tithes and to grant absolution to those who had not paid earlier. Early in 1279, Pope Nicholas III wrote that there could be no question of waiving any of the tithes that were due, but that the archbishop would have eight years, rather than six, to collect them.[35]

Just at that time, King Magnus was making major changes with potential implications for the Norse Greenlanders: church taxation was expanded to include every conceivable source of income.[36] Not surprisingly, resistance hardened among those asked to pay.

We can only guess how Bishop Olaf had reacted to the archbishop's two 'reliable men' and their errand, which took place prior to Olaf's death (1280 or '81) and to the expiration of the extended grace period for the Six-Year Crusading Tithes. The Greenlanders must have paid up in some fashion, because the archbishop complained early in 1282 that the tithes from Greenland – oxhides, sealskins, walrus tusks and walrus-hide ropes – were difficult to sell for a 'suitable' price. Unfazed, the pope told the archbishop to sell the regular tithes for gold or silver and send the money to Rome together with the Six-Year Tithes. A turning point had obviously been reached, because neither the king nor the archbishop and his bishops in Norway during this period scrupled to withhold money from Rome if they thought they could get away with it. Lay Norwegians had to be threatened with excommunication if they did not pay. One may therefore reasonably wonder about church discipline and tithing compliance in Greenland in the years following old Bishop Olaf's death, when the Greenlanders had no way of knowing when a replacement bishop might arrive. Had they been aware of the utter confusion in the Nidaros archdiocese during the next several years, they would probably have given long odds indeed. In any event, not until 1288, when the dust had settled and Archbishop Jörund was in place, was Bishop Thord of Gardar consecrated in Nidaros.[37]

After Thord's 1289 arrival in Greenland, he stayed for twenty whole years, which perhaps explains why church construction continued into the beginning of the fourteenth century. He may merely have been reluctant to face the disorganisation in Norway under Eirik 'Priest-Hater' Magnusson (†1299), followed by more confusion under Eirik's brother, Hákon V Magnusson. However, the speed with which Thord reacted, in the summer of 1308, to a letter he received from Bishop Arni of Bergen, suggests that lack of travel opportunities had played a substantial part in the Gardar bishop's unbroken attention to his duties. Clearly assuming that Thord had been out of touch with Norway for a long time, the Bergen bishop wrote that King Eirik had died in 1299, and that five Norwegian bishops had also died during the past few years. Those dead colleagues included the bishop of the Faeroes, who had passed away in Bergen just before Bishop Arni wrote his suspiciously bland letter asking Thord to pray for the dead bishops' souls. With the letter came a generous personal gift to Bishop Thord of a pale blue chaperon lined with black fur and a gown of the same material.[38]

The wealthy Bergen bishop's gift and letter were a thinly disguised invitation to his friend Thord to hurry home, dressed as was proper for a man in his position, and put himself forward for one of the vacant bishoprics. When the Bergen ship returned to Norway in 1309, Thord was on board, and for the next several years, Bishop Arni assiduously lobbied the Norwegian archbishop to have Thord appointed the new bishop of the Faeroes, but in vain. The most Thord achieved was to become a canon of Bergen before he and Arni both died in 1314, by which time the next Gardar bishop had already been consecrated in anticipation of Thord's death.[39]

Gardar See had been left to a steward for six years in 1315 when the new bishop, also named Arni, arrived in Greenland for a tenure that was to be remarkable for its length as well as for several events on his watch. He had been in residence for ten years when Bishop Audfinn of Bergen and his archbishop exchanged letters to discuss the taxes due on Greenland goods that had just arrived in Bergen aboard several private merchant ships. None of the letters mentioned what sort of wares the merchants had brought, however. The last known document specifically mentioning Norwegian import of Greenland walrus ivory in payment of church taxes dates from 1327, when a large consignment of walrus ivory, representing Peter's Pence and Crusading Tithes, arrived in Bergen and was later sold to a Flanders merchant for the equivalent of about 28 pounds of pure silver.[40]

It is surely significant that within a two-year period, the Greenlanders had been able to pay these dues while also making it worthwhile for private merchants to undertake the long voyage. It strongly suggests that when the Greenlanders subsequently ceased to meet the Church's demands, they were not suddenly short of exportable goods for payment, but increasingly felt no need to comply. In both Norway and Sweden there was widespread resistance to church taxes during this period, after several years with very poor harvests in large parts of Europe, but the Greenlanders never cultivated grain for trade or for the payment of tithes, so their reluctance to pay the Church hierarchy abroad must have had different roots.

The explanation for the Norse Greenlanders' attitude probably lies in a deep-seated cultural reservation that appears to have lasted much longer in Greenland than in either Norway or Iceland. In the traditional social organisation which the Norse settlers had brought with them to Greenland, people expected observable value in return for gifts and loyalty to a chieftain. If they failed to obtain this value, they would find a different leader. Put differently: a major reason why the Greenlanders stopped paying tithes and taxes to a distant Church and Crown may have been that further compliance promised precious little in return and little threat of retaliation from either ecclesiastical or secular authorities in Norway.

In Norway, struggles between Church and Crown were on the increase in the first half of the fourteenth century, especially in Bergen, the wealthy hub of ecclesiastical and mercantile contact with both Iceland and Greenland. In 1316 Bergen had not just one, but two royal ombudsmen responsible for collecting taxes and keeping accounts, and they and other servants of the Crown did not submit readily to competition from the Church. For instance, the Bergen bishop complained to his archbishop in 1328 that when he tried to collect tithes for some local property, he had been threatened by the lawman as well as by the sub-ombudsman and the seneschal.[41]

ÍVAR BÁRDSSON'S MISSION

Astute Greenland merchant-farmers would inevitably have been aware of the struggle for the authority to collect taxes of various sorts, therefore it is scarcely surprising that in the second quarter of the fourteenth century, while Bishop Arni resided at Gardar, Norwegian accounts show no further Greenland imports earmarked for tithes and taxes. In the Norwegian tithe collections of 1333, Gardar is not mentioned, and in 1340, the Bergen bishop complained to King Magnus that people arriving from 'the West' would pay their taxes only directly to the Crown, not to the king's fiscal representative, who was now the bishop himself. The Bergen bishop at the time was Hákon Erlingsson, a zealous royal servant who nevertheless did not neglect his own interests, and he soon decided what to do about the situation. The very next year, he sent his priest Ívar Bárdsson to Gardar as his officialis or ombudsman for financial matters. The office as such had existed in Norway since 1290, and now, sixty years later, it finally seemed urgently needed in Greenland.[42] Ívar sailed to Greenland in 1341, carrying a letter in Latin in which the Bergen bishop asked everyone to assist his priest, whose business in Greenland was on behalf of the bishop himself as well as of the Church generally.

This attempt to tighten Bergen's control is both another indication that the Greenlanders were balking at paying tithes and taxes and an example of the increasingly blurred line between royal and ecclesiastical finances in Norway, because Ívar came to Gardar as the ombudsman of the Bergen bishop with a share in the latter's office as royal tax collector. Ívar's 'Description of Greenland' referred to two royal farms in the Eastern Settlement – Foss ('Waterfall') and Thiødhijllestad ('Thjodhild's Place') – but it implied no relationship between these two farms and a royal ombudsman in Greenland.[43] The two documents mentioning a royal ombudsman for Greenland both date from several years after Ivar's return to Norway, which suggests that he may have attempted to establish the office to tighten up tax collection in accordance with Bishop Hákon's wish to separate royal tax collection from the duties of the Bergen bishop. If a local Greenlander had actually been appointed to the ombudsman office by Ívar, the incumbent would in any case have found it more profitable to side with local chieftains than to rely on support and advancement from a distant and increasingly impotent monarch.

It is anyone's guess how Bishop Arni reacted to Ívar's arrival and, soon afterwards, to the news that in 1343, Jón Eiriksson skalli ('the bald') had been consecrated Bishop of Gardar by the Norwegian archbishop, who claimed that he had no idea that old Arni was still soldiering on out there in Greenland. Considering that the ship that brought Ívar to Greenland presumably had returned to Norway with fresh news, such obliviousness seems peculiar at the very least and downright suspicious given the drying-up of Greenland tithes. The nearest explanation is that Ívar had sent back a report about Arni's failure to fleece his flock, and that the report had occasioned Jón skalli's appointment, news of which probably reached Greenland the very next year when the merchant Thord Eigilsson 'sailed to Greenland and the same year returned to Norway with a richly laden ship and much goods'. Old Bishop Arni left Greenland not long afterwards, became Bishop of the Faeroes in 1348 and died that same year. As for Jón skalli, he never came out to Greenland, but stayed in Norway until he went to Iceland as the Hólar bishop in 1357.[44]

Exasperated by Pope Clement VI's latest demand of a Three-Year Tithe from all ecclesiastical offices in Norway, the Provincial Council in Bergen in 1345 asked for a general reduction in Crusading Tithes and a complete exemption for the Faeroes and Greenland. Whatever Thord Eigilsson had brought back from Greenland the summer before may not have made the Norwegian Church authorities sanguine, but the Provincial Council's petition was more likely a sign that the clergy wanted to keep their own money and reasoned that the pope might find it easy to credit such distant communities with inability to pay. It is unlikely that they themselves had given up on those island societies just four years after sending Ívar off to handle Gardar See, particularly when the Greenland knarr had again had a most satisfactory cargo when it stopped in Iceland in 1346 and presumably continued on to Norway.[45]

When the small, anchorless Markland ship with seventeen Greenlanders on board reached Iceland's shores the following year (1347), Icelandic harbours also saw the arrival of thirteen oceangoing ships besides the six foreign ships already in the country. Probably helped along by the large number of foreign visitors, various kinds of non-plague epidemics raged in Iceland that year and the next, but there is no information about whether contagion spread to Greenland.[46] It is certain, however, that Ívar Bárdsson did not succumb to either illness or accident in Greenland, because he returned home in 1364 to social and economic conditions that had been profoundly changed by the Black Death, which struck in Norway, Shetland, the Orkneys, the Hebrides and the Faeroes in 1349 with as much devastation as in England and elsewhere in Europe the previous year. At the peak of the crisis, shipping in the North Atlantic came to a virtual standstill, so that the Skálholt bishop's ship *Thorlakssuðinn*, for example, which had arrived in Norway in 1347 on its annual trading voyage, was unable to sail home again until 1351.[47] Ívar might reasonably have expected to return home after eight or ten years, but the plague's effect on long-distance sailing would have forced a change of plans.

With Bishop Thord gone and no replacement bishop arriving, Ívar was nevertheless fully occupied during his entire stay, although his presence at Gardar was not for the purpose of providing the Greenlanders with Christian tutelage. He was a man of business and had been sent to determine parish boundaries and establish tithing districts that would speed the flow of goods back to Bergen. The parish system was just then being put into effect in both Norway and Iceland, and in Iceland this turned out to be uphill work indeed, because it ran counter to the country's tradition of private church ownership. Transfers of real property to the Church remained mostly nominal even after the passage of new laws of 1278, when the consent of heirs was no longer required for a bequest to a church, and, because wardship over a church was often inherited, the position of the big farmer with a church hardly changed. Laymen continued to administer church property, and the only advantage the church farmers eventually lost, some time towards the end of the Middle Ages, was the right to choose the priest. The individual church farmer's power in Iceland appears to have diminished only when the parish system finally became effective during the fourteenth century and people must have all church services performed by the church to which they owed tithes.[48]

When Ívar Bárdsson arrived to put administrative polish on the Norse Greenlanders, it is unreasonable to expect that Norse Greenland church farmers were eager to give up their ancient privileges, considering how poorly the parish system was functioning in Iceland despite persistent pressure from Norway. Although Ívar's original report on the state of Greenland's churches is lost, the account in its present state is considered a good guide to churches and farm sites in the Eastern Settlement, and its statements about land and tithes 'belonging' to various churches have therefore been interpreted literally as signifying that the Church owned outright about two-thirds of the best pasture land in Greenland by the mid-fourteenth century.

To Thomas McGovern, the large number of cattle and ample pastures said to belong to the big farms with churches suggested that people on the small-holdings eventually were reduced to 'alms status' from the Church in bad times.[49] However, there is a difference between parish boundaries established for tithing purposes and actual ownership of land. A number of passages in the 'Description' concern land that belongs to (hører till) a certain church or such-and-such a church that owns (eger or æger) a specific area. In this case, the expressions 'belongs to' and 'owns' do not refer to land owned by a particular church, but to the congregation belonging to a given parish – the people of a parish 'belong to' the church that has the cure of their souls.

If Ívar in fact had described Church-owned real estate, the Greenlanders would undoubtedly have been in a bad position, but for that to happen, landowners would have had to turn over their land in neat parcels around each church, rather than in the ancient, crazy-quilt pattern slowly stitched together from someone's dowry here, another's bequest there and a gift somewhere else. Instead, the orderly demarcations repeatedly noted by Ívar correspond to the early land-takes and reflect the fact that he merely described sensible parish boundaries, not a society sinking under ecclesiastical dominance.

Ívar returned to Bergen in 1364, and the very next year, Brother Alf from the Munkeliv monastery in Bergen was consecrated as the new Gardar incumbent. The Greenlanders finally saw their new resident bishop in 1368, after which Alf served at his post until he quietly died in

1377 or '78. The news of his demise did not reach Norway until the Icelandic ship *Ólafssúdinn* sailed directly from Greenland to Bergen in 1383.[50] Communications with Norway were thus demonstrably in decline, but the Greenlanders were used to waiting many years for their bishops and could not have anticipated that no more resident bishops would come their way. By the time they had reason to accept this possibility, the Western Settlement was gone, although not in the manner implied by Ívar's 'Description', which gave a picture so dismal that it supposedly explained the removal of that northern community from the Church ledgers, and which was a marked contrast to Ívar's report of prosperity in the Eastern Settlement. The latter's sanguine account of the region's economy, implying the ability to pay proper tithes, was what had prompted the appointment of Bishop Alf.

NO MORE RESIDENT GARDAR BISHOPS

Intractable lay control over churches and trade goods was likely a significant reason why Gardar bishops were increasingly reluctant to live in Greenland. Although corruption and favouritism in the Norwegian Church influenced episcopal appointments, this would not have prevented later Gardar bishops from going out to Greenland if they had thought that this would bring them more wealth and social status than they could command at home. They could function in Greenland only on the inhabitants' own terms, and if those were now unacceptable, the news would soon have spread. Even so, as late as in 1402, Gardar diocese was among the Norwegian bishoprics from which out-of-touch Rome expected papal tithes to be collected.

A number of circumstances outside the Greenlanders' control would also have contributed to the changing situation. The situation was so bad in Norway after a fresh outbreak of the Black Death that in 1371, the archbishop received papal dispensation to ordain and promote twenty men born out of wedlock, as well as ten sons of priests, because the number of ecclesiastics in his see had been reduced to about forty old and decrepit priests.[51] Furthermore, the Church hierarchy in Norway had long reflected the growing contention within the papacy, and the Great Schism beginning in 1378 certainly did not help, nor did the death of King Olaf and the accession of Queen Margrethe.

On hand in Oslo in 1388 for the celebration of Queen Margrethe's assumption of sole power in Norway was Bishop Henrik 'of Gardar' (a Dane), who had been consecrated some time before 1386 – presumably soon after the Norwegian authorities had learned about Bishop Alf's death. He never made any effort to go to Greenland, but spent his time in Denmark and Norway except for a visit to Rome in 1391. By 1394, he was the bishop of the Orkneys, where his predecessor had been killed a few years earlier. Henrik was understandably no keener on going to the Orkneys than to Greenland, but his death in 1396 relieved him of any further career dilemmas.[52]

Confusion grew steadily to the point that just in the period 1431–34, there were four nominal bishops of Gardar. One of the four, Bartholomeus de St Ypolito, was provided with six official letters testifying to his appointment, including one missive addressed to the 'city and diocese of Greenland'.

Underlying the developments that led to the eventual rupture between Greenland and Norway were the politics of the Crown. Hákon VI Magnusson had tightened restrictions on trade both with and among Norway's Atlantic colonies, and his policy was continued by Olaf Hákonsson, who ruled from 1380 to 1387. When Hákon's widow Queen Margrethe – the daughter of King Valdemar of Denmark – took the reins after her son Olaf's death, she steered a tighter course still. She effectively united the three Scandinavian kingdoms by means of the 1397 Kalmar Treaty, at which time she had her young nephew Eirik of Pomerania accepted as her legitimate heir. Subsequently, both Greenland and Iceland were at the mercy of Denmark both economically and politically. The two countries continued to experience royal power differently, but neither was immune to the disastrous turn brought by Eirik's governance after his aunt's death in 1412. His actions caused widespread misgiving in his three kingdoms and forced him to flee from Sweden in 1436 and relinquish his Danish home base in 1438. Throughout that whole period, the last thing on his mind was concern for the Greenlanders' spiritual and physical well-being, and his successors likewise preferred to concentrate on opportunities for prestige and money closer to home.

DID THE GREENLANDERS LOSE THEIR CHRISTIAN FAITH?

If the Church had formed the core of the Greenlanders' existence, their communities would have suffered devastating deprivation during the increasingly long periods when there was no resident bishop, but there is no sign that this was the case. By demonstrating that not only big churches, but large festal halls, were attached to the four most prominent farms in the Eastern Settlement – Brattahlid, Gardar, Hvalsey and Herjolfsness – archaeologists have shown that secular power survived in Greenland for many decades after Ívar's time. The large festal hall at Herjolfsness was built so late that a piece of early fifteenth-century Rhenish stoneware, found in the depth of the foundation, 'lay at such a considerable depth compared with the building that it cannot date from the last Norse period at Herjolfsnes', as Nørlund wrote after his excavations there. The festal hall at Hvalsey is also a late addition, as is the one at Gardar, which is the biggest of the four known halls and which architecturally resembles those at Hvalsey and Herjolfsness.[53] By the early fifteenth century, Greenland had been without a resident bishop for some decades, therefore this late-date evidence of expensive, secular construction again conflicts with the notion of a fatal ecclesiastical stranglehold on the Greenlanders.

The Greenlanders nevertheless seem to have adapted to ritual Christianity without too much struggle. Although the hierarchical chain of ritual sacred power ruptured within fifteen years of Ívar's departure from Greenland, many Christian rituals endured as an ingrained part of Norse Greenland's social fabric long after the last episcopally ordained priest had died. Regrettably, efforts to judge the Greenlanders' deeper religious commitments have often been derailed by interpretations of two fifteenth-century papal letters concerning appointments for ostensible Gardar bishops. Both letters were written at a time when the Greenland Church had already been abandoned by the Church hierarchy for some generations and will therefore be discussed in Chapter Ten, but they also warrant a mention here, because Nicholas V in 1448 referred to 'the fervent piety of the peoples of this island [Greenland]', while in 1492, Alexander VI drew a sad picture of a people abandoned by the Church for so long that they had reverted to heathen practices.[54]

Unfortunately, throughout the whole Middle Ages the Curia's knowledge of Greenland was so flimsy that these letters do not indicate either religious or material conditions in Greenland at any time. Suffice it to say that the Greenlanders had accepted the Christian religion along with everyday church rituals, and that their spiritual life seems to have operated somewhere between 'fervent piety' and 'heathen practices', judging from the mix of pagan and Christian symbols recovered by archaeologists.

In Norse culture, the line between religion and magic as well as between Christianity and heathendom is often blurred, one example being a casting mould for a combined Thor's hammer and a cross, to be used in amulets. In Greenland, the Christian symbols range from simple crosses or runes carved on everyday objects to tombstones and sometimes elaborate crosses and crucifixes found in Norse graves. At the same time, the pragmatic colonists' reluctance to abandon heathen safeguards is also evident, an example being two graves which Nørlund excavated in the nave of the Herjolfsness church. One grave contained a bear's tooth amulet, while the second burial featured grave goods of a sort normally associated with heathen burials. In addition to the Thule-culture oval box noted in Chapter Five, which was placed under the dead person's head and contained some sort of animal substance, there were also the remains of a dagger.[55]

Excavations of the Herjolfsness churchyard uncovered graves dating from the late twelfth century to about AD 1500, but mostly from the fourteenth century and later. Throughout the period, even infants had been buried with as much Christian care as in Europe, wrapped in shrouds and occasionally placed in coffins, and with their heads facing west. There were less favourable conditions for preservation in the Gardar churchyard, but the burial customs there had clearly been similar to those at Herjolfsness. About his Herjolfsness finds, Nørlund wrote emphatically: 'On the whole neither dresses nor other objects bear the stamp of a culture that is degenerating into barbarism.'[56]

Modern archaeologists are increasingly following up on Nørlund's long-ago excavations, but I have yet to hear anyone question the heart of Nørlund's judgment here.

7

FOREIGN TRADE

The Norwegian mid-thirteenth-century work *The King's Mirror* claimed that men who braved the dangers of the voyage to Greenland did so to satisfy their curiosity, to win fame and to gain wealth through a trade from which a good profit might be expected in a place that 'lies so distant from other countries that men seldom visit it'.[1] To believe that this description represented reality is to overlook the work's lavish references to huge monsters, horrendous ice conditions and other impediments to safe and profitable travel in the seas around Greenland – fantasies common in other medieval literature intended to inspire awe about the outer limits of the world most Europeans knew. *The King's Mirror* is not a guide to how actual Greenland-farers approached their undertakings or to the nature of Norse Greenland trade.

Eirik the Red knew that his Greenland settlement would need an economy capable not only of meeting domestic needs, but of producing goods for export. Having claimed the choicest farm site for himself and his family when he explored the inner Nuuk fjord regions during his initial Greenland reconnaissance, he urged the start of the Western Settlement because he saw its northern location's advantage to northern hunts focused on goods for foreign trade. In every way, the Norse Greenlanders' culture relied on the resources found in northern regions. Even the grapes discovered in Vínland took a back seat to sustaining life and trade by well-tested methods.

Exports would pay for grain and honey, or for finished articles of iron and other metals – imports that were not necessary to the colony's survival, but that constituted luxuries for display and for privileged consumption. A fondness for show was an important component of medieval Norse culture, and there is no reason why the Norse Greenlanders should have been different. As for Eirik himself, he would have been aware, furthermore, that controlling the exchange of prestige goods, which could be used as bribes, rewards or other forms of social and political manipulation, would be essential to maintaining his own social and political standing in the new community.[2]

MARKETABLE GREENLAND COMMODITIES

Markets for produce from the Far North had long existed in Europe. Eirik, coming from an ancient trading culture, would therefore have been confident that he and his fellow colonisers could count on foreign buyers for surplus goods, including farm products such as butter, cheese, hides and homespun wool cloth (vaðmál). Indeed, Greenland wool cloth became prized for its quality, and vaðmál generally was so central to the medieval Scandinavian economy that after the union with Norway in 1263, the Icelanders' tax to the Norwegian king was assessed in homespun cloth. A wide variety of articles harvested in the wild would have played at least as important a part in the Greenlanders' economy. Dried strips of walrus hide provided tough, resilient mooring lines that fetched a good price abroad and were also needed for domestic purposes, while meat and blubber from walrus and other marine mammals were used for food and fuel at home. Blubber from sea mammals was also a dependable export article in the unglamorous category, just like wool cloth. In the luxury line there would be tusks of walrus and narwhal, polar bear skins and other furs, eiderdown and falcons.

White gyrfalcons, called Greenland falcons because they were so rare elsewhere, were difficult to catch even in Greenland and worth a small fortune by the time they reached Europe. For example, King Magnus's many petitions to Pope Clement VI in 1347 included a request for permission to send falcons to the Sultan and other countries in order to sell them and pay off the king's debts, and in 1396, the Duke of Burgundy is said to have ransomed his son from the Saracens for twelve Greenland falcons.[3] These and other examples of distinctive treatment accorded the trade in luxury articles suggest that people of high rank were often directly involved in the transmission of choice Arctic items, whether these had been obtained from taxes and tithes or through private trade.

As a special treat in 1276, the king of Norway sent his English colleague three white and eight grey gyrfalcons, a quantity of ermine pelts and a complete whale's head with all the baleen still attached. Edward II of England dispatched a special messenger to Norway to buy hawks and falcons in 1315, and in 1337–40 (just when the Norse Greenlanders were becoming increasingly reluctant exporters to Norway) the Bergen bishop confessed himself unable to provide King Magnus with the white and grey gyrfalcons the king had specifically requested from him and his contacts. The role of Flanders merchants in disposing of walrus ivory and exotic furs and other valuable goods emerges both in the five-year trade treaty which the Norwegian Crown made with Flanders in 1308 and in the 1338 letter which Bishop Hákon of Bergen sent to a contact in Brussels, accompanying his message with a polar bear skin, seven walrus tusks and other prestigious Arctic items. The bishop's letter referred to these articles as 'gifts', but they were clearly a consignment of valuable goods which the bishop wished to have sold on his behalf by an experienced Flemish merchant – again at a time when Greenland imports were becoming increasingly rare.[4]

MARKET FLUCTUATIONS

Walrus ivory was well suited to the luxury trade, and secular merchants and Church authorities alike appreciated both its value in the European market and the fact that the tusks were nonperishable and took up little shipboard space, thus lending themselves to transport over long distances. This Arctic ivory, widely valued by craftsmen for its beauty and the relative ease with which it could be carved, had long served as a raw material for both useful and decorative objects, and being cheaper than elephant ivory in northern Europe was also part of its charm. It was never cheap, however. Even after 1500, when the Portuguese had broken the Muslims' North African trade monopoly and elephant ivory could be shipped directly to Europe aboard Portuguese ships from both African coasts, walrus ivory retained its value, and so did African ivory. The Arabs had never been able to obtain enough elephant tusks to satisfy the demand, and any expansion of the ivory catchment area increased the cost of transportation on the vast African continent, thus adding to the cost of the material, both before and after 1500. Elephant ivory remained a true luxury and a desirable material for objects which lay and ecclesiastical magnates in Europe could use to display their wealth. When the Gothic style became prevalent and artists and craftsmen wanted larger pieces with which to work, they found elephant ivory especially appealing, but that did not mean an end to walrus ivory's attraction among northern Europeans with ancient traditions for its use, nor among craftsmen in the Near and Middle East. The latter actually preferred walrus ivory to other kinds of ivory when decorating knives and other weapons, because when walrus tusks are sliced lengthwise they exhibit a delicate flame pattern.[5]

In northwestern Europe, walrus ivory was still widely used for liturgical and other purposes throughout the fourteenth century, but by about the middle of that century there was an observable change in the material's availability due to diminished supplies from Greenland – a development which is supported by Thomas McGovern's finding that late-phase Norse middens appear to contain relatively fewer walrus elements than earlier ones. The fact that the Norse Greenlanders were no longer collecting walrus ivory in the former quantities was not due to either European disinterest in the product or falling prices for elephant tusks, however. In the Nordic countries, walrus ivory was clearly still appreciated in 1479 when the powerful Icelander Thorleif Björnsson gave the royal governor of Iceland a large sum of silver and a horn made of walrus ivory, to be passed on as a gift to King Hans of Denmark in order to obtain a licence for Thorleif to marry his cousin Yngvild and legitimise his many children by her.[6] Elsewhere in Europe, walrus ivory also remained a coveted commodity well into the Renaissance, and so did narwhal tusks, another Arctic speciality. Although narwhal ivory was too brittle to be suitable for carving, narwhal tusks were peddled as unicorn horns and preserved their reputation for medicinal and magical properties well into the seventeenth century.

Trondheim was the final destination for much of the Greenland walrus ivory that reached medieval Norway through secular as well as ecclesiastical channels. After the foundation of the Trondheim archiepiscopal see in 1152, first-rate craftsmen had created a thriving walrus ivory industry serving both ecclesiastical and secular needs; the famous chess pieces from the Hebridean island of Lewis were very likely made there.[7] Two Norwegian art historians familiar with the products of the Trondheim walrus tusk industry have noted a drop-off in activities around the mid-fourteenth century – a change which they attribute to a lack of interest in walrus ivory once the Gothic style had put a premium on larger pieces of material, which elephant tusks could provide and walrus tusks could not.[8] Exquisite Scandinavian artworks made after that time do not support that assumption, however. Instead, they suggest that walrus tusks, either carved whole or made into elaborate composite works, were still highly valued. Taken together with developments in Norse Greenland during this period, a more convincing explanation for the diminished number of walrus ivory objects in Norway and throughout Europe would be that the steady supply of Greenland walrus tusks had dried up at the source.

As with so much else concerning Norse Greenland, the documentary material is spotty. Much of our sparse information about Greenland exports, particularly of walrus ivory, comes from Norwegian church records, which makes sense, given that tithing is likely to have been a feature from the first in the Greenland Church – it was already instituted in Iceland when Bishop Arnold arrived at his Greenland See in 1126. The Greenland Church reached its zenith during the thirteenth and early fourteenth centuries and for a long time appears to have encouraged Arctic voyages in search of walrus tusks for tithes, but by the mid-fourteenth century, when the Norse Greenlanders became increasingly resistant to paying Peter's Pence and other church taxes, voyages to Norðrseta started petering out, judging from the lack of Norse objects found in the High Arctic and datable to a later time.

In light of recent archaeological research, the notion that the Norse Greenlanders had lost an important market share to elephant ivory, receiving a death blow to their colony's economy, makes no more sense than the long-held conviction that Ívar Bárdsson's 'Description of Greenland' constitutes gospel truth about the end of the Western Settlement sometime around 1350. Excavations of the 'Farm Beneath the Sand' in the Western Settlement demonstrate that the site was finally abandoned around 1400. Moreover, there is evidence that walrus were hunted for local purposes throughout the whole terminal period.[9]

EARLY MARKETS AND TRADE ROUTES

No record exists of how the Norse Greenlanders marketed their export commodities during the first century and a half of their colony's existence. Despite the dearth of written sources there are nevertheless literary hints of early trade connections between Norway and England before 900. For example, there was the 789 event on the English south coast in which a local official insouciantly rode down to greet newly arrived Vikings, mistaking them for some of the peaceful Nordic traders to which the region had become accustomed (Chapter Six). In 'Egil's saga', whose action takes place in the ninth century, we learn that after Egil Skallagrimsson's uncle, Thorolf Kveldulfsson, had helped himself to the so-called Finn tax in northern Norway, his enemies assumed that this treasure would be taken straight to England and sold there. There is also the story about the North Norwegian chieftain and trader Ohthere, who visited at King Alfred's English Court towards the end of the ninth century and described for the Anglo-Saxons his recent voyage around the North Cape and into the White Sea region.[10]

Foresightedly, Ohthere had brought gifts for King Alfred, walrus tusks included among them. One might be forgiven for thinking that Ohthere had several more tusks in his cargo and expected to sell them in England, and that trade was the actual reason for his long voyage south. Collecting tribute with a view to subsequent trade had plainly been behind his voyage past the North Cape, because he did not boast of having killed walrus and fur animals himself during that voyage, only of having extracted tribute from the results of other people's hunts.

Equally important to a discussion of early trade in products of the Far North is Ohthere's description, in King Alfred's Anglo-Saxon translation of Orosius's history, of his visit to a trading centre called 'Sciringes heal' in southern Norway. Ohthere's account of its location and sailing approaches was fairly detailed, but scholars wrangled for years about just what place he had in mind because the received wisdom was that no organised trading centre or town, comparable with Hedeby in Denmark and Birka in Sweden, had existed in Norway before the late tenth century and certainly not in Ohthere's day.

During the years 1950–57, the Norwegian archaeologist Charlotte Blindheim led excavations of thousand-year-old graves near the towns of Larvik and Sandefjord on the western side of the Oslofjord, where natural conditions for a meeting of trade routes had likely been present before the sea level dropped. The results of their investigations were so encouraging that Blindheim and her team widened their search to the surrounding area, and seventeen years later, there was little doubt in anyone's mind that the site, dubbed 'Kaupang' (from Old Norse kaupangr – town or market place) represented a trading centre, and that it very likely was Skiringssal ('Shining Hall') and thus Ohthere's 'Sciringes heal'. But had it really been an early market town, a place that attracted artisans and other year-round denizens?[11]

After more excavations during the years 2000–07, the answer was an unequivocal affirmative. Beneath the farm fields lay evidence for houses, graves, shops and workshops as well as the remains of piers to accommodate shipping. Starting around 780 and petering out sometime in the tenth century, when the growing urbanisation of Tønsberg to the northeast was siphoning off Kaupang's commercial activity, 'Sciringes heal' was a lively centre for Norwegian exports and imports and constituted a vital link in the Viking Age trade routes for raw materials as well as for manufactured objects.

Remains of walrus tusks and soapstone articles at Kaupang spoke of northern produce in transit to wealthy buyers elsewhere and, during the past twenty-five years, archaeological investigations much farther north in Norway have revealed the nature of the trade network that accommodated the exchange of luxury goods along Norway's long coast from very early on. This recent research has also shown Ohthere was not unique but represented just one of the many enterprising chieftains in northwestern Norway whose seats functioned as trading hubs, more than a dozen of which are now known to have existed during the Iron and Viking Ages. Only at Borg in Lofoten have the actual ruins of such a site been uncovered by archaeologists. They found the remains of a chieftain's huge longhouse, almost fifty-five metres long and eight metres wide, dating back to the fifth or sixth century. Just as significant is the Borg site's abundant evidence of the same kind of luxury articles Blindheim and her colleagues found at Kaupang.

The family graves in the Kaupang area, which appear to date mostly from the second half of the eighth century to about 940, were richly equipped with primarily western-style grave goods that had made their way to Kaupang from a large part of the Continent as well as from the British Isles. However, there was also a scattering of silver coins and items that had come from the east. In addition, bits of turned ceramic of foreign origin and shards of glass vessels were discovered, both of a type unknown from Norwegian Viking Age sites other than at Kaupang and Borg. Among the materials gathered from the Kaupang's dwelling area, the archaeologists found a large quantity of very fine ceramics from Denmark and the Continent, of a sort found nowhere else in Norway except at Kaupang and Borg; such material is missing even from the farms located fairly near the Kaupang centre. The foreign silver coins found among the town remains were Kufic, Frankish and Anglo-Saxon, while the artefacts generally point to the south and east. Despite an obviously busy exchange of goods, and despite Kaupang's importance as a collecting and storage point for domestic wares that had come long distances, the market town had no fortifications. Its people had probably relied on the protection afforded by a tricky access from the sea.[12]

Borg and Kaupang have clear links with Ohthere's purveying of Arctic goods to the south, and both places are evidence of a lively general trade in Norway by means of a network that reached far and wide and that would obviously have been part of the practical lore on which Eirik the Red based his own plans for exchanging walrus ivory, lustrous furs and other Arctic goods for foreign luxuries. No Norse archaeological sites in Greenland have yielded evidence of such elegant articles as the ceramics and glassware found at Kaupang and Borg, but nonessentials were brought to Greenland from abroad, and defining the extent and nature of these imports awaits future excavations and scientific progress in capturing tiny samples. Gone forever, though, are imports such as honey and malt, which were happily consumed at the table.

CONSOLIDATION OF THE EUROPEAN MARKETS

Norse trade during the Viking Age had mostly focused on luxury articles that took up relatively little space during transport and lent themselves to large markups – which gave further prestige to the buyer. From the early eleventh century, trade with ordinary consumer goods also increased, and for a century and a quarter more after Eirik had founded his Greenland colony and laid the foundation for foreign trade, merchants in Northern Europe took their cargoes to small markets around the North Sea, including to England. Around 1115–20, for example, the Orkney earl Rognvald Kali returned to Norway after a trading voyage to the English village of Grimsby, which was rapidly developing into a notable trading and fishing port town. King Henry II therefore took it for granted that during his grandfather's reign (1100–35), Norwegian traders had paid customs in Grimsby. The Norwegian scholar Egil Mikkelsen reasons, moreover, that trade between Norway and England and other North Sea countries probably increased during the reign of Harald hardrádi Sigurdsson (1047–66).[13]

Just around 1123, when Einar Sokkason availed himself of walrus tusks and other Arctic products to persuade the Norwegian authorities that the Greenlanders deserved their own bishop, a consolidation of English and other European markets and trade routes began. Somewhat later still, Bergen took over Trondheim's significance as a trading port and became the destination not only of furs, dried fish and other major export items from northern Norway, but from Greenland and Norway's other Atlantic outposts as well, due to the Bergen bishop's responsibility for the ecclesiastical concerns of these outlying societies. Once the new Gardar See had become a part of formal Church organisation, Bergen became the Greenlanders' chief Norwegian contact point for Church matters, and its mercantile importance was further enhanced by the passage of such laws as King Hákon's Rettarbót (amended law) of 1302, which King Magnus renewed in 1348. This law prohibited foreigners from trading north of Bergen or to Iceland and any of Norway's other tribute-paying countries.[14]

Trondheim nevertheless remained the organisational centre of the Norwegian Church and its link to Rome. Moreover, the archbishop was a major force in trade, because he had to market his share of the tithes, which were paid in naturalia. By virtue of his office, he was therefore the single biggest businessman in Norway in the second half of the thirteenth century, with huge investments in shipping and commerce, especially in the codfish trade.[15] As noted earlier in this chapter, the archiepiscopal establishment in Trondheim also became a major centre for receiving and using Greenland walrus ivory.

For ships carrying produce in payment of tithes from the distant Norse island communities, Bergen was the chief port of arrival, however, and collecting colonial tithes for the Church was the Bergen bishop's job, while assessing import and export taxes was a royal prerogative. It nevertheless fell frequently to the Bergen bishop to uphold the Crown's privileges as well, therefore he was likely to find himself engaged in a balancing act involving not only his archbishop, but royal functionaries who might or might not see eye to eye with what the bishop considered his own and the Church's privileges. This was especially true after 1343, when the Norwegian nobles – bishops included – felt the need to guard themselves against an increasingly unpopular king. During the period when Bishop Hákon of Bergen (d. 1342) and King Magnus were negotiating about falcons, their correspondence reveals considerable irritation on the bishop's part. He no longer wanted the responsibility of accounting for the king's tax receipts, he wrote; the money he earned from the privilege did not compensate him for the trouble caused him by the changes and confusion in the tax collecting system.[16]

THE HANSEATIC LEAGUE

It further complicated the lives of the Bergen bishops, as well as of many foreign and native merchants, when Bergen became a major hub of the Hanseatic League, which reached its peak in the fourteenth century. Although well-established Atlantic and North Sea trade routes insured wide circulation of manufactured goods and raw materials both before and after the Hanse trade hegemony had taken hold, shifts in the distribution pattern for Arctic luxury commodities such as walrus ivory and premium furs were probably unavoidable when trade with regular consumer goods in large quantities anchored the increasingly specialised Hanse business activities.

Under those circumstances, walrus tusks were liable to marginalisation in the marketing processes, the more so because walrus ivory's traditional travel companion, costly furs that appealed to Mediterranean people who wanted them for prestige reasons, gradually came to include large quantities of cheaper furs. In colder regions, where furs were valued for their warmth as well as for their looks, both day gowns and night clothes might be lined with rabbit skins, cat fur or squirrel fur, all of which were cheap and plentiful. When sold in large quantities, inexpensive furs were lucrative, and as this trade grew in volume it became a part of the well-organised Hanse distribution network that also serviced bulk shipments of stockfish, salted fish, cloth and grain. Increasingly, the trade went through Lübeck, Bruges and Novgorod. By the second half of the thirteenth century, German merchants were so entrenched in Novgorod that they soon dominated the fur trade from the Far North, and Norwegian commerce in exportable Arctic luxury products, which had grown out of the 'Finn taxes' and barters from northernmost Norway and the White Sea region, suffered in consequence.[17]

Even when the Norwegian Church was still the channel through which much (but not necessarily all) Greenland goods passed, private merchants had the option of bypassing Bergen and officialdom altogether. They are unlikely to have done so with non-luxury consumer items such as fish products, blubber, hides, wool and wool products, however. As the nearest port-of-call for ships from either Greenland or Iceland, Bergen's market place was prepared to handle such everyday goods both before and after the Hanse merchants had made an impact on the city's commercial life. In that connection, it needs noting that Icelandic and Greenlandic export goods intended for everyday consumption would have been so similar to each other (and to Norwegian produce of the same kind) that a specifically Greenlandic identification in the market place was unlikely. Precisely such a lack of differentiation characterised a 1316 decree in which King Hákon V established the tolls payable on commodities exported from Bergen to other Hanseatic trading centres. It is clear from the list that the anticipated export goods included wares that had first been imported, because it specifically mentions sulphur, a product for which Iceland was the sole supplier. The regulations otherwise spanned a wide variety of goods, ranging from stockfish and whale meat to furs, wool and wool cloth. Walrus tusks were in the same taxable category as wool cloth and furs from fox, beaver, otter, lamb and seal, all of which were considered more valuable than cow hides or marten fur.[18]

NORSE GREENLAND AND NORWEGIAN TRADE LEGISLATION

Three years later after proclaiming his tax categories, Hákon was dead, leaving the economic and political reins to the regency of his three-year-old son Magnus, who reached his majority in 1331 (a twelve-year period for which the source material is particularly poor). His son, again, Hákon VI Magnusson (1340–80) faced a greatly reduced Crown income after the devastations of the Black Death, and foreign merchants, especially those in the Hanseatic League, became more important than ever as trading partners and creditors, and also as a political power the king could not afford to offend.[19]

Given Iceland's greater vulnerability to coercion, due to its shorter distance from Norway, Iceland and Greenland were likely to react differently to Hanse manoeuvres and to the Norwegian Crown's responses to market conditions threatening to interfere with royal trade and taxing privileges, as well as to the economic problems caused by the Black Death. While Chapter Eight will examine how Iceland was affected by these changes in medieval trade within the Norwegian orbit, the present chapter will consider why the developments in Norway did not spell disaster for the Norse Greenlanders – not even when the devaluation of the Norwegian coinage accelerated in the 1340s. There is no evidence that the Norse Greenlanders ever used coin in the first place, therefore devaluation would merely have increased the value of the raw materials that formed the basis for Norse Greenland barter. If the bottom had dropped out of the market for most Greenland produce as early as in the fourteenth century, it would certainly be hard to explain Archbishop Valkendorf's eagerness to cash in on Greenland wares when he made plans for a voyage there in 1514–16 (Chapter Eleven). In any event, Norse Greenland society weathered these changes well enough to survive long after their loss of formal contact with Norway.

Evidence that profitable foreign trade had continued in Norse Greenland comes from the pieces of fifteenth-century Rhenish stoneware that turned up in front of the Hvalsey church wall as well as at a farm ruin in the Vatnahverfi district, while another piece was found at Herjolfsness below the foundation level of the farm's large festal hall. Other evidence comes from the existence of late-stage festal halls at three of the four major Greenlandic trading centres (the one at Brattahlid being of an older date and style). Those halls reflect continued prosperity into the fifteenth century, with the wealth no longer spent on church buildings, but on showy structures with a purely secular purpose. It is not surprising, therefore, that when Poul Nørlund excavated at Herjolfsness, he found the bodies shrouded in costumes, made from homespun Greenland wool, that included clothes showing influence of fifteenth-century styles elsewhere.[20]

Demonstrably, therefore, medieval Greenland had remained economically visible to merchants who were aware that the colonists produced a wide spectrum of staple goods for the foreign market. Walrus ivory had never been their only export article any more than walrus hunting had been the sole focus of their domestic economy in either the Eastern or Western Settlement. Of particular interest in that context is a tiny Eskimo woodcarving, of unknown provenance (but from the general Disko Bay region), which the Danish archaeologist Jørgen Meldgaard showed me during a private discussion in Copenhagen in May of 1991. The carving was an exquisitely detailed miniature bust depicting a mid-fourteenth-century European dandy, whose tight-fitting cap with a rolled brim rested on on carefully curled, earlobe-length hair. Meldgaard observed that the lack of proof that other Europeans besides the Greenland Norse had sailed in those waters at such an early date was all that prevented this carving from being seen to represent a non-Norse European.

There is actually very suggestive evidence of outside visitors at least as far north as to the Western Settlement. Pieces of chain mail found at medieval Eskimo sites as well as in the midden at a Western Settlement farm (site V54) likely point to travellers from the outside, because chain mail was so cumbersome to wear that it would have been of little use to people who fished and hunted for a living. It was also so expensive that, even in the other Nordic countries, it seldom turns up in archaeological excavations.[21] At the very least, one must ask what business such well-equipped travellers may have had in those northern waters!

A traveller's tale from the Western Settlement region around 1360 has a definite English connection, namely the *Inventio fortunata* described in Chapter Five. Even the few surviving fragments of the work as retold by Jacobus Cnoyen of 's-Hertogenbosch make it clear that Cnoyen was not unduly surprised that an Englishman had travelled to Greenland. The crux of the story was that the English Minorite had continued to explore northwards once he had reached Greenland. The *Inventio* voyage was obviously not unique. A late-phase Western Settlement farm site at Nipaatsoq yielded not only a small clump of silver, but a small silver shield of a shape associated with the first half of the fourteenth century.

Engraved on it was the coat-of-arms used by the Scottish Campbell clan in the period 1330–50.[22] Either a member of the Campbell clan had stayed on this Norse Greenland farm and created this symbol of his heritage (replicating it on other objects also found in the midden), or a Norseman belonging to the farm had seen a similar shield while abroad, unless he had simply taken a fancy to the pattern after seeing it in a visitor's possession.

Whichever scenario one chooses, the shield points to contact with the Scottish islands in the mid-fourteenth century. One possible reason for such contact would be the risky profession of falcon-catcher. That explanation comes to mind because it was during the period 1337–40 that Bishop Hákon of Bergen, in complaining to King Magnus about the difficulty of procuring white and grey gyrfalcons, groused that he had turned in vain to 'the Scottish page'.[23] The ancient connection between Norway and Scotland was still important – the Orkneys and the Shetland Islands belonged to Norway until Christian I of Denmark and Norway pawned both groups of islands to the Scottish king in 1468 (Orkney) and 1469 (Shetland) as a dowry for his daughter.

THE ART OF 'DRIFTING OFF'

For the fourteenth century, an overall picture emerges of political and economic developments in Norway that were bound to affect the Atlantic societies of Iceland and Greenland. The monarchs were increasingly eager to make money on the sale of licenses and to exercise tight control over trade monopolies with the Atlantic colonies. Hákon VI Magnusson's Rettarbót of 1360 further tightened restrictions on trade with and among Norway's Atlantic colonies – a policy continued by his son Olaf (reign 1380–87). When Olaf's mother, Queen Margrethe, took the reins after his death, she not only proved relentless herself, but instructed her heir, Eirik of Pomerania, to follow her example.[24] The cumulative effect of these royal efforts was to encourage evasiveness and secrecy and put a premium on illicit trade with Greenland, especially if a shipping hiatus of some years had left the inhabitants hungry for imported goods and with an accumulation of valuable barter goods.

Once a cargo had landed in Norway, it was not feasible to ignore the increasingly harsh Norwegian restrictions on trade with or among the Atlantic Norse societies, but it was always possible to cook up stories to avoid getting caught, especially given Norway's increasing neglect of those communities during the reigns of Margrethe and Eirik. Subterfuge was very successfully employed in each of the last recorded voyages between

Greenland and Norway, when Norwegian efforts to supply Greenland with a resident bishop had already ceased and official contact with Norway was dwindling steadily.

When Bishop Alf died at Gardar in 1377 or '78 (Chapter Six), the news did not reach Norway until 1383, when the Icelandic ship *Ólafssúdinn* sailed directly from Greenland to Bergen. The news about the bishop was not the only reason the ship's arrival earned a notice in the annals, however. The *Ólafssúdinn* was carrying a cargo of Greenland goods and also remaining crew members from the Skálholt bishop's ship *Thorlakssúdinn*, who claimed to have had a narrow escape in their ship's boat after being shipwrecked on the Greenland coast in 1381. It eventually transpired that neither the *Ólafssúdinn* nor the *Thorlakssúdinn* had had any lawful business in Greenland, and they were cited for having brought back export goods obtained without a royal licence. In defence against this accusation, the Norwegian tax authorities were told that both ships had 'drifted off course' while Iceland-bound and had fetched up in Greenland much against the crews' will. Luckily for the Icelanders, the king's chief financial officer in Bergen, Erlend Philippuson, claimed to believe their hardship story, despite the fact that they had not bothered to stop off in Iceland first on their eastbound voyage to reassure kith and kin that they were alive and well. Erlend exonerated them and did the same for the prominent North Icelander Björn Einarsson 'Jerusalem-Farer' six years later, when Björn was accused of illegal trade with Greenland and he, too, claimed to have drifted off.[25]

The common interpretation of these incidents has been that weather conditions must have worsened in the North Atlantic in the late fourteenth century, but nobody has explained why the wind directions and currents had changed to such convenient purpose that westbound mariners would be carried safely around Cape Farewell to the Eastern Settlement before being tossed ashore among people to trade with and in conditions pleasant enough to warrant a stay of a year or more. A ship coming from Iceland or Norway might well run into trouble on Greenland's east coast, which would have been as good as a death sentence, but only someone familiar with Greenland conditions would have known that. Erlend Philippuson and anyone else in Norway without direct experience with voyages to Greenland would have had only a hazy concept of Greenland's general shape, size and geographical orientation and therefore would not have been in a position to question these tall tales on the grounds of their absurdity. Instead, the discussion focused on whether or not these voyages to Greenland had been involuntary or planned mercantile ventures, and on the degree to which the royal tax authorities ought to benefit. In particular, the valuable cargo of Greenland export goods which Björn Einarsson brought to Bergen in 1389 occasioned a high-profile law suit that also elicited additional information about the voyages that had led to the Bergen inquiries in 1383.

Björn and his wife Solveig counted among the most prominent people in Iceland, and his social standing was no doubt known to his accuser Hákon Jónsson, a pugnacious money collector for the Crown who insisted that Björn and his men had gone to Greenland on purpose; had traded in Greenland without a royal license; and had bought Crown goods illegally. The well-born Erlend Philippuson, defending the 1389 visitors just as he had shielded the Icelanders six years earlier, would have been equally well aware of Björn and his social connections in both Norway and Iceland. He convinced the court to drop the charges, stating his belief in Björn's claim that he and his men had drifted off to Greenland in 1385 with no intention of violating royal privilege. Moreover, they had now paid ordinary import duty on their cargo. Two former *Ólafssúðinn* crew members also testified in Björn's favour, telling the 1389 court that when they themselves had been marooned in Greenland, the Greenlanders had *forced* them to trade their Norwegian goods for food and lodging and to buy Greenlandic export goods. Piously, they noted that they had obeyed the royal ombudsman in Greenland in every way.[26]

The mariners' reference to a dutiful and supposedly resident royal ombudsman in Greenland constitutes one more reason to disbelieve their account of their Greenland sojourn, because by the time Ívar Bárdsson left Bergen for Greenland in 1341, the ombudsman system was already blurring in Norway, and there is no evidence that the system had ever applied to Greenland (Chapter Six) or even that it should have applied, given the odds against the Greenlanders' submission to the Norwegian Crown.[27]

Björn's own story might have been less suspect in posterity if he had not had the opportunity to talk with crew members from the *Ólafssúdinn* and the *Thorlakssúdinn* before he left Iceland for Norway in 1384, and if his subsequent Greenland visit had not involved *four* ships laden with Norwegian goods and a stay of two whole winters in the Eastern Settlement (he returned to Iceland first, in 1387, and continued on to Norway two years later). There is even less reason to look for veracity in the work known as *Reisubók Bjarnar Jorsalafara*. It includes an account of Björn's stay in Greenland and supposedly originated with Björn himself, but it is known only in a confused seventeenth-century version.[28]

Erlend Philippuson's solution was a Solomonic one under the circumstances. In medieval Bergen, the issue of fiscal control always simmered just below the surface of any controversy involving the local power élite with the institutional powers of Church or Crown. Individual Norwegian officials were more likely to be interested in collecting money they themselves could control (and skim) than in defending the monarch's prerogatives at any cost, and they would no doubt have welcomed an excuse to collect regular duty and thus avoid a situation entailing fines or confiscation handled by other officials.

For Björn and his companions, paying the usual Norwegian import taxes on goods from Greenland and Iceland was obviously preferable to heavy fines or having one's cargo confiscated, therefore they would have had every reason to be pleased when they returned home to Iceland, where the big social and economic changes that were to shake the country from 1400 onwards were still in the unknown future, and where Björn's voyage to Greenland spawned events that reverberated in the Eastern Settlement and became part of the permanent lore about the colony's final phase.

8

CONTACT WITH ICELAND

The wide-reaching North Atlantic network, which kept the inhabitants of both Greenland settlements in touch with other Atlantic societies, produced an especially strong bond with Iceland, Greenland's nearest neighbour to the east. For centuries after Eirik and his fellow settlers had succeeded in forming their own separate society, the Greenlanders' cultural and familial bonds with Iceland remained close, with direct voyages between the two Norse outposts continuing well into the fifteenth century.

The Icelanders' experience with the wider North Atlantic network was somewhat different from the Greenlanders' in large part because they were closer than their western cousins to Norway and the rest of Europe and therefore more vulnerable to political and economic pressures, especially from Norway. They were also far more exposed to the European disease pool.

DISEASE: AN UNWELCOME TRAVEL COMPANION

Neither the Icelanders nor the Greenlanders would have been protected against leprosy, which was endemic in the Far North from the eleventh century until the Norwegian physician Gerhard Armauer Hansen (1841–1912) identified the cause of the illness and systematic prevention and cure could begin. Before that medical breakthrough, the port city of Bergen had been especially afflicted, which is a reminder that being a port was a mixed blessing until the arrival of modern medicine. Not surprisingly, medieval sagas and annals often refer to epidemics in Iceland and sometimes in Greenland, both countries with small populations and completely dependent on ships for contact with the rest of the world.

In Iceland, the number of arrivals from abroad fluctuated considerably throughout the Middle Ages, often as a consequence of circumstances related to Norwegian politics or economic conditions. For the year Queen Margrethe died (1412), the 'Lögmanns-annáll' noted ominously that no news reached Iceland from Norway. By contrast, the year 1347 had been a very busy one in Icelandic harbours, with thirteen oceangoing ships arriving to join six that were already there, making a total number of eighteen foreign ships set to winter in Iceland when seventeen Greenlanders, coming from Markland, hobbled into port aboard their small, anchorless ship. Starting the following year and beginning in the south, epidemics of various kinds raged all around Iceland for two years.[1]

Among the nasty surprises a visiting ship might bring were influenza and dysentery. Typhus, transmitted by body lice and at least as ancient as leprosy in the Far North, was often a scourge on long voyages with inadequate food stores and minimal opportunities for personal hygiene, and it was also a threat ashore whenever another disaster, such as famine, was already present.[2] The *Icelandic Annals* tell of volcanic eruptions, earthquakes and mudslides, or of skies so darkened by ash that the sun had no power even during the summer. The grass did not grow, birds and beasts died and famine stalked the unforgiving land. Such circumstances created optimal conditions for the spread of contagious illness. The resilient Icelanders have nevertheless to this day weathered both imported illnesses and the natural disasters heaped upon them by their country's extraordinary geological conditions. The Norse Greenlanders lived much more safely among their stable granite mountains.

Although the medieval Greenlanders were better protected than their Icelandic cousins from imported viruses, grave finds of parents and children buried together in both the Eastern and Western settlements do suggest invasions of virulent disease. Archaeologists have not found any evidence that a devastating epidemic put an end to either colony, however, nor did such a fate befall the medieval Icelanders despite their more frequent contact with the rest of the world, and despite ships that entered their harbours after voyages just short enough for diseased crews to survive and bring their troubles ashore. That was what finally happened when the Black Death reached Iceland in 1402, a little over half a century after devastating Norway and causing a reduction in the number of ships going out to Iceland and Greenland.

At least as far as Iceland was concerned, the reduction was temporary and obviously not enough to protect the country from the plague in the long run (an event to which we will return later in this chapter). Private and official shipping enterprises in Norway were equally hard hit, but it is obvious from the written record that after the initial shock, ships continued to sail the northern seas on both public and private business. In the same spirit, Bishop Vilchin of Skálholt sailed to Iceland from Bergen in 1394, just a year after German warships with about nine hundred men had attacked Bergen, burned all the churches and terrorised the inhabitants for eight days, before sailing off with as much plunder as they could fit on their own and stolen ships.[3] For those with money, ships and power, it was a question of priorities and of where their interests lay, not of whether they would be able to travel at all, as was amply illustrated by the voyages of the *Ólafssúdinn* and the *Thorlakssúdinn* in the 1380s, soon followed by the equally flexible enterprise of Björn Einarsson 'Jerusalem-Farer' and his friends (Chapter Seven). One would never know that during the years 1380–81, just before the *Ólafssúdinn* and the *Thorlakssúdinn* put to sea, Iceland had suffered a bad smallpox epidemic.

NORWEGIAN POLITICS IN ICELAND

Throughout almost their entire medieval history, the Icelanders needed to be alert to demands coming from Norway. Concerted Norwegian meddling in Icelandic affairs began before AD 1000, when King Olaf Tryggvason (who may also have hoped to add the Greenlanders to his slate of missionary triumphs) made the Icelanders feel the full force of his Christianising ambitions. Possibly, the king reasoned that, unlike their neighbours' fledgling society, the Icelanders were already well along, with orderly conditions founded on property, income and social organisation – the very basis for an institutional church that could also serve a secular administration.

If this was indeed King Olaf's perception of Iceland, it differed from that which Adam of Bremen expressed almost a century later:[4]

> [Iceland] is so very large that it has on it many peoples, who make a living only by raising cattle and who clothe themselves with their pelts. No crops are grown there; the supply of wood is very meager. On this account the people dwell in underground caves, glad to have roof and food and bed in common with their cattle. Passing their lives thus in holy

simplicity, because they seek nothing more than nature affords, they can joyfully say with the Apostle: 'But having food, and wherewith to be covered, with these we are content.' ... Blessed, I say, is the folk whose poverty no one envies; and in this respect most blessed because all have now adopted Christianity.

Adam was certainly correct in observing that the Icelanders had 'adopted Christianity', an event that had taken place in 999 or 1000. In response to King Olaf's demand for Iceland's public conversion to Christianity, the Law Speaker of the Althing, a chieftain and pagan priest named Thorgeir Thorkellsson, was asked to mediate between the Christian and non-Christian factions in his country. After meditating long and well on the likely consequences of domestic polarisation as well as of alienating the Norwegian ruler, whose aggressive stance had already made him hold the sons of several Icelandic chieftains hostage and deny Icelandic mariners access to Norwegian ports, Thorgeir concluded that all Icelanders henceforth should take the Christian faith and let themselves be baptised. In token of his decision, he threw his own heathen cult objects into the North Iceland waterfall which ever since has been called Góðafoss – the heathen priest's waterfall. About a thousand years later, my husband and I sat by that waterfall while first one, then another, young Icelandic couple came to watch the frothing waters for a long time in utter silence. In the late afternoon light, droplets from the rushing water mingled with a light rain to make the air shimmer, and the silence and solitude of the place made Norway seem as far away as the moon. Thorgeir had obviously seen things differently.

Adam's perception of the eleventh-century Icelandic lifestyle may owe something to the Icelander Isleif Gissursson (1006–80), who had been educated in Westphalia from when he was a small boy until he returned to Iceland in 1020s as a priest, and who became the first native Bishop of Iceland in 1056, serving under the Hamburg-Bremen archbishopric. Isleif's European education and subsequent career were direct consequences of his being the youngest son of the chieftain Gissur the White of Skálholt. As King Olaf's friend and a prosperous Icelandic farmer Gissur had, together with his fellow Christian Hjallti Skjeggjason, played an important part in Iceland's official conversion. Luckily, Isleif had clearly also inherited his father's personal abilities along with his wealth and determination.[5]

Bishop Isleif's son Gissur likewise studied in Saxony and later succeeded his father as Iceland's bishop. When he returned home after his 1082 consecration in Magdeburg, he gave his family farm at Skálholt as a permanent residence to the Skálholt bishopric and founded a school at his see. One of his students, Jón Ögmundsson, in 1106 became the first bishop of Hólar in the north, where there was soon a second centre of learning in Iceland. Jón had travelled extensively in Europe, including in France – indeed, the head priest at his Hólar cathedral school was referred to as 'French'.

Despite the considerable travelling distances involved, a strong appetite for foreign learning coloured Icelandic culture altogether in the eleventh and twelfth centuries. Bishop Jón's kinsman Sæmundr Sigfússon (who was so learned that Ari Thorgilsson submitted his *Book of Icelanders* to him for corrections) studied in France and subsequently founded a school at Oddi, where the famous historian and politician Snorri Sturluson became a student. With no fewer than three schools in Iceland by the end of the eleventh century, the literacy rate among privileged Icelanders soon was considerable. One product of these educational opportunities was the priest Ingimund Thorgeirsson, who was shipwrecked on Greenland's east coast in 1189 (Chapter Six) and left wax tablets inscribed with the story of his and his shipmates' ordeal.[6]

Ingimund had been a good friend of the Norwegian archbishop's, but relations between the archbishop and high-ranking Icelandic clergymen were otherwise not always the best. One example is Archbishop Sigurd's curt response to the newly minted Bishop Bótolf of Hólar's complaint that he lacked the outward trappings of his position; another instance is the fate of the previous Hólar bishop, Gudmund Arason, which demonstrated that it took more than outward trappings for a local bishop (Chapter Six) to be able to count on humility among the local farmers. More significant here is the fact that Bishop Gudmund then sought refuge with Snorri Sturluson, which was as good an indication as any that the bishop's troubles were not caused by liturgical issues, but political ones. That was also the case with the two bishops the archbishop had sent out to Iceland after rejecting the Icelanders' own candidates. When Sigvard of Skálholt and Bótolf of Hólar arrived in Iceland to assume their duties, the country was torn by local power struggles and quarrels between Icelandic farmers and Norwegian traders, as well as by the feud between King Hákon Hákonsson and Skuli Bárdsson for supremacy in Norway. The two bishops joined the fray and supported King Hákon's liege man in Iceland, Gissur Thorvaldsson, who killed his former father-in-law Snorri Sturluson in 1241.[7]

END OF THE ICELANDIC COMMONWEALTH

Snorri Sturluson (1178–1241) was the youngest son of the wealthy chieftain Sturla Thórdsson and, from the age of about three, the foster son of the even more powerful Jón Loptsson of Oddi (†1197), who offered to raise and educate the boy as compensation for an injury done by one of his own relatives to Snorri's father. The arrangement was greatly to young Snorri's advantage, because Jón was not only related to the Norwegian royal family and the most influential Icelander of his day, but trained in the law and very well educated in general, as befitted the grandson of Sæmund the Learned. Although Snorri never returned to his parents' house, his old and new family backgrounds, coupled with his intellectual gifts and fine education, an advantageous early marriage and fierce ambition, made him (along with his older brothers Thórd and Sighvat) one of the most powerful Icelanders in the thirteenth century. Snorri relocated to his wife's property in the southwest after his marriage, which lasted only a few years. Soon, he acquired a number of properties and chieftaincies on his own. The Sturlungar family and four or five other equally influential families essentially came to dominate the fractious political scene in mid-thirteenth-century Iceland.[8]

Trained as a lawyer, Snorri became the Lawspeaker of the Althing in 1215, but just three years later he received a royal invitation to go to Norway and left his country as well as his high position. King Hákon Hákonsson (King Hákon Sverresson's illegitimate son) was still a teenager and had a co-regent, Earl Skúli, who ruled over about a third of Norway. The situation was fraught with intrigue and divided loyalties, because the earl was the half-brother of Inge Bárdsson who had held the Norwegian throne from 1204 until 1217, and Skúli now wanted the kingship for himself. When Snorri arrived in Norway in 1218, the legitimacy of the young king as a royal son was therefore very much in dispute. Skúli was still Norway's de facto ruler, and as such he threatened to send a navy to Iceland in order to settle a dispute between Norwegian merchants and the Oddverjars, another of Iceland's most powerful families. Snorri averted this action by offering to persuade the Icelandic chieftains to submit to the authority of the Norwegian Crown. Upon his return home in 1220, however, he appears to have done little or nothing to convince his peers that such a move would be to their advantage, although he was the Lawspeaker again from 1222 until 1232.[9]

King Hákon made a fresh attempt to assert himself in 1235 through Snorri's nephew Sturla Sighvatsson. This time, the plan was for Sturla to capture all the Icelandic chieftains and send them to the king, who would then make them hand all their chieftaincies over to himself. Sturla and his allies decided to begin by sending a thousand men against Snorri, who fled to Norway in 1237, where relations between the king and Skúli had deteriorated further by the time Snorri arrived. Skúli's violent death in 1241 put an end to over a century of civil wars in Norway, but not to King Hákon's ambitions in Iceland. Disregarding royal orders against leaving Norway, Snorri had returned to Iceland and now found himself in a dangerous spot. On the one hand, he had sworn fealty to the king while, on the other, his close association with Skúli was sufficiently well known for him to be considered a traitor. The king now wrote to another of his liege men in Iceland, Snorri's estranged son-in-law Gissur Thorvaldsson (a direct descendant of Gissur the White), asking him to capture Snorri and send him to Norway. Failing that, Snorri was to be killed outright. And that was what happened. Far from living happily ever after, however, Gissur continued his high-stakes game in both Iceland and Norway, until the king sent him out to Iceland in 1258 with orders to bring about the Icelander's submission to Norwegian rule. When nothing happened for three more years, the king sent along another emissary, a Norwegian this time, to put pressure on Gissur. The result was that a number of Iceland's chieftains and farmers' representatives swore allegiance to the aging King Hákon and his son Magnus at the 1262 Althing. The rest of the country followed suit, and by 1264 republican Iceland was no more.[10]

ICELAND UNDER THE NEW RULE

Magnus Hákonsson, king of Norway 1263–80, went down in history with the cognomen 'Law Mender' because, in 1276, he succeeded in creating a unified law code that included all of Norway as well as Shetland and the Faeroes (the Hebrides and the Isle of Man had been sold to Scotland ten years earlier). A different version (Járnsíða) was sent to Iceland in 1273, where a circa 1280 revision called Jónsbók served Iceland for more than four centuries. A particularly important aspect of this new law code was that its enactment placed Iceland squarely outside the unified law district of Norway.[11] It is also notable that nowhere do the written sources suggest that Hákon intended his new Iceland law code to serve for Norse Greenland as well – a circumstance that makes it even more doubtful that the Greenlanders had accepted Norwegian rule in the manner of the Icelanders.

Magnus also provided a separate law code for Norwegian cities, with a specific section given to an orderly succession to the throne. At the age of five, his eldest son Eirik was given the title of king, while his little brother Hákon was given his position next in line. This was in 1273. Seven years later Magnus was dead and Eirik became king, remaining on the throne until his death in 1299. He had no sons, therefore his younger brother succeeded him as Hákon V Magnusson. During a reign that spanned two decades, Hákon V made his policies felt both domestically and in Norway's North Atlantic satellite communities. At home he (and his regents during his minority) curtailed the power of the nobles and shifted the capital city from Bergen to Oslo, thus changing the centre of power at home and signalling an attitude towards Norway's connections westwards that was fully expressed when Hákon's Rettarbót of 1302 prohibited foreigners from trading north of Bergen, to Iceland or to any of his other tribute-paying countries.

Troubled by the new version of the old covenant between Iceland and Norway, the Icelandic chieftains attending the 1302 Althing wrote a letter to the king in which they acknowledged Hákon's good will and his right to rule over them, but which also registered several serious complaints. Too much wealth was now leaving their country, too few goods were received in return, and the earlier promise of six ships arriving annually with imported goods was not being honoured. Moreover, the chieftains reminded the king that only Icelanders were to be appointed to the administrative offices of lawmen and sheriffs in Iceland.[12] This last point was naturally of major importance to the chieftains, who expected to fill such positions themselves, but it also mattered greatly to other Icelanders.

The chieftains' unease did nothing to shift Hákon V's view that his realm was not primarily a North Atlantic kingdom, but one that ought to expand its influence towards Denmark and the Baltic region in the south and towards Sweden in the east. To the latter end, he betrothed his toddler daughter Ingeborg to Erik Magnusson, the son of the Swedish king.[13] Born in 1301, Ingeborg was only eleven years old when she was married to the nineteen-years-older Erik in 1312, and when she was fifteen, she bore him a son, Magnus. A daughter, Euphemia, came a year later. By 1318 she was a widow with two small children. When her father, Hákon V, died the following year, her four-year-old son inherited the Norwegian throne, and shortly afterwards he was also proclaimed king of Sweden. The two countries had now achieved a personal union that endured until all three Nordic countries were formally joined by the Kalmar Union of 1397.

Far from fulfilling his Norwegian grandfather's ambitions for a powerful Norway, Magnus Eriksson's reign openly favoured Sweden to such a degree that both secular and ecclesiastical nobles in Norway rebelled repeatedly and in the end succeeded in placing Magnus's younger son Hákon on the Norwegian throne in 1343. In 1355, when the boy reached his majority while Norway and Sweden were still reeling after the Black Death, Magnus ceded power to his son. He found his power waning also in Sweden, and when he attempted a return a year after he had been driven into exile, he was imprisoned in Stockholm for four years. It is unlikely that he was heavily mourned, especially by the Bergen bishop and the Icelanders, when he drowned in Norway in 1374.

The switch to Hákon VI Magnusson was not an easy one, however, especially given a precarious financial situation that led to further restrictions on trade with and between Norway's Atlantic colonies with Hákon's Rettarbót of 1360. As noted in Chapter Seven, his policy was continued by his son Olaf (reign 1380–87), and Olaf's mother proved equally relentless when she took the reins of state after her son's death. Queen Margrethe also instructed Eirik of Pomerania, her appointed heir, to follow her example.

The Crown's efforts to maintain a strong royal trade monopoly placed increasing stress on both Icelandic and Norwegian traders and, by extension, on exporters of Greenlandic goods. By the 1380s, the situation had created such a premium on illicit trade with Greenland that several enterprising Icelandic mariners resorted to blaming the wind and the weather for the Greenlandic goods they had obtained and carried back to Norway. Their 'drifting off' excuse, coupled with a pretence of having obeyed a royal ombudsman in Greenland, spared them from punitive action by Crown authorities, although they still had to pay import taxes before they could go ahead and sell their Greenland goods for a handsome profit in the Bergen market.

For Björn Einarsson 'Jerusalem-Farer' and his friends, who had sailed to Greenland with four ships in 1385, the proceeds from their 'drifting off' are likely to have been very nice indeed – nice enough for Björn's methods to be emulated by a group of highborn young Icelanders some years later.

BJÖRN EINARSSON 'JERUSALEM-FARER' AND HIS CIRCLE

Björn's profits from his recent voyages to Greenland and Norway were no doubt useful when he arranged the 1391 marriage of his daughter Kristín to Jón Guttormsson, a man as prosperous and well connected as his bride.[14] It is also a safe assumption that Kristín's Vatnsfjord wedding was a grand affair attended by important people in Björn's orbit. That year, both Björn and Sigmund hvítkollr (White-Pate), Björn's friend and travel companion on his Greenland venture, were reckoned among the chief men in Iceland, and so were Björn Brynjolfsson *hinn ríki* (the

Wealthy/Powerful) and the *hirðstjóri* (royal governor) Thorstein Eyjolfsson, whose immediate descendants became closely involved in events related to the last recorded news about the Norse Greenland colony.

Thorstein Eyjolfsson had produced a number of children in the midst of a busy life that involved a fair amount of time abroad and that constituted a high-stakes game in which he had cultivated the friendship of both King Magnus and his son Hákon. Both his children and grandchildren benefited from those relationships. Throughout the fifteenth century, while the Middle Ages drew to a close, Thorstein's descendants and other powerful North Iceland families formed a tight ruling class able to avoid the economic hardships visited on their less fortunate countrymen. By the time Thorstein's grandchildren reached adulthood, they had nevertheless tasted turbulence and danger, especially the four grandchildren of particular concern to our story here: Thorstein, Arni and Hall Olafsson, who lost their father, Olaf Thorsteinsson, to drowning in 1380, and their cousin Steinunn Hrafnsdaughter, who lost her parents, uncle and siblings during 1389/90.[15]

As male members of North Iceland's most prominent families, Thorstein Eyjolfsson and the two Björns were accustomed to dealing with one another in property transactions, legal disputes, marriage agreements and other matters.[16] All three men were alive and well in 1391 and would have attended the wedding of Thorstein's granddaughter Kristín, sole fruit of the union between Thorstein's daughter Solveig and Björn Einarsson 'Jerusalem-Farer'. Much of the talk during the festivities would inevitably have been on the topics of most interest to both men and women in that stratum of Icelandic society: property transactions, legal disputes and marriage arrangements. Not only was this a wedding where financial agreements would have played a substantial part, but Thorstein Eyjolfsson's grandchildren were now coming into adulthood and Björn Brynjolfsson's eldest daughter, Sigrid, born around 1380, was entering her teens.

Like Thorstein Eyjolfsson and his kin, Björn Brynjolfsson of Great Akrar and his relatives figure prominently in medieval Icelandic documents. They were financial managers of religious houses (among other offices), they took part in a number of recorded property transactions, and their wealth and its attendant power had them serving as lay judges or witnesses in property disputes that often involved friends or relatives. Significantly, not only Björn and his brother Benedict, but also their father Brynjolf, were described as *hinn ríki* many years before mortality from the Black Death had placed large numbers of farms in the hands of a few people.

The property inventory for the church at South Akrar from 1382 to about 1600 shows that Björn made generous donations to that church in 1392, and that the lands at Akrar, Grof, Gegnishól, Vellir, Mid-Grund and South Grund were among his many farms at the time. Responsible for arranging his sister Jorunn's marriage after their father's death, Björn did it with due diligence and then had the complicated business transaction written up and witnessed. His habit of circumspection is equally evident in a document he drew up towards the end of 1392, in which he formally granted his children Olaf, Sigrid and Málfrid equal shares in their inheritance, but with a detailed provision that reveals that he was actively planning for the marriage of his eldest daughter, Sigrid.[17] Her marriage is central to our story here, because it took her to Hvalsey in Greenland, where she was still living in 1406 when Thorstein Eyjolfsson's grandson Thorstein arrived with a number of his friends after having 'drifted off'.

SIGRID BJÖRNSDAUGHTER

Sigrid was a most eligible potential bride, and her father was not a man to leave the choice of her future groom to chance or to ignore suggestions from trusted friends such as Björn Einarsson 'Jerusalem-Farer.' Björn knew his way around the Norwegian tax authorities and had recently visited the big farmers in Greenland's Eastern Settlement, and while he had not revealed to the 1389 Norwegian Court just where he stayed during his two-year Greenland sojourn, the demonstrable fact that his close friend's young daughter found herself at Hvalsey just a few years later suggests that he had spent enough time at the prosperous Hvalsey farm to examine the prospect of a match between Sigrid from Akrar and the Hvalsey farm's owner or his son. Nothing but the best would have done for such a wealthy North Iceland bride, but there is no reason to suppose that Sigrid's father had gone to Greenland to negotiate personally, because he does not appear to have been much of a traveller.

In the written property dispositions Björn Brynjolfsson made on 13 December 1392, witnessed by his brother Dádi and several other men, he did not indicate why he decided to settle property on his children at that time. A sense that death was imminent cannot have been the reason, because documents show that he was still alive and well in 1396. (It is likely that he died in the Black Death of 1402–04, because he was not involved in a 1405 property transaction involving other members of his family and Björn the 'Jerusalem-Farer'.) In addition to giving his three children equal shares in a number of named farm in his 1392 document, he designated Sigrid as the sole owner of Thorleiksstead, a sizable property that had belonged to her wealthy mother.[18] No maternal inheritance was specified for Sigrid's brother and sister, although they all had the same mother, and that leaves determining Sigrid's dowry as the only discernible reason for drawing up the document.

Björn had a very good reason for avoiding a publicly witnessed document that could be interpreted as part of a marriage contract with a Greenlander. Such a deal, a business arrangement pure and simple, would be a violation of the royal trade monopoly forbidding Icelanders and Greenlanders from trading directly with each other. Any financial agreements made in conjunction with Sigrid's forthcoming marriage would have had to be spoken in the presence of witnesses. The same curtain of documentary silence blankets Sigrid's transfer to Hvalsey and her first wedding, both of which events must obviously have taken place.

We know absolutely nothing about Sigrid's life in Greenland for the next ten years or so, but we do know that being far from home, she was spared the Black Death, which arrived in Iceland in 1402 and raged for two years, killing huge numbers of people, a disproportionate number of priests among them.[19]

THE BLACK DEATH

The Black Death struck Iceland twice in the fifteenth century, first in 1402–04 and again in 1494–96, but it evidently did not become endemic in between onslaughts, as had happened elsewhere, and it did not affect Greenland, as already noted. The explanation is the same for both phenomena, namely that the Plague experienced in Iceland was not primarily the bubonic version, diffused through flea vectors with or without rat hosts, but pneumonic plague, which spreads through direct human contact. Pneumonic plague, the most common form of the Black Death in northern cold and damp climates, was ninety-five to a hundred per cent fatal. It circulated swiftly and killed just as swiftly, and it is vividly described in a fifteenth-century Icelandic source: 'It was the nature of the pestilence that men lived no more than a day or two, with sharp, stabbing pains in the chest, after which they haemorrhaged and expired.' No ship's crew thus afflicted would have survived a voyage to Greenland, and it took half a century, plus advances in English shipbuilding, before it reached Iceland.[20]

With the first onslaught of the Black Death came a watershed in Iceland's economic, political and social history. The learned North Icelander Jón Espólín (1769–1836) observed that when the Plague caused a great deal of land to fall into a few hands, it produced many rich people who had no incentive to add to their wealth by hard work, but who sought out other avenues to promotion and power. Great feuds developed among the leading families, and first English, then German interests replaced Norwegian ones. Even worse – the Icelanders soon forgot how things used to be, learning was neglected and nobody any longer wrote down various events as they occurred, Espólin grumbled.[21] Despite Espólín's exaggerations, a modern historian will likely complain right along with him about the dwindling of written sources, but that dearth had less to do with situational sloth than with political expediency, both in Iceland and elsewhere, while fifteenth-century Icelanders who had hit the double jackpot of survival and huge inheritances did what they could to sweeten their personal pots.

Among those who died in the 1402–04 epidemic were Thorstein Eyjolfsson, Sigrid Björnsdaughter's father, sister and brother and Björn the 'Jerusalem-Farer's son-in-law. Björn and his wife survived, however, as did their young nephew Thorstein Olafsson (grandson of Thorstein Eyjolfsson), and they put their survival to good use. In the late summer of 1405, at least three ships left Iceland bound for Norway, one of them with Björn the 'Jerusalem-Farer' and his wife aboard. Two others carried Thorstein Olafsson and several of his equally well-born friends. The written sources name among them Snorri Torfason, Sigrid's relative Sæmund Oddsson, Thorgrim Sölvason and Thorgrim's wife Steinunn Hrafnsdaughter, who was Thorstein Eyjolfsson's granddaughter and thus young Thorstein Olafsson's cousin.[22] There were apparently no other wives along on that voyage. Thorstein Olafsson was unmarried, as will shortly become clear, and we know that Snorri's wife Gudrun had stayed behind in Iceland, because she eventually gave her husband up for dead and remarried in 1410.

THORSTEIN OLAFSSON PLANS HIS FUTURE

As prominent Icelanders interested in trade and eager to stay in royalty's good graces, all of these Icelandic travellers had good reason to head for Norway in 1405. Not only were Princess Philippa of England and young King Eirik of Pomerania supposed to marry then, but a year earlier the groom's uncompromising aunt, Queen Margrethe, had written him a long letter whose contents would have sparked attention in wide circles as soon as it became known. After advising her nephew on how to receive his bride in Bergen, she told him to be sparing with privileges for his Norwegian subjects and illustrated her intention by noting that the last time the bishop of Bergen visited her, she had ordered him to recall all licenses for sailing to Iceland. Those who wanted these or other privileges must get new ones from herself or from Eirik.[23]

Thorstein Olafsson's brother Arni, the future bishop of Skálholt, was already in Norway at that time, serving as chaplain to Queen Margrethe's trusted retainer Magnus Magnusson, whose father-in-law Erlend Philippuson had been such a useful friend to the weather-tossed Greenland-farers in 1383 and 1389. Arni would have known well ahead of time about both the wedding and Queen Margrethe's efforts to put starch in her nephew. However, not even Arni could have anticipated that, almost at the last minute, the royal wedding would be postponed until the summer of 1406.[24]

Björn, Thorstein and the rest of their party spent the winter in Norway, which they may have planned to do in any event, and when the wedding had finally taken place, they set sail again, this time heading in separate directions. To reach Jerusalem via Rome and Venice, Björn and his wife set out on the trip that eventually earned him his cognomen 'Jerusalem-Farer', while the two ships with Thorstein and his friends headed west.[25] In Norway four years later (see further below), they explained that while Iceland bound, they had been caught in a dense fog and had drifted off course to Greenland.

Thorstein had presumably benefited from his uncle Björn's counsel and was well provisioned with saleable Norwegian goods, but given that he also had his closest friends and a relative of Sigrid's on board when he made his way to Hvalsey for a stay of four years, his agenda appears to have encompassed more than a bit of illegal trade topped with fresh news from Norway. In this case, news from Iceland would have been more important. With Sigrid's kinsman Sæmund Oddsson along to confirm his story, Thorstein could tell Sigrid that her whole family had died, and that she was now the sole heir to her father's wealth.

By that time (1406), Sigrid would have been in her mid-twenties and some ten years married, but the sparse written sources are so selective in the information intended for outsiders in posterity that they never mention her husband's name or disclose whether she had children by him. Nor do they reveal whether she was a widow when Thorstein and his friends arrived, whether she was made to divorce her husband – or whether her husband's death was hastened. This last is certainly not impossible, because the Icelandic visitors reacted with great savagery when Thorstein's cousin Steinunn took a young Greenlander named Kollgrim as her lover within a year of her arrival. Her father had been an Icelandic lawman, and her husband Thorgrim and his friends were of equally good stock, but Kollgrim evidently was a common sort, which made matters worse. To save face for the visitors, a local, lay-dominated court of Icelanders and Greenlanders held at Hvalsey blamed Steinunn's infidelity on Kollgrim. Accused of having seduced her by means of black arts, he was sentenced to be burned at the stake at Hvalsey. Steinunn presumably watched his execution, for she reportedly lost her wits, and she died not long afterwards. Her husband Thorgrim was still flourishing in Iceland in 1438.[26]

Although Thorstein Olafsson's connections were with the rich and famous from childhood onwards, he had to make his fortune by his wits. He had been very young when his father drowned in 1380, and it seems that he had little or no land of his own. As the husband of a rich woman, however, he would have effective control over her property and thus be in a very favourable position in a society where wealth and power were closely connected, and where a man of his social class was expected to pay fines and compensation if a political or economic gamble turned out badly. Thorstein had much to gain and little to lose by going to Greenland to see if he could persuade Sigrid to marry him. And marry him she did, on 16 September 1408, with blessings spoken over the bride and groom in Hvalsey church (Figs. 12, 13) after the bridal pair had pledged their troth and agreed on financial arrangements elsewhere on the farm.[27] If the large festal hall had already been constructed, both the financial negotiations and the wedding feast would have taken place there; otherwise, the farm's older hall would have been used. Parts of the hall's massive walls, still prominent in the landscape, reveal an architectural style different from that found elsewhere on the farm, and it is clearly a late addition, but a closer dating than 'early fifteenth century' (Chapters Six and Seven) has so far not been possible. For reasons which Chapter Nine will touch upon, that particular building may well postdate the 1408 wedding, but it would have been a grand wedding just the same.

Six hundred years later, I stood in the now roofless shell of Hvalsey church (Figs. 8, 9) together with fellow participants in a conference celebrating those events of a long-ago September day. Outside the church, the glitter dancing off the blue, sheltered fjord and the sheep dung recently deposited in the meadow produced an eerie sense of timelessness, but that feeling was soon put to flight by sweeping one's eyes over the ruins that were all that remained of the once prosperous farm and trading centre. Inside the church, however, time again ceased

Fig. 12   The remains of Hvalsey Church, where Sigrid Björnsdaughter and Thorstein Olafsson were married on a September Sunday in 1408

to matter while the archaeologist George Nyegaard from the Greenland National Museum described current knowledge about the building's former interior – a topic he knows better than most after his long involvement with maintaining the church ruin. Nyegaard explained that at the time of Sigrid's marriage, the inside walls may have been panelled in wood, with church vessels and glass windows adding to the impression of solid wealth, and he also noted that the Inuit name for Hvalsey fjord suggests that the church had once been whitewashed on the outside and visible at a great distance.

Both the whitewash and the inside frills are long gone, but excellent preservation measures, including work completed just a few years ago to shore up the sagging wall facing the sea, ensures that both the church and the farm ruins will be there for future generations eager to see the site of the last recorded events in Norse Greenland. Visitors should know, however, that Norse activities on Hvalsey farm and elsewhere in the Eastern Settlement were far from over when the last of the wedding guests left for home, and that is hardly cause for wonder. Sigrid's wealthy father would not have sent his eldest daughter off to a dying community, nor did Thorstein and his companions go there to 'rescue' Sigrid, but to profit in one way or another from their voyage. Thorstein's Greenland gamble paid off handsomely indeed the day he married Sigrid.

LEAVING GREENLAND IN 1410

Being foresighted as well as literate, in 1409 Thorstein obtained an affidavit about the wedding from the Gardar officialis Eindride Andreasson and the priest sira Páll Hallvardsson before he and Sigrid left Greenland in 1410, along with their companions and a cargo intended for Norwegian trade. Síra Eindride and síra Páll attested that three lawful banns had been published before the marriage took place and also noted that many people had been present at the wedding on an ordinary Sunday – again a sign that life was normal in the community.[28]

Neither the two clerics' letter nor two subsequent Icelandic affirmations, dated 1414 and 1424 respectively, mention the financial arrangements that had taken place before the church blessing was pronounced. In stark contrast to the widely documented property transactions involving Sigrid and Thorstein's descendants, all the written sources are completely silent about the agreements crafted at Hvalsey in 1408. As the newlyweds well knew, however, a spoken agreement witnessed by trusted Greenlanders and Icelanders would have carried sufficient weight in both countries, especially given that one of the witnesses was a male relative of the bride's. The plain purpose of all three affidavits was to ensure that all property transactions connected with the marriage were legal because the marriage itself was legal. Tellingly, the 1414 affidavit was discovered in a bundle with two other documents from the same

Fig. 13 View from inside the entrance to Hvalsey Church, looking across the fjord toward's Hvalsey ('Whale Island') on the right

year that concerned land transactions among Thorstein Olafsson's group of North Iceland chieftains, while the 1424 affidavit begins with Sæmund's affirmation that he, as Sigrid's kinsman, had consented to the wedding. Thus he confirmed that the marriage (and any property transfers connected with it) was in accordance with Christian practice and Icelandic law.[29]

When Thorstein and his friends left Greenland with Sigrid in 1410, theirs became the very last recorded voyage from Greenland. The record, such as it is, reveals that although the men had been absent from home for five years, they headed straight for Norway without stopping in Iceland first, therefore it is clear that they knew the sailing route perfectly well and that their cargo consisted of Greenlandic export goods suitable for trade in Norway. When they arrived in Bergen, they nevertheless avoided even a pro forma trial for having defrauded the Crown. The circumspect annalist who observed for 1406 that the party had drifted off course on their way to Iceland in a heavy fog, noted for 1410 only the travellers' high rank and mentioned no public concern over their voyage at all. This sanitised record in the *New Annals* is likely due to the probable author of that section of the work, namely Thorstein's well-connected and loyal brother Arni, who died in 1430, the same year the *New Annals* end.[30]

The administrative confusion in Bergen at the end of Queen Margrethe's reign may have helped Thorstein and his company to get off as easily as they did, but the chief reason would have been that they had had their way smoothed in advance by Thorstein's two brothers, Arni and Hall, together with their powerful friends. In 1409, the year before Thorstein and Sigrid left Greenland, Hall Olafsson had been one of the many chieftains at the Althing who signed a document affirming that, generally speaking, the Norwegian Crown owned one quarter of the space aboard ships going to Iceland *from* Norway, but also making it clear that exceptions might be made if, for example, the ship belonged to one person but had been rented to another, or if the king or his representatives had granted an exemption. At least one of the signatories to this document, Vigfus Ivarsson, was able to grant such exemptions in Iceland. Besides being a royal governor, Vigfus was a friend of Björn the 'Jerusalem-Farer' and belonged to the powerful group of chieftains consisting of the recent Greenland-farers' kinsmen. Others who signed this document held positions of power in Norway, including two members of the City Council in Bergen who had visited Iceland during the 1409 Althing meeting. They were clearly on their way home soon afterwards, for by 13 September that year, the three Icelandic versions of the document (dated 3, 7 and 13 July) had been transcribed and witnessed back in Bergen.[31]

FROM NORWAY TO ICELAND

Thorstein and Sigrid settled at Great Akrar in northern Iceland when they returned from Norway in 1411, just when English fish merchants and fishermen were establishing themselves in Iceland and the adjoining seas, setting in train a series of events which will be the focus of Chapter Nine. That same year, Björn the 'Jerusalem-Farer' also arrived home, fit and well, having completed his journey to the Holy Land and spent a winter in the Shetland Islands.[32]

From the moment Thorstein brought Sigrid home to her native land, he regarded her inherited property Great Akrar as his own principal seat, therefore his and Sigrid's only child, Kristín, became known as Akra-Kristín to distinguish her from Björn the 'Jerusalem-Farer's daughter Vatnsfjord-Kristín. He also considered Thorleiksstead, Sigrid's maternal inheritance, a desirable biproduct of his marriage; when he wanted to build a chapel there in 1431, the Hólar bishop's permission called the farm Thorstein's own property. His and Sigrid's heirs also found the property useful – in 1456, for example, Akra-Kristín's second husband, Torfi Arason, paid with his share in Thorleiksstead for a favour that had gained him the office of lawman. In 1489, Akra-Kristín sat at Thorleiksstead in her old age while selling off some of her land elsewhere, and when her wealth was to be distributed, her heirs held a meeting at Thorleiksstead to discuss the matter.[33]

A series of carefully recorded transactions undertaken within Thorstein and Sigrid's North Iceland circle focuses only on the properties Sigrid had inherited; the documents are completely silent about Sigrid herself. Only by inference is it clear that she was still alive in 1436, having survived the smallpox epidemic of 1431–32 that killed both Thorstein and his brother Hall (Arni had died abroad). Her life back home had seemingly been as quiet throughout as her husband's had been busy, but the wife of such an important man would inevitably have been touched by the growing English presence in Iceland, by the power grabs at the highest level in her own circle and by the policies of King Eirik of Pomerania.

ANOTHER TRANSFER OF ROYAL POWER

Just a year after Sigrid and Thorstein had returned to their North Iceland farm, Queen Margrethe's death marked the start of another downturn in Norway's economic situation and her relations with the Atlantic colonies. King Eirik of Pomerania, now thirty years old and in sole power in Norway, Denmark and Sweden, perpetuated his aunt's trade policies for thirty more years. He also engaged in a series of fruitless foreign wars that constituted a steady drain on the state coffers, and his increasingly desperate efforts to raise money diverted his attention further from the needs of his subjects in Norway and its Atlantic satellites.

Icelandic chieftains felt these developments keenly when their own powers were usurped at home and abroad, at the same time as they were preoccupied with the changes the English presence had brought in their country. Thorstein Olafsson played his chieftain's role for high stakes, cushioned by Sigrid's wealth and his tight network of powerful friends and kinsmen, until he disappears from the written record in 1431. At that time, he was the lawman for southern and eastern Iceland and in that capacity signed an Althing resolution, addressed to King Eirik, of which he had probably been the chief instigator. It gave vent to the Icelandic chieftains' sense of having been betrayed by the English, whom they had befriended, and by King Eirik, to whom they had sworn fealty. Those who signed the petition were almost all from Thorstein's jurisdiction, and by signing such a document they had essentially become rebels against the king.[34]

Key events leading up to that moment were just as closely linked to Thorstein and Sigrid's circle of powerful Icelanders as were the events that followed, and they have the English presence in Iceland as their central theme.

9

THE ENGLISH IN THE NORTH ATLANTIC

Fish has always been a major source of protein in the Far North. Ari's Book of Settlements blamed the Norwegian pre-settlement visitor Flóki and his men for being so busy catching the abundant fish in the fjord that they failed to gather hay for their cattle; elsewhere the work tells about the early settler Ásolf, a good Christian, who had to move three times because his heathen neighbours took it badly that, no matter where he settled down and built houses, his farm creek was always full of fish. He went down in history as 'the holiest of men'.[1]

The Icelanders of six hundred years ago would have been as capable of pulling in the fish as their present-day peers aboard the small, one-man cod fishing boats that come in from the open sea with their catch already gutted, done by the boat's owner along with baiting and setting the lines, handling the boat and watching the sea. Nowadays, the fish mostly ends up frozen, but from the time they first arrived in their island, the Icelanders used the age-old Norwegian method of preserving their catch by wind-drying it without salt. Cod cured in this manner is called stockfish, as distinct from klippfish, the latter being cod that has been heavily salted before being laid out to dry, following a method that came in around 1500. The new method made it possible to complete the curing process so quickly that it could be used in a milder, damper climate than that required for producing the unsalted, wind-dried stockfish. Before that time, stockfish was essentially the only choice for consumers needing inexpensive protein with good keeping qualities, and for centuries, the stockfish trade was a steady source of income for Crown and Church in Norway. It brought riches to medieval Bergen and its bishops, and the Norwegian archbishop was still busily expanding his central position in the stockfish trade in the late Middle Ages. Stockfish was also the staple driving Hanse enterprise in Norway.[2]

After Iceland had submitted to the Norwegian Crown and its tax laws, exported Icelandic stockfish became a source of conflict not only between Norway and Iceland but, by extension, between the English and Hanse fish merchants vying for a product that was in increasingly great demand as European populations began to recover from the mid-fourteenth-century devastations of the Black Death. That recovery began at about the same time that the Plague of 1402–04 killed so many people in Iceland that the country was not only short of fishermen and other labour, but was poorly positioned to defend their fishing grounds when the English decided to catch much of the fish themselves off Iceland's shores. They also bought as much stockfish as the Icelanders could provide, but supplies were not inexhaustible, and the competition for cod soon became fierce. Some of the English visitors resorted to outright violence, while others looked for new fishing grounds farther and farther west, towards Greenland and beyond. This chapter will follow some of that development, especially as it relates to the possible consequences for the Norse in Greenland when, as magistrates, Thorstein and several of the friends who had gone to Greenland with him became involved with the relentless English pursuit of cod and cod products.

THE SWEET SMELL OF PROFIT

Until humans figured out how to take to the air, the sea was their perfect highway for long-distance trade. Ever since Iceland was settled, the route there was known to the English, who have seldom taken the back seat in commercial matters, and who were obviously well aware of the resources of the Far North from early on. The Anglo-Saxon world map dating from the first half of the eleventh century (although based on an earlier Roman map) depicts both Norway and Iceland in a realistic relationship to the British Isles.[3] Social and cultural connections among the three countries were important throughout the Middle Ages, as the written sources demonstrate, but the huge upswing in English sailings to Iceland shortly before 1400 had little to do with social niceties and everything to do with cod.

The English had long been buying stockfish in Norway, often in violation of royal prerogatives, and had become the middlemen for the stockfish trade to the Iberian Peninsula. Reacting to royal trade restrictions in Norway and the growing influence of Hanse merchants in Bergen, they decided around 1400 that going to Iceland might help them circumvent both the Hanse and the Norwegian monopoly restrictions. By then, they were in a much better position than earlier to exploit the sea lanes to Iceland, because they were now building two- or three-masted ships with high pointed bows that could counter strong head seas, and with improved rigging that enabled them to stay a course within six or seven points of the wind. These improvements also brought changes to the ancient pattern of seasonal sailing in the North Atlantic. Sailings between England and Iceland (and from Norway to Iceland and Greenland), had earlier taken place almost entirely during the summer, which usually made it necessary to overwinter before the return voyage, but now, at the very time when the Icelanders' needs were mostly ignored by the Dano-Norwegian authorities and contact with Greenland was left entirely to illicit private enterprise, the English could sail to Iceland and home again in one extended season and not be beholden to anyone for winter quarters.[4] In both Iceland and Norway, the 'spring' fishing season began amid ice, snow and howling gales in February. English fishermen, too, usually left England for Iceland between February and April, returning home in August-September at the latest. It would be an understatement to say that it was a risky business – in a Maundy Thursday gale in 1419, no fewer than twenty-five English ships were lost off Iceland.[5]

A brief entry for 1396 in the 'Gottskalk Annals' notes that six ships were at anchor in the Westman Islands when a local farmer was killed in the night. Assigning the incident to 1397, the *New Annals* observe that the ships belonging to the murderers were 'foreign' and that the visitors had caused much other damage besides. Most likely the visitors were English, especially as it is certain that English fishermen visited the Iceland Banks in the spring of 1408 or 1409 and soon started searching for other fishing grounds farther to the east and west of Iceland. At first, the Icelanders welcomed the English fish merchants. Bergen had never been a good market for Icelandic stockfish in the first place, because the Norwegians produced plenty of their own, and now the English were willing to pay almost fifty per cent more than the Norwegians for the Icelandic product. The fishermen who wanted to pull their own fish from Icelandic waters for their English salt barrels were another matter.[6]

The life of those fishermen was not necessarily rosy, however. English fishing vessels had been active off the Dyrhólaey Peninsula in southern Iceland during the summer of 1412, and that autumn five of the fishermen came ashore, starving, after having been left stranded when the ships went home. The Icelanders took pity on them and saw them through the winter.

KING EIRIK COMES TO POWER

While the Icelanders in the south were adjusting to an increasing English presence, Thorstein Olafsson and Sigrid Björnsdaughter up north had been given a year in which to accustom themselves to life at Great Akrar and to becoming the parents of a baby daughter, but if their lives that year were tranquil, that situation was soon to change. Queen Margrethe died in 1412, oblivious to the recent events at Dyrhólaey, and Eirik of Pomerania was now at the helm. Without wasting any time, Thorstein's brother Arni and Arni's powerful Norwegian employer rode off in search of King Eirik and finally located him in Hälsingborg in Scania, which was Danish at the time. Evidently in a good mood from having just had a counterfeiter shot and his hirðstjóri hanged, the king was well disposed towards Arni and lavished lucrative appointments on him. Arni returned to Iceland in 1415 aboard a ship of his own, not only as the bishop of Skálholt but as the royal governor of all Iceland. In addition, the merchants of Bergen had deputised him to collect their debts in Iceland for them, and he was appointed Church visitator for all of Iceland.[7]

In the three years prior to Arni's homecoming, several events had affected the English involved in the stockfish trade. King Eirik had allowed the Hanse grip on Norwegian trade to tighten in step with the Crown's restrictions on trade with Norway's Atlantic satellites, and in 1413, a house in Bergen belonging to Englishmen from Kings Lynn was burned to the ground, courtesy of the Hanse and the competition for cod. The incident gave the English additional reason to go to Iceland for stockfish as well as for salted fish, which they called 'wet' or 'green' fish. In 1413 alone, there were more than thirty English fishing doggers in Iceland. English fishermen also arrived in the north of Iceland that year and peremptorily took some cattle for which they 'left behind some money'. Those incidents would necessarily have involved Thorstein, his magisterial kinsmen and his friends with the English visitors.[8]

In the south, an English merchant named Richard arrived that same year, bearing a letter from King Eirik of Denmark-Norway with permission to trade in his realm without paying toll. Later that summer, Eirik also sent letters to Iceland forbidding the inhabitants to trade with foreign merchants except for those with whom they had traded in the past – a construction that suggests that this was not Richard's first visit to Iceland.

Richard rode off to present his letter to the *hirðstjóri* Vigfús Ivarsson while his ship sailed along the coast to the farm of the rich and powerful Gísli Andresson, who had married Gudrun Styrsdaughter when she had supposed herself the widow of the Hvalsey wedding guest Snorri Torfason (Chapter Eight). As luck would have it, 1413 also saw Snorri returning to Iceland after four years in Greenland and three in Norway. Gudrun had just ridden to meet him when Richard the Englishman turned up at her second husband's home, where delicate negotiations must necessarily have followed, in which case the English visitor would also have heard about Snorri's Greenland visit.[9]

THORSTEIN OLAFSSON'S CIRCLE AND THE ENGLISH

Snorri was probably still in the south of Iceland when the 1414 affidavit confirming the legality of Thorstein and Sigrid's Hvalsey marriage was signed at Great Akrar, because Snorri's name does not join those of his friends Thord Jörundsson, Thorbjörn Bárdsson, Jón Jonsson and Brand Halldorsson.

Like his good friend Thorstein Olafsson, Brand had been born into the centre of power in northern Iceland and was able to act as his own scribe. He was also rich and became even richer and more powerful after he married a daughter of the lawman Hrafn Gudmundsson. Through Brand, just as much as through Snorri, Thorstein and his other friends, the English had contact with the 1406 Greenland-farers from the beginning. Eventually, Brand had an unpleasant experience with some of the Englishmen, but when he signed the 1414 wedding affidavit at Thorstein and Sigrid's home, the English in Iceland were still enjoying a comparatively trouble-free period.[10]

Björn Einarsson 'Jerusalem-Farer', who had been back in North Iceland since 1411, soon found himself having to deal directly with the rapidly increasing number of English fishermen and fish merchants converging on his country. He was thrust into the centre of power in 1414 when Thorstein's brother Arni – newly made *hirðstjóri* (royal governor) of all Iceland – appointed him his ombudsman for a year. Arni himself arrived in 1415, replacing Vigfús Ivarsson, the governor who had permitted the English fish merchant Richard to stay and trade in 1413. Making the most of his friendly relations with the English, Vigfús went to England with his wife, mother and eight children aboard one of the English ships visiting in Iceland in 1415, bringing luggage that catered to what he had evidently learned about contemporary English tastes: forty to sixty lasts of cod and 'much burned silver'. That same October, the Prior and Chapter of Canterbury Cathedral announced that they had placed him and his entire family under their protection because Vigfús had assured them that he was related to Thomas Becket.[11]

Because Arni combined the office of governor with that of the Skálholt bishop, he had now become the most powerful man in Iceland. The *New Annals* are as discreet about the royal governor's business while Arni held that office as they had been about Thorstein Olafsson's 1406–10 voyage from Norway to Greenland and back. They are equally cautious about any dealings which Arni and his episcopal successor at Skálholt had with the English prior to 1430.[12] Nevertheless, we know that Arni was well disposed towards the English merchants and fishermen, and that this was an attitude which King Eirik did not share. He saw the English as intent on abusing both his royal monopoly and the privileges of the Hanse in Bergen.

The year Arni returned to Iceland, Eirik sent his chief official in Bergen and the bishop of Oslo to England with a letter to his brother-in-law, Henry V. Henry was busy at Agincourt just then, so the Duke of Bedford replied on his behalf to Eirik's complaint about the damage done by English fishermen in Iceland 'and the adjoining islands' with an assurance that all sailings directly from England to islands in King Eirik's dominions – *particularly* to Iceland – had been forbidden for at least a year. Hereafter, English ships would go to Iceland only via the Bergen Staple. Shortly after this message went out, Henry V returned from France, and King Eirik's ambassadors pleaded their cause directly with him. Henry responded with a letter to his 'beloved brother Eirik', repeating the Duke of Bedford's injunctions, which were to be read aloud in sixteen towns in England. The House of Commons disliked the ban against fishing in Iceland, however, and petitioned against it, saying that English fishermen had been going to Iceland to good purpose for the past six or seven years at least and that such a ban would have very bad consequences for the English.[13]

Unable now to get letters patent from either King Eirik or King Henry, the English contented themselves with procuring licenses in Iceland from the governor there, Bishop Arni, and continued to sail to Iceland to fish and trade.

MOVING WESTWARDS

Ashore, increasing competition caused heated tempers among the English cod merchants who had come to Iceland for the stockfish, and rivalry for fresh fish soon had so many English fishing doggers on the Icelandic coastal banks that enterprising fishermen explored the possibilities farther west. There is good reason to believe that fishermen from Bristol, well accustomed to searching ever farther north and west for fish, were soon fishing off the east coast of Greenland in the late summer, when the Icelandic fishing season would be on the wane, and that they had probably found the large banks off Newfoundland by about 1430. In the opinion of one Icelandic historian, trading doggers would have been among the first English ships to round Cape Farewell, and he also took it for granted that the Norse Greenlanders at Herjolfsness and in the Hvalsey fjord disposed over ships and had been able to trade in stockfish, but assumed that this activity would have been curtailed by English pirates operating in the waters around Iceland after about 1400.[14] There is every reason to believe that the Norse Greenlanders still disposed over ships and had stockfish to trade, but a number of documents testify that the risks facing non-English mariners approaching Greenland came slightly later, from about 1420 onwards, when the waters around Iceland were indeed controlled by English ships. Thorstein Olafsson and his company had certainly encountered no problems either when sailing from Norway to Greenland in 1406 or when leaving in 1410 with a cargo worth taking straight to Norway.

Thorstein and his friends knew the Eastern Settlement to be a normal, viable Norse community when they left it. Returning home in 1411 and learning that the English merchants paid up to twice as much as the Norwegians for dried cod, Thorstein, at least, would surely have found it natural to encourage one or more English merchants to become middlemen for trade in Greenland stockfish and other export goods, bypassing King Eirik's tax collectors altogether. Although Greenland may have been too distant to benefit from the Norwegian codfish trade when it began its rapid expansion in the early fourteenth century, English ships already in Icelandic waters could easily and safely provide a fifteenth-century link between Greenland and the growing English market for cod.

Such an arrangement would have been particularly tempting if Sigrid still had farm property in Greenland and could expect an income from accumulations of stockfish and other export wares. It is hard to believe that she and Thorstein never thought of Greenland again after they left in 1410. They could not have predicted Greenland's eventual isolation from Iceland, and Sigrid may even have left behind an heir to the Hvalsey farm, in which case she would have wanted to go back in order to be present when the child came of age or got married. Both kinds of occasions would have involved property settlements requiring witnesses.

An indication that Sigrid did retain property interests in Greenland occurred ten years after the 1414 confirmation that Thorstein's and Sigrid's Hvalsey wedding had been proper and legal. Like its predecessor, the affidavit signed at Great Akrar in 1424 ultimately concerned property, but with the important difference that this time it was Sigrid's kinsman Sæmund who testified that he had been present at the Hvalsey wedding; Thorstein's friends merely witnessed Sæmund's testimony.[15] This suggests that the 1424 document was prompted by concern about property belonging to Sigrid alone, not by a transaction or dispute involving land she owned jointly with Thorstein. However, supposing that an event at Hvalsey had renewed the focus on Sigrid's property dispositions at the time of her marriage to Thorstein, did the couple themselves make it back to Greenland in connection with the event? The known record for the time that had passed since their marriage indicates that they did go back, and the time span involved suggests that the coming of age or the marriage of a child from Sigrid's first marriage was the likely cause of their visit.

WHERE WAS THORSTEIN IN 1419–20?

Thorstein was fully integrated into the North Iceland power élite in 1419. That year, he was the only layman on a panel of judges appointed by the bishop of Hólar; in 1420 he was on the list of the most important North Iceland chieftains; and as *hirðstjóri* he supervised a property dispute involving his cousin Vatnsfjord-Kristín in the spring of 1421. Despite his prominence, however, his name does not appear on the letter addressed to King Eirik, signed on 1 July 1419 by a number of North Iceland chieftains attending the Althing, nor did he sign a letter to the king written at the Althing a year later to complain about the English. Thorstein's brother Hall and his uncle Arnfinn Thorsteinsson signed both letters, and so did Sigrid's kinsman Sæmund Oddsson.[16]

The reason Thorstein did not sign the second (1420) letter might conceivably have been that he disagreed with his peers about the threat posed by the English, but it is harder to explain why his name is missing from the 1419 letter, although this, too, refers in passing to English violence in Iceland while it mainly shows the chieftains' mixed feelings about their Dano-Norwegian superiors and the English in their country. After formally stating their allegiance to King Eirik, those who signed the 1419 letter complained that Norway's 1362 covenant with Iceland, which stipulated the arrival of six trading ships annually, was now so badly abused by the Crown that the Icelanders found it necessary to trade with foreigners who had come on peaceful and legitimate business. The chieftains duly added that owners and crews of fishing doggers had robbed Icelanders ashore and also caused trouble at sea, but they were also careful to observe that the Icelanders themselves had punished these offenders. The message to Eirik was clear: the Icelanders wanted him to permit peaceful trade with the English to make up for the neglect of the Norwegian authorities, a situation for which the Icelanders could not be blamed. The chieftains also showed considerable political shrewdness by first expressing deference to the king and then noting that they themselves had dealt with the most violent English *fishermen*, as opposed to those peaceful and welcome merchants. Taken together, their statements would have made it hard to accuse them of having acted against the king's wishes on purpose or to claim that they could not maintain law and order on their own.

It is difficult to see why Thorstein would have objected to this letter, which had satisfied his relatives and other peers whose economic and political views he is likely to have shared. The most reasonable explanation for the absence of his name on the 1419 document is that he did not attend the 1419 Althing, where his presence would have been mandatory unless he was gravely ill or out of the country. Between May 1417 and the autumn of 1419 the written sources are so silent about him that he may well have been out of the country, off to Greenland while his brother Arni was still the most powerful layman and churchman in Iceland and his brother Hall and his uncle Arnfinn yet again dealt with the Crown in Norway and Denmark.

If Thorstein went back to Greenland, he may by this time have found the intrusive presence of English ships in Icelandic waters a good reason to undertake his voyage aboard an English ship. Finding an English merchant happy to beat the growing competition for fish in Iceland would surely have been easy, particularly because the existence and general location of Greenland had been known to northern seafarers for centuries.

Any English fish merchant undertaking such a voyage in defiance of King Eirik's prerogatives would have been unlikely to share the information and his profits with others or to make it part of the written record. The absence of written mention about any part of this enigmatic interval in Thorstein's career provides only part of the reason for suspecting that he (and possibly some of his North Iceland friends) had acted as liaison between the Eastern Settlement farmers and one or more English stockfish merchants, and that he and Sigrid had found occasion to go back to Hvalsey at least once because a child of Sigrid's had reached adulthood/marriageable age.

Archaeological finds also come into play here, with artefacts of English origin discovered in late-phase Eastern Settlement strata, including at Hvalsey, and with some remarkable women's garments found in Herjolfsness graves.

THE GROUND SPEAKS CLEARLY

Nørlund's excavations of the Herjolfsness churchyard have been widely discussed since the 1920s, but it has received surprisingly little scrutiny that among some of the garments used as shrouds were women's dresses in styles similar to those used elsewhere in Europe in the first half of the fifteenth century. The models for these garments would not have been worn by male sailors from either England or the Nordic countries; they would not have belonged in any known inventory of English merchant ships in the northwestern Atlantic during the fifteenth century; and it is improbable that English wives had been brought along on trading or fishing voyages that lasted for several months aboard cramped and smelly ships.[17] Given the rupture of official contact with Norway even before 1400, the woman or women whose clothes had inspired the more recent Herjolfsness dresses are therefore likely to have been Icelandic.

Nørlund, an historian by training, thought the sad tales of devastation resulting from ruptured Norwegian communications with Greenland must have been greatly exaggerated, and he noted that the fifteenth-century dresses he found at Herjolfsness mostly belonged to a higher social level than the dresses of common people known from contemporaneous European images. One Herjolfsness woman had gone to her grave wrapped in a particularly elaborate dress, made from Greenland wool twill, in a style datable to the first half of the fifteenth century. The dress had a bodice shaped by stitched-down, narrow pleats in front, a deep V-neck and set-in sleeves wide at the top and tapering at the wrist – the unknown Norse Greenland woman who made it had spared no effort while copying a garment she had seen on a woman coming from abroad. Thorstein's luckless cousin Steinunn had possibly worn something like it when she arrived from Norway in 1406 – the first woman to arrive in Greenland since Sigrid came there to be wed in the 1390s, as far as one can tell. However, the elegance of the Herjolfsness dress, the general circumstances of the find and the time it would have taken for any new European court fashion to catch on elsewhere, let alone be copied in Greenland, all point to a somewhat later date. And that suggests the possibility that the wealthy Sigrid Björnsdaughter had come back for a visit in Greenland dressed in the latest Icelandic fashions, perhaps inspired by English clothes worn by some of her peers.[18]

How Sigrid had arrived in Greenland the first time must be inferred from circumstantial evidence, and the same is true concerning the story of Thorstein and Sigrid's likely activities during the period 1417–20 as well as with any assumption that Thorstein had encouraged English trade with Greenland. Fortunately, the evidence for English visitors in the Eastern Settlement is concrete. Artefacts of English origin in late-phase strata at Norse Greenland farms testify to direct contact with the British Isles in the fifteenth century. These discoveries involve three of the four major trading sites in the colony. A pendant cross made from an English pewter alloy has been found at Hvalsey. A late-medieval manufactured table knife, with a typological twin found in London, was discovered in a late stratum at Gardar (allowance should probably also be made for the likelihood that the cutlery used aboard ships in the far northern codfish trade was not in the very latest style). From the Herjolfsness shore (Fig. 14) comes a crucifix made of jet, suggesting an origin from the area around Whitby. Also worth noting is the discovery, in the uppermost stratum of a late-period Norse ruin in the Vatnahverfi region, of four pieces of semi-manufactured iron that would fit the description of 'osmunds', small pieces of iron scrap, which the fifteenth-century English used to barter for cod in Iceland. They obtained their good-quality iron chiefly from Sweden (the home of real osmund iron), Normandy and Spain. One of the four pieces found in Greenland was recently analysed by the Danish scientist Vagn Fabritius Buchwald, who judged it to have been produced in Sweden.[19] He did not examine the other three pieces.

IN ICELAND MEANWHILE…

A couple of other events in Iceland during the summer of 1419, when Thorstein failed to sign the Althing letter to King Eirik, add to the circumstantial evidence for Thorstein's absence from Iceland around that time.

The lucrative career of Thorstein's brother Arni came to a sudden and rumour-encrusted end in 1419, when he departed Iceland by way of the Westman Islands, never to return. Before he left Iceland, he made his and Thorstein's uncle Arnfinn his ombudsman as *hirðstjóri* (later that summer, King Eirik replaced Arnfinn with his own man). Arnfinn therefore called himself *hirðstjóri* of all Iceland when, two weeks after he had put his name to the 1 July letter to King Eirik, he signed a letter giving two English

Fig. 14   The lovely harbour at Herjolfsness with ruins from the medieval farm in the foreground

merchants permission to trade in the Westman Islands and all over Iceland, and also to fish for one year with as many men as they pleased. Had Thorstein been present at the Althing in 1419, he would presumably have been a good candidate for Arni's temporary replacement. As it turned out, he was appointed *hirðstjóri* in 1421 when Arni had been absent for two years. It is also striking that Thorstein's name does not appear in connection with any other business at the 1419 assembly, nor in last-minute transactions connected with Arni's departure.[20]

Bishop Arni may have agreed to carry to the king both the 1 July letter and the one written two weeks later. Both documents are still in Danish archives. Because his departure was so abrupt, scholars have generally assumed that he had had a falling out with King Eirik over money or politics, but this is unlikely to have been the case. Just a year later, when Arni acknowledged a debt while at Laaland in Denmark, his guarantors were the king's chamberlain and four others who counted among the most important people in the Dano-Norwegian realm. Arni had reportedly brought goods earmarked for the king with him from Iceland, which he had sold in Bergen because he feared an attack by the pirates who, due to King Eirik's quarrels with Schleswig, were now increasingly frequent in the waters between Denmark and Norway. Arni's successor at Skálholt, the Dane Jón Gerreksson, was appointed in 1426. Nothing is known about Arni's last years, except that he died abroad sometime between 1425 and 1430.[21]

A FURTHER SEA CHANGE

The summer of Bishop Arni's departure marked a turning point in the Icelanders' relations with King Eirik as well as with the English. While the Icelanders welcomed the English merchants on the one hand and decried the violence of English fishermen on the other during the turbulent years 1419 and 1420, King Eirik's attention was focused elsewhere. Two things nevertheless remained unchanged: the mixture of opportunism and personal loyalties that characterised Icelandic chieftains' dealings with each other as well as with the king, and Sigrid and Thorstein's inner circle's grip on power. Yet even the mightiest Icelandic chieftains must have worked side-by-side with King Eirik's personal representatives, especially in situations involving the English.

The two groups did not necessarily have common goals when weighing royal trade privileges against the Icelanders' own expectations or against large-scale acts of violence perpetrated by English visitors. In the summer of 1420, for example, men from Hull – including the sea captain Richard of 1413 fame – killed and looted at Hólar See in the north and elsewhere in the Skagafjord region, in fights so savage that a number of English lives were lost as well. During the next few years, they reportedly pillaged the countryside and burned churches, and during the years 1422–24 they robbed the royal farm at Bessastaðir annually.[22]

There is no reason to suppose that Greenland suffered similar attacks by the English. For one thing, the English who sailed deep into the Eastern Settlement fjords would not have been fishermen, whose operations were along the outer coasts. Instead, they would have been merchants, quite few in number, with more to gain from trade than from threatening people who outnumbered them. For another, by this time Norse Greenland chieftains did not interact directly with Norwegian authorities and therefore would not have been manoeuvering for personal notice as their Iceland peers did, nor did the Eastern Settlement have the kind of royal officials and sycophants whose efforts to curb English enterprise, both in 1419 and for several years more, caused much of the violence in Iceland.

King Eirik evidently was not reassured by the two letters that reached him from Iceland in the summer of 1419, because later that same summer he sent along his replacement for Arnfinn *hirðstjóri* in the person of his royal chaplain, Hannes Pálsson, who clearly intended to keep an eye on both the Icelandic chieftains and the English visitors. Hannes arrived in the company of 'many other Danes' and Bishop Jón of Hólar. Thorstein Olafsson was familiar with both men (for example, Bishop Jón asked Thorstein, Hannes and four more clerics to judge a property transaction made while Bishop Arni had been the ombudsman at Hólar See). Another of King Eirik's men, a German named Stephan Schellendorp, was also in Iceland that spring of 1420. He reported to the king that the English merchants and fishermen in Iceland were behaving very badly, and unctuously he observed that while both he and Hannes were working very hard to control the situation, it might be advisable for more of the king's men to come out to Iceland to prevent the English from taking over.[23]

In April 1420, Hannes and the local royal official in the Westman Isles charged six English merchants and their men with having traded and overwintered illegally and ordered them to appear before the next Althing. The Englishmen never showed up, but this and similar situations were the background for the 1420 Althing and to the new letter from the chieftains to King Eirik which Arnfinn, Hall Olafsson and several others of Thorstein Olafsson's kinsmen and friends signed, but not Thorstein himself. The letter stated that Thorleif Arnason (Björn the 'Jerusalem-Farer's son-in-law) and Hannes Pálsson would soon be setting out to see the king to tell him about the difficulties the Icelanders faced. Among the Icelandic chieftains, Thorleif was one of the people most likely to benefit hugely from the Englishmen's trade, but choosing him to complain to King Eirik nevertheless made sense if his peers sent him along as a counterweight to Hannes, an outsider who could not be trusted to relay the Icelanders' own concerns and who may in fact have made the chieftains write the letter. Hannes and Thorleif travelled separately on their errand to the king; Thorleif was so wealthy that he had a ship of his own. Near the Faeroes, his ship was attacked by a large English vessel marking English control of those waters, but Thorleif and his men fought them off and went on to Norway, where people were complaining not only about Englishmen trading illegally north of Hålogaland, but also about attacks by Russians and 'heathens' (Carelians) in the north.[24] King Eirik paid attention to those activities only when his income or his honour abroad might be at stake.

SHARPENED CONFLICT WITH THE ENGLISH

The winter of 1423 was a very bad one, according to the *New Annals*, which also noted a shortage of fish that year. In the summer of 1424, a furious

Englishman named John Selby attempted to solve the shortage problem for his own part by capturing Thorstein Olafsson's wealthy friend and neighbour Brand Halldorsson, exacting from him a ransom of four lasts of dried codfish. Brand's temper was not the best, however (he had mortally wounded a man in a fight at the 1421 Althing), so it is quite possible that he had either refused to honour a business agreement with Selby or else had used his clout as the king's man to bully the Englishman. In any event, Hannes Pálsson, also a very violent man, took note of Selby's deed. Hannes and another of King Eirik's men, Balthazar von Damminn, were captured by the English in the Westman Islands in 1425 and taken to England – an act for which few men in Iceland were sorry, the *New Annals* sourly noted. Hannes used his English captivity to draw up for King Eirik a list of thirty-seven outrages committed by the English in Iceland between 1420 and 1425. The king responded with a decree which, translated into English, was made public in Kings Lynn in Norfolk in February 1426. It reiterated that all Englishmen sailing to Iceland without Eirik's permission would be called to account. By this time, Hannes had lodged his complaints with the English Council, and an English injunction against voyages to Iceland had also been issued in consequence. The Kings Lynn merchants and fishermen therefore knew what they risked if they kept going to Iceland. Blithely ignoring both injunctions, John Vache brought his ship into Kings Lynn that autumn at the end of a voyage to Iceland.[25]

The factual basis for several of Hannes Pálsson's complaints is dubious, but reality dominates in his claim that the English had taken a number of children and youths from Iceland, either by force or by paying their naive parents a pittance. These youngsters were now living in greatest misery in England, and Iceland was becoming depopulated in many places, according to Hannes. Just four years after he lodged his complaints, eleven Icelandic boys and girls were in fact offered for sale in Kings Lynn. Bishop Jón Gereksson of Skálholt was visiting the town just then (1429), because he was already in England as King Eirik's representative to negotiate with Henry VI about the continuing violations of their agreement to limit the English fish trade to the Bergen Staple. It was very likely he who got the local merchants to promise that they would send the children back home the following spring.[26]

Hannes was merely the first to assert that the Icelanders gave or sold their children to foreigners, displeasing big landowners who complained about a shortage of labourers. In 1432, King Eirik ordered the English to free any people they had abducted from the northern countries, especially Iceland, Finnmark and Hálogaland and 'any other territory in the

Norwegian realm' (hverju ödru landi Noregs rikis) – a frequently used term that was so imprecise that it could also have included the Greenlanders, should anyone still be worrying about them. Many Icelandic children were indeed sent home, but the English economic historian E. M. Carus-Wilson noted that some must have remained in England, voluntarily or involuntarily, given the number of Icelandic men and women who show up in the Subsidy Rolls, or the people 'born in Iceland' who swore fealty to the English king. Martin Behaim, whose 1492 Nuremberg globe bears witness to more than a little confusion about the geography of the Far North, demonstrated that in some form, the notion of these English abductions survived in Europe for a long time. A legend near the upside-down turnip shape representing Iceland reads: 'In Iceland are handsome white people, and they are Christians. It is the custom there to sell dogs at a high price, but to give away the children to [foreign] merchants, for the sake of God, so that those remaining may have bread.'[27]

A good many of the English outrages in Hannes Pálsson's list concerned disputes with Danish officials and alleged thefts of fish from them, rather than the theft of children. Half of the complaints involved the same few people, many of them from Hull, which was always more of a centre for piracy than Kings Lynn and Bristol, which do not show up at all in the *hirðstjóri*'s report. Carus-Wilson took that as an indication that the English mostly 'carried on a peaceful trade to the advantage of all concerned'. 'Peaceful' is a relative quality, however, in a violent age in which the English did not have a monopoly on looting and killing. It is also debatable just how law-abiding men from Kings Lynn and Bristol were compared with those from Hull. For example, Bristol merchants held foreign merchants prisoners for ransom during the period 1424–25, by which time Bristolmen had already found their way to Iceland.[28]

THE ENGLISH TIGHTEN THEIR GRIP

There was less and less chance that King Eirik would interfere with the growing English hegemony at sea, no matter how much he wanted to control the stockfish trade. Both in Denmark and on the continent, his disastrous foreign policies had him enmeshed in problems, and as a financial milch cow the Norwegian economy was in deteriorating health. Norwegian naval power – already reduced – received crushing blows in 1428 and 1429 when Hanse pirates attacked Bergen and devastated the ships in its harbour. For a long time afterwards, few ships were sent out from Norway, and English codfish merchants considered the Bergen Staple less desirable than ever. Nevertheless, in 1429 the English government issued a decree stating that English codfish merchants could go *only* to the Bergen Staple, where King Eirik had given the Germans and the English equal rights, and not to Finnmark or any other place in the Danish kingdom prohibited to foreign merchants.[29]

Unfazed, the English continued to defy both their own king and King Eirik, but to document their activities in detail is not possible. English documents for the fifteenth century pertinent to the English expansion into the northwestern Atlantic mostly concern power politics and relations with the Dano-Norwegian Crown, not the activities of lowly fishermen, and tracking English codfish merchants becomes an increasing challenge as trading licenses grew increasingly vague about actual destinations. There are also serious gaps in the medieval records from Bristol, the English city that became most closely associated with early English westward expansion, and records of voyages from Iceland to Bergen ceased for a long time.[30]

While direct communication between Norway and Iceland dwindled, many ambitious Icelanders looked for advancement in Denmark rather than at home. Englishmen and other foreigners were appointed bishops in Iceland, the first one being Jón Vilhjalmsson (John Williamsson Craxton) of Hólar. He was appointed in 1426 and arrived in Iceland aboard an English ship the following year, but when he read his letter of appointment at the Althing, he got such an unfriendly reception from the North Icelanders that he decided to leave Iceland again that same summer. He seems to have been an astute merchant, however. Before going out to Iceland in 1427, he had obtained a licence from the English king to trade with wheat, malt or barley to Iceland, on a ship departing from either Kings Lynn, Hull or Newcastle, and when he returned home that same autumn, it was presumably with a satisfying quantity of stockfish. He was back in Iceland in 1429, this time for a stay of several years at Hólar, which was within easy distance of Thorstein Olafsson and Sigrid Björnsdaughter at Great Akrar. His letter-book shows that he became well acquainted with them both. Indeed, it would have been impossible for Thorstein and the bishop to avoid constant meetings on business, for Thorstein was then at the peak of his wealth and power. He was the *hirðstjóri* of northern and western Iceland when Bishop Jón of Hólar arrived in 1429 and held that office again in 1431, concurrently with being the Lawman for southern and eastern Iceland.[31]

One might reasonably ask how well Thorstein or his peers trusted Jón and their other cod-merchant bishops, including Bishop Jón Gereksson of Skálholt, who arrived in Iceland in 1430 after a winter spent in England.

He came with a retinue of roughneck foreigners and accompanied by two priests, one of whom returned to England that same summer with a large cargo of cod. These bishops represented outside officialdom, thus threatening the chieftains' power, and they were probably the last people a native leader would have told about Icelanders acting in violation of Dano-Norwegian trade laws. Furthermore, the greed and violence they spread in their wake was so unprecedented that it seemed as if Church and Crown together had sanctioned a period of lawlessness that represented a foreign power grab at the highest level. And that is the light by which one must read the resolution addressed to King Eirik and passed at the Althing by Thorstein Olafsson and his peers in 1431 (Chapter Eight), the last year of Thorstein's life.[32] It is uncertain whether King Eirik received this petition, but his concern was in any case not with the Icelanders' well-being. He was fighting for his political survival at home.

Untroubled by royal decrees, the two English-backed bishops continued their activities in Iceland in the name of God and cod, but not for long. Jón Gereksson of Skálholt was hauled out of his cathedral and drowned by angry Icelanders in 1432 or 1433, and Jón Vilhjalmsson of Hólar found himself replaced while he was abroad in 1435.[33]

PASSING THE GENERATIONAL TORCH

In the second half of the fifteenth century, the part played by the central government in Copenhagen in the affairs of Norway and its satellites was increasingly destructive and narrowly focused on obtaining money for the Crown's European power politics. Icelandic farmers, fishermen and labourers, who exerted little or no influence on politics, were impoverished by relentless demands for taxes and tithes, preferably payable in stockfish, while their number was reduced by epidemics and natural disasters. The country's animal husbandry economy had deteriorated to the point that butter, formerly a common export article, was now imported on English ships.[34] The Icelanders who did well were the wealthiest landowners; they became royal proxies and were rarely called to account for their brutality towards either natives or foreigners. Prominent among these domestic power mongers were, as before, Thorstein Olafsson and Sigrid Björnsdaughter's friends and relations and their descendants.

Arnfinn Thorsteinsson, Thorstein's uncle, had continued to play an important part in Icelandic politics and was eventually knighted, as was his son Eyjolf after him.[35] Thorstein Olafsson and Sigrid Björnsdaughter's only child, Akra-Kristín, married twice and married well. Her first husband was

Helgi Gudnason, who traced his ancestry to Thorfinn Thordsson Karlsefni and Gudrid Thorbjörnsdaughter of Vínland fame, and after Helgi's death, Kristín married Torfi Arason, who gained prominence through power play at home. Carefully cultivating his relations with King Christian I of Denmark-Norway, he gained a knighthood in 1450 – the same year the king signed his Löngurettarbót (Long Law Code Amendment), in which he threatened all Englishmen and Irishmen who sailed to Iceland with arrest and confiscation of ship and cargo. Torfi fell ill while in Bergen in 1459, and he drew up a will in which he remembered Bishop Andres 'of Gardar', among others, and concluded with: 'I wish Kristín Thorsteinsdaughter and all my friends and kin in Iceland a very good night and ask that they will pray for me.' The very next year, Bishop Andres 'of Gardar' was throwing his weight around in Iceland as ombudsman for the Skálholt bishop and a friend of Thorleif Björnsson's (for Thorleif, see below).[36] Akra-Kristín showed herself over the years to be a tough negotiator over property rights on her own behalf as well as that of her two daughters, Yngvild Helgadaughter and Málfrid Torfadaughter. Málfrid entered into a properly arranged marriage, but Yngvild carved out a niche in contemporary lore by becoming the concubine of her third cousin Thorleif Björnsson, the son of Björn Einarsson 'Jerusalem-Farer's daughter Vatnsfjord-Kristín by her second husband. The liaison between Thorleif and Yngvild tightened the connections among the North Iceland chieftain families discussed so far and added considerably to that inner circle's number, because Thorleif had at least thirteen children by Yngvild before he finally obtained permission to marry her.

Thorleif's father was the notorious Björn Thorleifsson, whom Christian I knighted and made a *hirðstjóri* in 1457. It says something about the king's temperament that he thus honoured a man he had blamed four years earlier for the English refusal to pay harbour fees in Iceland, and whom he had more recently accused of stealing the income of Skálholt See while supposedly looking after the bishopric's affairs. Björn had both plundered and debauched as the Skálholt bishop's ombudsman, but this was a case of the pot calling the kettle black, because in 1455, Christian I had taken for his own use, from the sacristy in Roskilde Cathedral, the money collected for a joint Dano-Portuguese war against the Turks and for the relief of the king of Cyprus. All was clearly forgiven between Björn and the king, however. Björn had been high in the king's favour for ten years when he was killed in 1467 by some men from Kings Lynn, in an event that exacerbated Anglo-Danish relations further. A two-year peace treaty between Edward IV and Christian I, signed in Utrecht in 1473, attempted to defuse the situation, but the effort got little help from Björn's son Thorleif, who had been captured by his father's killers. Ransomed by his mother, Thorleif took furious revenge on the English, and then he and his mother went to Copenhagen to complain to Christian I.[37]

THE ENGLISH ENCOUNTER A HEADWIND

The Hanse had been slow to establish direct trade with Iceland, but that had changed by 1469, when men from Bremen and Braunschweig made ready to go there. Two years later, two Dutch ships from Amsterdam arrived in Iceland, and so did a German Bergen-trader. Predictably, the English felt squeezed, and vicious fighting broke out in Hafnarfjord between the Hanse and Englishmen from Hull and Bristol in both 1474 and 1475. The Danish king, now Christian I's son Hans, responded in 1478 by sending a man named Didrik Pining to Iceland as royal governor, endowed with the new title of höfuðsmaðr. Pining's apocryphal career in Greenlandic waters will be discussed in Chapter Ten; his actual job qualifications for the governorship included years of service as pirate for the king as well as his friendship with Thorleif Björnsson, who may or may not have been hirðstjóri still when Pining arrived. As observed in Chapter Seven, Pining supported Thorleif's efforts to marry Yngvild and was entrusted with silver and a horn made of walrus ivory to pay for a licence from King Hans.[38]

The 1484 nuptial agreement between Thorleif and Yngvild, which merged two of Iceland's greatest fortunes and political dynasties, came just two years before Thorleif died, but at a time when both he and Pining still had great influence with the Danish Crown. Usefully disguised as loyal to the king, they aimed to keep foreign merchants trading directly with Iceland and paying their taxes directly to the local royal representatives – themselves – rather than to Bergen, but those foreigners also had to be controlled. The two brothers-in-greed were unable to control events, however. The few sources we have for Pining's dealings with the English suggest that while he systematically forced them out of the best Icelandic harbours, he precipitated a series of English raids along the coast and attacks against the governor's residence.[39]

After one of his frequent absences from Iceland, Pining returned in 1490. King Hans had just signed (and Henry VII of England was about to sign) a treaty in which King Hans allowed the English to trade and fish in Iceland provided they obtained a licence every seven years. This provision was deleted by Pining and the chieftains at that summer's Althing when they confirmed the treaty. Instead, in what became known as the Piningsdómur (Pining's Judgment), they set their own rules for foreign merchants in Iceland, the main points of which remained in effect for a long time. The rules forbade any foreigner to spend the winter in Iceland except in an emergency and prohibited Icelanders from taking jobs as servants or sailors on a foreign ship. The following year saw even stricter measures enacted against foreign fishermen, now forbidden to operate in Icelandic waters at all unless they also engaged in trade – a restriction that obviously favoured the Hanse.[40]

These laws coincided with the waning of Pining's career in Iceland at a time when Thorleif Björnsson had been dead for four years, but there was no danger of a domestic power void. Thorleif's brother Einar, as greedy and ambitious as any man in Iceland, regarded himself as his brother's heir in more ways than one. For example, when his sister-in-law Yngvild inherited one-third of Akra-Kristín's property in 1490, Einar claimed that he was entitled to another third. A letter written at the Althing in 1491, in which twenty-five chieftains led by the husband of Yngvild's sister Málfrid asked King Hans to make Einar his new governor, makes it clear that Sigrid Björnsdaughter's huge inheritance continued to grease the biggest power wheels in Iceland almost a century after Thorstein had fetched Sigrid home from Greenland.[41]

By 1500, there was an improvement in the unstable Icelandic conditions that had made it increasingly awkward for English traders and fishermen to go there, but Bristol entrepreneurs had found a direct route to the 'Isle of Brazil' (their name for Newfoundland and its rich fishing banks) about twenty years earlier. Merchants had profited from the resurgence of Bristol's trade with France after 1475, and with further progress in shipbuilding, the conditions were evidently right for Bristol navigators to replace a triangular course to Newfoundland, by way of Iceland or Greenland, with one heading straight west-northwest from Galway.[42] Prevailing winds and currents made for an even quicker voyage home along the fifty-third parallel – the latitude of Galway – with barrels full of salted fish.

Those English navigational strides encouraged the Italian John Cabot to make Bristol his point of departure in his 1496, 1497 and 1498 Atlantic crossings. After his 1497 voyage to the 'Island of the Seven Cities'/'Isle of Brazil', the fecundity of the Newfoundland Banks could no longer be kept from common knowledge. Cabot's mostly English crew said that there was so much fish in the new land that Iceland would no longer be needed. While this optimism was wasted on Cabot, who was on a quest for a short northern route to the riches of Cathay and not for codfish, European fishermen who descended on the Newfoundland Banks in droves smelled silver of a different sort.[43]

10

WHERE DID THE NORSE GREENLANDERS GO?

The Norse Greenlanders, who were gone by the time the Dano-Norwegian authorities got around to looking for them, appear to have left on their own accord. So few artefacts have been found in the ruins of both farms and churches that it points to a community decision to move on and bring their valuables with them, and to their final departure being as deliberate as the settlers' arrival some five centuries earlier. We don't know why they left, however, nor where they went and how many people were involved in the final decision to move on. We don't even know the timing of that last move or when the last Norse bodies were buried in Greenland.

New research is now shaking up old dogmas, including the dictum that the Western Settlement was defunct around 1350. As Chapter Seven described, recent excavations at the 'Farm Beneath the Sand' demonstrated that the site's last occupation had ended around 1400. Reverence for the 1350 date is rooted in Ívar Bárdsson's 'Description of Greenland' and its account of an expedition to the Western Settlement, supposedly to aid local farmers threatened by the 'heathens'. The surviving version of Ívar's report says that the expedition found neither Christians nor heathens, only deserted farms where horses, goats, sheep and cattle grazed untended, but there is no reference to ruined houses or to a proper search by the expedition members. The account notes only that Ívar's men slaughtered as many animals as they were able, loaded the kill aboard their ships and sailed home.

This story gained additional credence from the claim made by Bishop Gísli Oddsson of Skálholt (1593–1638) that in 1342, the Greenlanders had left for North America. Gísli wrote:

> The inhabitants of Greenland of their own free will abandoned the true faith and the Christian religion, having already forsaken all good ways and true virtues, and joined themselves with the folk of America. Some consider too that Greenland lies closely adjacent to the western regions of the world. From this it came about that the Christians gave up their voyaging to Greenland.[1]

When Gísli concocted his explanation for the Norse Greenlanders' disappearance, the European colonisation of North America was well under way, and several attempts to contact the old Norse colonies in Greenland had failed. Supposedly, his information came from the Skálholt archives, but many documents were lost when the Skálholt Cathedral burned in 1630, which makes it impossible to check if the archives once contained notes about the Greenlanders' reluctance to pay church taxes – a matter likely to have been brought to the attention of Jón Sigurdsson of Skálholt when he was abroad to be consecrated in 1343. By themselves, Gísli's assertions primarily reflect his Copenhagen education and the thinking of many in his own time, and are neither evidence of the Norse Greenlanders' wholesale departure nor proof of their apostasy.

The date Gísli assigned to that final Norse migration falls five years before the 1347 Markland ship incident reported in the Icelandic annals and one year after Ívar's arrival in Greenland. Nobody would guess from Ívar's account that he came to a depopulated country or that, far from cowering from the Thule people, the Norse Greenlanders still disposed over ships and were calmly going about their business. But what should one make of Ívar's claim that a rescue expedition to the Western Settlement had found only abandoned farms and animals? As if to stress the eeriness of the scene, Ívar's 'Description' says twice that the expedition members saw neither Christians nor heathens.

Citing the need to save the Christian Norse from the heathen Skrælings as the reason for going up there in the first place, would have fit the current fashion for pious locutions in Ívar's own time, and it could equally well have been an interpolation made in the early sixteenth century, when Archbishop Valkendorf was preparing to visit Greenland and reclaim the Norse inhabitants for Church and Crown (Chapter Eleven). However, for Ívar and his contemporaries, heathens and black magic would have been so closely connected that the unexpected sight of deserted homesteads would have frightened them enough to forgo a search and get back on ship as soon as they had done their butchering.

The Gardar contingent were reportedly armed and must have looked so menacing when approaching that the Western Settlement farmers, who would very likely have understood why they were honoured with a visit, hurriedly went into hiding, leaving their defenceless animals untended. They still had contact with the Eastern Settlement and would have known about Ívar's arrival in Greenland to collect tithes and taxes for Crown and Church, and they would naturally also have been aware of their own growing reluctance to pay up. They clearly did not intend to leave their animals alone for long, however, if both horses and cattle were among them. Sheep and goats have been known to survive for several seasons by themselves, but one winter out in the open would have killed the horses and the cows.[2]

PAPAL LAMENTS

Gísli Oddsson's assertions about apostate Greenland émigrés and Ívar's gloomy description of the Western Settlement are not alone in creating befuddlement about the Norse Greenland colony's end. Two fifteenth-century papal letters concerning appointments of ostensible Gardar bishops share much of the blame.[3]

In the fifteenth century, Rome's information about the Far North had not progressed noticeably since 1192, when a Church document listing the bishoprics in the Norwegian archdiocese noted that the Faeroese See was one of two bishoprics in Greenland. As late as in 1464, the Roman Curia issued a receipt to the Norwegian bishop Alf of Stavanger – 'in Ireland'. Small wonder, then, that a 1448 letter written by a proxy for Pope Nicholas V in response to a 'pitiful lament', described Greenland as 'situated We are told at the extreme limits of the Ocean....' With good reason, the papal proxy sounded another cautious note: 'Touched as We are...by the desires expressed by the indigenous people... of this island of Greenland nevertheless We do not have at Our command sufficient information about the described situation.'[4]

Without mentioning their names, the letter asked the bishops of Skálholt and Hólar to find and consecrate a suitable bishop of Gardar. Its language suggests manipulation by someone with little information about Greenland but with a will to deceive for profit's sake, and that someone was almost certainly Marcellus de Niveris, whom Nicholas V had just appointed to succeed Gottsvin as the bishop of Skálholt at the urging of the freshly minted King Christian I of Denmark-Norway. Marcellus (who never set foot in Iceland) had already accumulated an impressive twenty-year record as a scoundrel and impostor by the year of his appointment, at which time he was hustling in Rome and gathering perquisites such as the right to collect all papal income in Scandinavia.[5]

According to the 1448 letter, the Greenlanders had been Christians for nearly 600 years and had supported their 'fervent piety' with regular divine services until 'thirty years ago'. But then

> barbaric pagans came by the sea from the neighbouring coasts and invaded the country, bringing low all the people established in this island with their bloody aggression, devastating their native land and its sacred edifices by fire and the sword until there was nothing left in this island (which is said to be very extensive) but nine parish churches difficult of access to the raiders because of the steepness of the mountains. The unfortunate indigenous people, men and women, particularly those who looked strong and fit enough to withstand the yoke of slavery, were deported into captivity in their own regions, as if they were under the sway of this tyrannical power.[6]

Many of the captives reportedly returned to their country years later and rebuilt their villages. Finally overcoming poverty and hunger well enough to 'supply the needs of a few priests or a bishop', they now wanted to re-establish divine worship after thirty years and had petitioned the pope to 'fill the spiritual void' in which they found themselves.

Generations of historians have mined this document for information about the final chapter of the Norse Greenland colony, but it is a blind alley, because not one of the letter's supposedly factual statements holds up under scrutiny. The pope's proxy himself admitted his inability to visualise Greenland's location – he knew only that it was in a distant region vaguely reported to contain Iceland as well. That is why the atrocities supposedly committed by 'barbaric pagans' in Greenland around 1418–20 actually refer to events involving the English in Iceland during that same period, partly catalogued in Hannes Pálsson's complaints. The letter's history of the Roman Church in Greenland should also give one pause. When Christianity supposedly arrived in Greenland six centuries before 1448 (that is, around 850), even Norway was still determinedly pagan, while Eirik's colonising venture lay another century and a half in the future, and the Greenlanders had been without a resident bishop from about 1378, not 1418–20. The nine 'inaccessible' parish churches supposedly left standing would have been at least three quarters of the known number of churches in the Eastern Settlement, most of them well accessible for obvious reasons. Last, but certainly not least, archaeologists have found no sign at all of large-scale burning and destruction at any Norse sites in Greenland, whose topography would have required a sizable and single-minded army to do as much damage as the papal letter described.[7]

Forty-four years after the request to Nicholas V that he meet the Norse Greenlanders' renewed wish for a bishop, Pope Alexander VI (reign 1492–1503) painted an even more dismal picture of the Norse Greenlanders, who had been so long abandoned by the Church that they had reverted to heathendom. Alexander expatiated in a 1492 letter to his Chancery and Apostolic Chamber on the need to nominate Matthias Knutsson, a poor Benedictine, to the Gardar See. Greenland had seen no ship arrive for eighty years because sea ice permitted access only in the month of August, the letter said, and

> it is also thought that no bishop or priest has dwelled in this country for about the last eighty years. The absence of Catholic priests has alas resulted in most of the parishioners, formerly Catholic, repudiating the baptism they had received. It is said that a communion cloth on which the last surviving priest in the country consecrated the Body of Christ, over a hundred years ago (and which is presented to the faithful once a year) is the last witness to Christian worship.[8]

Other Vatican documents reveal that Brother Matthias, who had no intention of going to Greenland, flourished as a confidence man in Rome in the autumn of 1492, just as Marcellus had done before him. The pope's letter about Matthias's episcopal appointment is merely another example of his success. The date assigned to the last ship believed to have called in Greenland strongly suggests that Matthias had fed the Curia hearsay – either from Bergen or his native Denmark – about the arrival in Bergen of Thorstein Olafsson and the other Greenland-farers eighty years earlier. Several Danes and Norwegians would have known that no ship had sailed directly from Norway to Greenland since 1410 and that no bishop or priest had been sent out there; moreover, the death of the last ordained Greenland priest could easily be estimated from the date of the Hvalsey wedding. It was also part of Greenland sailing knowledge that the Eastern Settlement was most accessible during the month of August, when the fjords were unlikely to be blocked by ice. The detail about the communion cloth was just another deft touch by a practiced confidence trickster.[9]

OTHER END GAME SCENARIOS

It is safe to say that the stories that reached the Curia's ears in 1448 and 1492 do not constitute evidence of conditions in Norse Greenland at any time in the fifteenth century. A number of other dire descriptions have surfaced in modern times – many, but not all, now discarded by scholars. Chapter One discussed several proposed reasons for the end of the Norse Greenland settlements, including that the Greenlanders had brought dire conditions upon themselves and had no hope of escape. Scholars currently favour a more complex approach, however, and look for a combination of circumstances that could have persuaded the Norse to leave their Greenland farms, rather than assume that the settlers had suffered as a group because of a final, disastrous development in a small, isolated community.

A harsh life kills individuals but is unlikely to exterminate an entire population, otherwise we would not still have Icelanders, Faeroese and Norwegians. The oft-made suggestion, by McGovern, Diamond and others too numerous to list, that climate deterioration contributed to the Norse Greenlanders' ultimate failure to survive, presupposes reliable data about fluctuating local climate conditions as well as about Norse ability (or inability) to cope with changing conditions, but such information is not yet available. One must nevertheless ask if, soon after 1410, when all was reportedly well in the Eastern Settlement, the Greenlanders had lost the ability to adapt to their challenging environment, and whether their society thereafter went downhill so fast that they were forced to give up by around 1450.

The likely answer to the first question is negative, and both common sense and fragmented evidence point to an end date of no later than about 1500. Some modern scientific observations may also be helpful in searching for an answer to the second question.

In a seminal 1978 palaeo-botanical study made in the Eastern Settlement, the Danish scientist Bent Fredskild concluded that by about 1450, or somewhat later, home fields and pastures near Eirik the Red's old farmstead were receiving less care than before and were reverting to wild meadows.[10] Forty years ago, radiocarbon-dating was considerably less sophisticated than now, but there was and is no uncertainty about the pollen graphs Fredskild provided, only about the applicable dates, about the validity of his data for areas he did not sample and about his underlying assumption that his results showed actual abandonment of the area by both people and animals. There are several alternative reasons why formerly cared-for fields had reverted to wild meadows, among them unusually inclement weather, soil erosion from excessive grazing or simply a lack of available labour to maintain the haying fields.

Later studies have added further nuance to the discussion about the Norse and their farms during their last period of tenure in Greenland. Pollen studies at Norse Greenland sites by the University of Aberdeen scientists Kevin Edwards and Ed Schofield have produced fascinating new information about Norse Greenland agriculture, including preliminary data that could suggest that the farm at Hvalsey was still functioning as late as around 1500.[11] Also quite recently, the Icelandic biologist Ingvi Thorsteinsson observed that land deterioration in southwest Greenland in the Middle Ages was not nearly as severe as in Iceland, 'which experienced similar effects of human habitation and cooling climate'. He also noted that while soil erosion has been demonstrated in some areas in southwestern Greenland, the physical properties of the soils in the region make it seem unlikely that large areas were damaged in Norse times. In the former Eastern Settlement, he found undisturbed areas with a rich natural vegetation – 'grazing lands of the highest quality'.[12]

CHANGES IN ANIMAL HUSBANDRY

Cows need better summer grazing than either sheep or goats and will survive a sub-Arctic winter only with adequate shelter, hay and other fodder, but they also yield more human food relative to pasture acreage than sheep do, as discussed in Chapter Three. Because both sheep and goats manage with far more spartan conditions in every way, less effort goes into building shelters, fertilising haying fields and gathering hay and other winter fodder. Under certain circumstances, therefore, a sheep farmer might have an advantage over one priding himself on his cows.[13]

One cannot suppose that the Norse Greenlanders were less flexible than their Icelandic cousins or less able to balance needs against resources. In their domestic economy, cows were expendable, but sheep were not. If, towards the end of their colony, it required a disproportionate amount of labour to fertilise and harvest home fields for the sake of keeping cows, those home fields would soon have shown neglect of the kind suggested by Fredskild's pollen analyses. Nevertheless, if the Norse reduced the number of cows and neglected their home fields, it does not mean that they also eliminated their flocks of sheep and closed up shop. Instead, Eastern Settlement farmers may well have decided to keep those tough animals producing meat, milk, and wool while roaming the hills with minimum supervision, and to use the freed-up labour elsewhere. Whatever the reason Norse Greenland home fields fell into disuse, it would at the very least signal a changing domestic economy.

In Iceland, where medieval land deterioration was more pronounced than in southwest Greenland, and volcanic eruptions frequently affected the weather and the crops, the farmers neither died off nor moved away. Instead, they increasingly focused on keeping sheep and freed up labour for the intensive fishing industry ignited by English buyers. From studies of Norse Greenland skeletal and midden material comes evidence suggesting that medieval Greenland may have undergone similar economic changes, tilting the available labour towards increased maritime exploitation and away from activities on land. During the final phase of the Eastern Settlement, in some locations there was a substantially increased reliance on marine food resources. Radioisotope readings on skeletons have confirmed the dietary change, while midden evidence primarily shows an increased proportion of seal bones relative to terrestrial mammal bones. It is surely also significant that no modern skeletal studies indicate that the Norse faded away from malnutrition; instead, these studies provide evidence of hard physical work and of common ailments such as arthritis, middle ear infections and bone fractures.[14]

CHOICES

There is no way to estimate how many people were left in the Eastern Settlement when it closed down, but there is a general and reasonable assumption among scholars that there had been a gradual attrition for some years. It is also reasonable to suppose that a few elected to stay when the rest left, as has happened in efforts to move people off remote Scottish and Norwegian islands to integrate them into modern society. Regardless of how many Norse Greenlanders participated in that momentous decision, however, they had obviously been able to function both individually and as a society until, after centuries of adjustment to life in Greenland, they abandoned their farms. Archaeological evidence also indicates that right into their colony's last phase, the Norse Greenlanders had maintained contact with the outside world, which suggests that they would still have had the vigour and the means to go elsewhere. But where did they go? And what prompted them to leave?

It is a commonly held theory that the Greenland Norse returned 'home' to Iceland and/or Norway.[15] That is akin to suggesting that in an economic downturn, today's denizens of Boston, Massachusetts, would go 'back' to England, which the Pilgrim Fathers left in 1620. An eastbound exodus by the Norse Greenlanders is highly unlikely for several weighty reasons, quite apart from the fact that throughout the medieval Norse colonisation in the North Atlantic, the settlers each time soon regarded themselves as belonging to their new homes, not to their former one.

For one thing, economic and political developments in Norway and Iceland in the fifteenth century had made those countries less than congenial for landless immigrants without powerful connections. For another, not a single extant Icelandic document indicates that people who inherited large numbers of farms after the Black Death turned property over to rank outsiders. Nor does it appear that regular contact between Iceland and Greenland endured past the first few decades of the fifteenth century. Another argument against crediting the Norse Greenlanders with a final eastward migration is that such an action would have come to the notice of royal officials who, even before the second half of the fifteenth century, were as numerous as they were obtrusive in both Iceland and Norway. If word had reached Danish, Norwegian or Icelandic officials that the Norse Greenland colony had ceased to exist, it would have been noted somewhere by somebody, but there clearly was no such report. Had there been, Archbishop Erik Valkendorf of Nidaros, who mined every available scrap of information about the Norse Greenlanders during 1514–16, would have known about it, but he obviously did not do so, because he planned an expedition to reconnect with the Norse Greenlanders he still believed to be living out there (Chapter Eleven).[16]

For the Norse Greenlanders to settle farther north in their Arctic homeland would have made no sense, and there is no indication of a wholesale movement south, such as to the British Isles. That leaves only the option of going west, but exactly where and to what end? Even a partial answer requires another look at how the Eastern Settlement fared after Sigrid Björnsdaughter and Thorstein Olafsson had left in 1410.

GREENLAND AND THE NORTH ATLANTIC ECONOMY

The Norse Greenlanders had participated actively in North Atlantic trade since their colony's inception, and they must have adapted successfully to ongoing changes in the general North Atlantic economy, because they carried on with foreign trade in the fifteenth century after their loss of contact with Norway. As described in earlier chapters, the biggest change involved the trade in fresh and cured cod, a business which the English dominated in Iceland for many decades despite Hanseatic competition.

When Thorstein Olafsson and his friends returned to Iceland, they were well placed to encourage contact between the Greenlanders and one or more of the English fish merchants already in Iceland. Such an arrangement would have been increasingly attractive when the stockfish trade in Iceland became a tangle of political and economic strictures and the competition on the fishing banks grew increasingly fierce. One might suppose that the flurry of stockfish licences issued to English merchants, by both Danish and English monarchs, as the fifteenth century wore on, would give historians a documentary window on possible trade voyages from Bristol to Greenland, but that is unfortunately not the case. As licences became more numerous for the benefit of empty royal coffers, they also became increasingly vague. For example, in 1461 John Shipward of Bristol obtained a licence from Edward IV to bring the *Julian* of Fowey back to England from Iceland, where it had gone with a cargo of merchandise allowed by a letter-patent from Henry VI (since deposed). In Iceland, the *Julian* was said to have exchanged their Bristol cargo for 'other merchandise of no little value' – but when the ship actually returned to Bristol in late summer, the Customs Accounts showed it as having arrived from 'Norbarn' (Bergen).[17]

At that time there would have been little reason for the ship to sail to Norway after first going to Iceland, and official records that adaptable could easily have covered the bringing back of stockfish from Greenland instead. English import duty on the stockfish would have been the same regardless of the cargo's point of origin, and anyone bringing in goods from Greenland without the knowledge of the Dano-Norwegian authorities would have been a fool to let on about it, lest trade and fishing restrictions involving Iceland were also redefined to include Greenland.

The English were in fact as ready to lie about the origin of a returning cargo as they were to sail without any licence at all, and John Forster and his partner in Bristol in 1470 obtained a licence so vague that they needed no subterfuge of any kind. It allowed them to sail to Iceland or any other parts for fish and other goods, exporting any wares except English staple goods.[18] According to the historian David Quinn, forty per cent of the English royal licences issued between 1439 and 1484 for trade in Iceland were to Bristol men for Bristol ships, and that number represented only a fraction of those who went north without a licence. Nothing could stop them from sailing wherever they saw an opportunity to fish or trade in the large areas over which the English exercised control, which included the approaches to Greenland.[19]

Scattered archaeological and cartographic evidence (Chapter Nine and below) supports the assumption that English vessels called in Greenland while the Norse were still there. Although the English gradually explored opportunities beyond Greenland, they continued to buy stockfish from both Iceland and Norway also during the later part of the fifteenth century, and the considerable friction this caused between the English and the Germans in both places appears to have triggered our only hint of documentary evidence for English trading voyages to Greenland until at least the early 1480s. In Copenhagen, the learned Ole Worm (1588–1655) told the Frenchman Isaac de la Peyrère (1596–1676) about an old Danish document – since lost – which he had read personally, and which stated that in Bergen in 1484, some forty sailors claimed that they made annual voyages to Greenland and obtained valuable merchandise. Hanse merchants, enraged at these mariners' refusal to trade with them, reportedly invited all forty of them to supper and then killed them. The Frenchman discounted Worm's tale on the grounds that the Norwegians had long since stopped sailing to Greenland, which was certainly the case, but there is solid documentary evidence of bad German–English relations in Bergen in both 1475 and 1476, when merchants from Hull and Bristol were accused of plundering Hanse merchants there. Worm's story may therefore have involved English mariners, because no other nation would have been sailing to both Greenland and Norway.[20]

It stands to reason that such visits may have become markedly less frequent by 1480 or so, when Bristol mariners had learned how to navigate directly from western Ireland to the Newfoundland-Labrador banks without sailing the familiar outward route by way of Iceland and/or Greenland. Without their remaining foreign contact, the English, the Norse Greenlanders would have faced complete isolation, although other Europeans were now feeling their way north into the Davis Strait. That European expansion, coming just when the Greenlanders were faced with the gravest threat to their colony yet, is the likely key to what they did next.

JOHN CABOT'S SUCCESSORS

Three kinds of explorers succeeded John Cabot in the northern Atlantic. Some, like John Cabot and his son Sebastian after him, sought a northwest passage to the spices and silks of the Orient, through what was still seen as northeasternmost Asia until it became known as the northern part of a vast American continent. Others hoped to find gold or silver right across the Atlantic. The third kind focused on non-glamorous commodities along the east coast of North America and in its adjacent waters, expanding the quiet reach of fishermen and whalers since time immemorial while including merchants who hoped to exchange wool cloth, tin kettles, hats, lace points and other manufactured goods for exotic indigenous merchandise.

Most of the Europeans who ventured into the Davis Strait in that early period were English or Iberian, and all relied on pilots with some previous experience from northern voyages. A few were also familiar with Greenland, because it is clear from surviving descriptions of their ventures that they were well aware of the sailing route going towards Iceland first and then using southern Greenland as a navigational marker. Regardless of the motives behind those early expeditions, they got little or no help from contemporary maps. That was also true of writers who commented on various feats of exploration at the time, including Francisco López de Gómara in the mid-sixteenth century when he reflected on those who had headed north:

> Many undertook to continue and complete the discoveries initiated by Christopher Columbus; some at their own cost, others at the King's expence, hoping thereby to become rich and famous... But as most of those who made discoveries were ruined thereby, there is no recollection left by any of them so far as I know, particularly those who steered northward, coasting the Bacallaos region and Labrador.

In singling out the special dangers that brought grief to so many northern expeditions, López de Gómara's notions about the physical configurations of that faraway region were necessarily vague, but he was accurate in reporting that those northern entrepreneurs left practically no records for posterity. Much more recently, David Quinn lamented: 'From the point of view of the sources on which it is founded the history of North America emerges from its dark ages some time in the second decade of the sixteenth century.'[21]

THE EARLY CARTOGRAPHIC RECORD

European map makers were apt to mix explorers' reports and rumours with their own theories as they struggled to form a picture of newly observed territories, including that alien land across the Davis Strait, but no useful reports reached them about the strait's eastern shore, Greenland. Although the new fisheries along Newfoundland and Labrador involved both big business and international conflicts and therefore warranted public attention, the day-to-day activities of fishermen and whalers were generally beneath notice. For example, because Queen Elizabeth's factotum Dr John Dee (1527–1608) believed that the *Inventio fortunata*'s description of a voyage to Greenland and into the Davis Strait in the year 1360 (Chapter Five) had produced valuable information about the polar regions, he showed great interest in the expedition, but otherwise he saw nothing exceptional about this northern voyage by an Englishman. Dismissively, he observed that from Kings Lynn to Iceland 'it is not above a fortnights sayling with an ordinary winde, and hath beene of many yeeres a very common and usuall trade'.[22]

In the fifteenth century, the Norse Greenlanders still mattered to some outsiders with an economic interest in going out there, but awareness of their existence and of their settlements' actual locations vanished from general European knowledge long before the inhabitants had decided to close down their communities. The disappearance of that knowledge is made indelibly clear for posterity in the work of the Danish map maker Claudius Clavus 'Swart' ('Black'), born on the island of Fyn in 1388 and professionally active around 1410–30.

CLAUDIUS CLAVUS

Claudius Clavus (Klaus Klaussøn) is known to have produced a textual description of the north in addition to a map that represents Greenland's cartographic debut. Having received his education at a Danish monastery school, he went abroad around 1412–13 and in the winter of 1423–24 reached Italy, where the recent translation into Latin of Ptolemy's *Geographia* was encouraging new approaches to world mapping. Clavus was evidently caught up in the excitement and complied with requests to delineate and describe his own remote northern region.

His known effort, an extant map of the north created around 1424–27, is allegedly only as a copy. It is called the 'Nancy' map because, together with a textual description also attributed to him, it was discovered in Nancy attached to Cardinal Guillaume Fillastre's personal manuscript copy of Ptolemy's *Geographia* in Latin, completed in 1427 but remaining unknown until 1835. Subsequent reports of the existence and contents of a second Clavus map, supposedly drawn somewhat later, are based only on two 'Vienna texts', which are mid-sixteenth-century copies of earlier works. Axel Anton Bjørnbo and Carl Petersen, who discovered the manuscripts quite by chance in 1900, made conscientious efforts to trace the descriptions' journey from Claudius Clavus to the Vienna archive, and their work strongly suggests that there had been plenty of room for errors in copying as well as for changes and additions born of new information.[23]

Bjørnbo provided a reconstruction and analysis of Clavus's second map based on the descriptions and geographical coordinates in the Vienna texts. Having found a reference there to the place name 'Thær' on the farthest northeastern Greenland shore, Bjørnbo put that, too, on his reconstruction. No such name is associated with Clavus's earlier map in the Nancy copy, however, but Nicolò Zeno's 1558 faked map of the North Atlantic (Fig. 2) has a 'Ther promontorio' far up north on the East Greenland coast. That is a fair indication that this 'promontory' had first entered geographical lore – including in the Vienna texts – sometime in the first half of the sixteenth century.

Bjørnbo's belief that medieval people had conceived of the world as laid out on a disc (Chapter Five), not as a sphere, marred his painstaking work on Clavus, but scholars are nevertheless in his debt. On the extant Clavus map at Nancy, which shows no west coast for 'Gronlandia provincia', only Greenland's *east* coast as it arches over Iceland to join Arctic Norway, Bjørnbo spotted a small, red bracket indicating 'town' in the middle of that east coast. No place names were provided either there or elsewhere in Greenland, but Bjørnbo reasoned that the bracket signified Gardar. He was certain that Clavus had visited the Greenland Norse in person by the time he made his second map of the north, therefore he assumed that his fellow Dane had made the mistake of putting the bishop's seat in the wrong place because he had not yet been to Greenland when he drew this *first* map.[24] Clavus was never anywhere near Greenland, however, and was quite ignorant in general about any regions north of Denmark. Nevertheless, he knew that the Norse had colonised Greenland from Iceland and had their own bishop's seat, and because he was also aware that Greenland was located west of Iceland, he simply assumed that the Norse colonists had chosen the shortest route and settled on Greenland's eastern shore. Chapter Eleven will discuss some other consequences of this theoretical approach.

Clavus had a lasting impact on fifteenth-century European cartography and provided plenty of room for confusion, especially since Cardinal Fillastre probably did not have the only copy of Clavus's textual description, which appears to have inspired later Ptolemaic maps of the north defining Greenland as a long peninsula coming down from the northwest of Iceland, in a concept that became known as the A-redaction. If Clavus himself expressed himself similarly in a second map, nobody has ever seen it and described it.

At Wolfegg Castle in southern Germany, Father Josef Fischer, SJ, in 1901 identified a Nicolaus Germanus manuscript from 1468 as the forerunner of the Nicolaus Germanus maps of the north in the 1482 and 1486 Ulm editions of the *Geographia*, heralding what became known as the B-redaction.[25] In that version, Greenland lies well to the *east* of Iceland as a large peninsula named 'Engronelant', north of Norway and Sweden and connected by 'Pilappelanth' to the land mass below. A duplicate 'Engronelanth' northernmost on the Scandinavian peninsula demonstrates the German map maker's debt to Claudius Clavus in another way, because the Nancy map has 'Engromelandi' in relatively that same position, but referring to the northeastern Swedish region of Ångermanland. From 1482 onwards, twin Greenlands continued to show up on many a map of the north.

Right after AD 1500 it is also possible to see the cartographic impact of increased European sailings into the Davis Strait. Before considering a couple of important examples of this development, let us dispose of yet another tenacious myth about northern exploration involving Greenland.

LARSEN'S FANTASY

The wealthy Azorean João Vaz Corte Real had three sons: Gaspar, Miguel and Vasco Annes. They were apparently enterprising mariners like their father, who had reportedly received the captaincy of Angra in Terceira as his 1474 reward for a voyage (undated) to North America under the orders of King Alfonso V.

To this travel supposition, the Danish librarian Sofus Larsen in 1925 added Didrik Pining and his fellow Hanse privateer Hans Pothorst, crediting both men with a career as North Atlantic explorers before 1478 and with an interlude as pirates in Greenland waters around 1494, headquartered on the (nonexistent) island of 'Hvitsark' between Iceland and Greenland. Larsen was evidently unaware that Pothorst and Pining had not been assigned to this pirate's nest until 1548, when the Parisian publisher Henri de Gourmont printed a map of Iceland that drew heavily on the 1539 *Carta marina* by the Swedish archbishop Olaus Magnus and included Olaus's general reference to pirates on 'Hvitsark'. The mayor of Kiel, Carsten Grypp, saw De Gourmont's map and described it in a sycophantic letter to Christian III of Denmark, to which he added that, at the request of the Portuguese king, Christian III's grandfather had sent Pining and Pothorst with some ships to look for new lands and islands in the north, and that these gentlemen had erected a defensive structure on 'Hvitsark' against the pirates roaming those seas.[26]

From Grypp's letter and the other intertwined myths, Larsen concocted a tale, still alive in certain circles, that has Pining and Pothorst participating in a 1473 voyage of northern discovery which the Portuguese king had requested and the Danish king had organised, and on which a certain Jon Skolp (alias Scolvus) had been the pilot. One might think that the Norse in Greenland would also have had a place in these fantasies, but the general view in Larsen's generation was that the Norse colony had folded soon after contact with Norway was lost. Instead, Larsen topped off this fictional expedition into the Davis Strait with claiming that it had been the very one for which the Portuguese king had rewarded João Vaz Corte Real.

PORTUGUESE EXPERIENCE AND THE 1502 'CANTINO' MAP WITH GREENLAND

When João's son Gaspar in 1500 obtained a royal licence for northern discovery, giving him and his heirs broad rights to any lands he might discover, the patent also noted that he had made earlier voyages towards the north. It has therefore often been speculated that he had accompanied his father João Vaz (†1496), which is possible, but it is equally likely that Gaspar had ventured out on his own soon after coming into his patrimony. One may in any case assume that there had been previous Portuguese voyages in the waters to which Gaspar was heading, and that he knew approximately where he wanted to sail in 1500, because it would have made little sense to pay for a licence and mount an expensive expedition without a reasonable expectation of success.[27]

It is not possible to document Gaspar's original goal or what he had told King Manoel in order to get his patent, but both his own account of his voyage and the 'Cantino' map (see below) suggest that he set a course much like the one English fishermen had been using to reach the banks off western Iceland and in southeast Greenland. Following the current south and sighting the mountains of southern Greenland, Gaspar rounded Cape Farewell and continued up along the Greenland west coast until the current and the ice urged his ships westwards across the Davis Strait. He clearly made no effort to land on either Greenland coast.

Across the Davis Strait, he found another northern land, cool and green and with many trees, which he called Terre Verde ('Greenland'), seemingly unaware that the name already applied to the mountainous, barren land he had observed earlier on his voyage. This western discovery appealed to him so well that the following year, he and his brother Miguel set out with three ships and a fresh royal licence. They followed the same route as before until they reached southern

Greenland, where large amounts of ice made them sail straight west across the lower Davis Strait. Apparently, they then coasted south along Labrador and headed down the outer coast of Newfoundland, possibly exploring parts of Nova Scotia as well. Two of the expedition's three ships returned to Lisbon in October without Gaspar, who had kept sailing south.[28]

Still without news of Gaspar's fate, Miguel Corte Real set out in 1502, with three ships and a fresh charter from Manoel, to look for his brother. When Miguel failed to show up at their Newfoundland meeting place, the other two ships sailed back to Lisbon to inform the third and eldest brother, Vasco Annes, of what had happened. The armed search expedition which the Portuguese king sent out in 1503 (without Vasco Annes) failed to find the two brothers, and all the patent rights fell to Vasco Annes, who renewed them several times through at least 1522. The Corte Real exploits still live on in a beautiful manuscript map which the Duke of Ferrara's agent in Lisbon, Alberto Cantino, commissioned in 1502 and smuggled out of the country.[29]

The work of an anonymous Portuguese author, the 'Cantino' is the earliest extant map to show the imaginary line running north–south in the mid-Atlantic, about 50°W of Greenwich, which was decreed by the 1494 Treaty of Tordesillas to prevent Spanish–Portuguese arguments over newly discovered territories. Everything west of the Tordesillas line supposedly belonged to Spain, while everything east of it fell to Portugal. On the 'Cantino' map, the line bisects a free-floating, unidentifiable part of North America, placing Gaspar Corte Real's Terra Verde safely to the east of it and naming the region Terra del Rey de Portuguall, with an inscription that attributes its discovery to Gaspar. A Portuguese flag is attached for good measure. Two Portuguese flags also appear on a very recognisable peninsular Greenland, coming down from the north with ample water separating it from Gaspar's discovery. The flags are placed at either end of a region running from Greenland's southernmost point some way up along the east coast, with a legend noting that the area had been discovered by order of King Manoel by explorers who had not disembarked. They had, however, observed jagged mountains, which reportedly suggested to some cosmographers that this might be 'the peninsula of Asia'.[30]

The 'Cantino' map reveals no awareness of English sailings in the northwestern Atlantic, and the angle and position of the unnamed Greenland peninsula on the map demonstrate that the 'peninsula of Asia' was thought to be northwesternmost Eurasia. That traditional notion was soon to be discarded by another man who sailed to the Newfoundland region during the period of the Corte Real voyages, and who drew a map that reveals both personal observations of the general northern area to which the Portuguese laid claim in the 'Cantino' map (Greenland included) and information gained from English mariners long involved in the northern codfish trade.

ENGLISH EXPERIENCE AND THE 1507/08 RUYSCH MAP

In 1502 or 1503, the German map maker Johannes Ruysch sailed to the Newfoundland fishing banks with an English ship that set out from southern England and followed the fifty-third parallel west 'somewhat northerly'. By 1507 he had completed a world map (published in the 1508 Rome edition of Ptolemy's *Geographia*) depicting the southern half of Greenland with sufficient realism to belie any notion that Greenland was essentially unknown to Europeans. In contrast to the 'Cantino' work, the Ruysch planisphere shows 'Grvenlant' as an immense, northeastern outgrowth of Asia, completely separated from the European side of the Atlantic, just as a mariner would experience it on a westward course from the British Isles. The Newfoundland-Labrador region is named 'Terra Nova'.

Three details in particular confirm that Ruysch, who otherwise based much of the rest of his map on Portuguese knowledge, had access to English fishermen's cumulative information about Greenland and Iceland. Off western Iceland, a small island said to have been consumed by fire in 1456, is in an area of considerable underwater volcanic activity to this day. An upwelling of magma would certainly have impressed fishermen observing it from out at sea. The connection between cod fishing and Ruysch's English companions is also evident in northernmost Norway, where a tiny symbol for a church and the name 'Sancti Odulfi' refer to St Olaf's Church at Vardø, dedicated by the Norwegian archbishop in 1307. Along with a fortress erected at about the same time, the church marked the importance to Church and Crown of this codfish-rich region, with which English cod merchants would long have been familiar. Last, but certainly not least, one state of the Ruysch map gives the name 'Sinus Gruenlanteus' – the 'Bay of Greenland' – to the wide bay separating Greenland from the New World's northeastern coast. In other words, to the English fishermen Ruysch credits with his information about this region, the familiar entity here was not 'Terra Nova', but Greenland, which implies that his companions were accustomed to crossing *from* a known Greenland *to* the relatively new fishing grounds on the other side of the strait.[31]

PORTUGUESE AND ENGLISH EXPERIENCE MEET

In a 1506 lawsuit, the Azorean landowner Pedro de Barcelos of Angra in Terceira complained about property and privileges which had been usurped during his three-year absence on a voyage of northern discovery on which his partner had been João Fernandes, also a Terceiran llavrador (landowner), for whom Labrador was named (the name was first applied to Greenland and then gradually moved west). João warrants our attention here, because his Bristol connections place him at the centre of activities that are likely to have involved the last generation of the Norse Greenlanders.[32]

JOÃO FERNANDES, LLAVRADOR

João Fernandes seems to have followed a separate track from that of Pedro de Barcelos by 1499, because later De Barcelos documents do not mention him. João's name was sufficiently common that we cannot know for certain if he is the man to whom the customs records for Bristol refer when noting 'ffernandus and gunsalus' as having traded in Bristol in 1486. Nor do we know whether he was the Portuguese merchant 'Johannus Fornandus' who brought sugar from Lisbon to Bristol on 12 November 1492 and took Bristol cloth back with him to Lisbon on 26 January 1493. An early trading association with Bristol by 'ffernandus' together with 'gunsalus' makes sense, however, when we know that João Fernandes and his Azorean companion João Gonsalves were members of the Anglo-Azorean syndicate in Bristol in 1501 (see further below). We know definitely that he was the João Fernandes (Joham Fernandez) of Terceira who, in 1499, obtained a charter from Manoel I's official in Lisbon 'to seek out and discover at his own expense some islands lying in our sphere of influence', over which he would then have full authority.[33]

While this patent did not refer to grand family connections or to previous voyages, it implied an earlier voyage by João by noting that he had convinced the Crown that he had a particular region in mind, and that it lay within the Portuguese sphere according to the Treaty of Tordesillas. In other words, like Gaspar Corte Real he had a good idea of where he was going and did not intend to pay for a charter and sail 'at his own expense' if he might have to hand his newly discovered territory over to Spain. The charter's allusion to previous experience most likely refers to his three years of exploration with Pedro de Barcelos, because a voyage of that duration could not have been accomplished between 1499, when documents for João appeared that never mention De Barcelos, and 1506, when De Barcelos was already involved in his Azorean lawsuit.

By the end of the fifteenth century, the Portuguese were so far ahead of the English in navigational skills and instruments that the English, right to the end of the sixteenth century, preferred to have a Portuguese pilot along on their explorations.[34] As far as knowledge of the northwestern Atlantic was concerned, however, the English had the advantage, as John Cabot clearly knew when he chose to set out from Bristol with a Bristol crew in order to search for a northwestern passage to India. When João Fernandes went exploring with De Barcelos, he may already have been visiting Bristol for ten or more years, picking up information about the sailing route to Greenland and Newfoundland, and if the two men had followed the North Atlantic fishermen's route, their voyage may explain why the 'Cantino' map claimed southeastern Greenland for Portugal without specific reference to the Corte Reals.

Soon after 1500, João Fernandes evidently became directly associated with Greenland, but there is no telling the exact year and on what information map makers made the connection. The earliest known map with a reference to the llavrador is the anonymous 'King-Hamy' sea chart, which depicts Greenland as an attenuated island on an east-west axis, named 'Terra Laboratoris'. West of it lies the Newfoundland-Labrador region with a number of bays and capes that include an area named 'Terra Cortereal', thus distinguishing between the llavrador's discoveries and the Corte Reals'. On the 1529 world map by Diogo Ribeiro (a Portuguese in the service of Charles V of Spain) and on a similar map from a couple of years later (most likely also by Ribeiro but usually just called the 'Wolfenbüttel' map), the name Tiera de Labrador is applied to what is clearly Greenland, although shown as the northernmost part of North America. On the coast is this legend: 'The English discovered this country. It produces nothing of any value. It was discovered by the English from the city of Bristol.' The 'Wolfenbüttel' map adds: 'As he who first sighted it was a farmer from the Azore Islands, this name remains attached to that country.' Ribeiro had this to say about Newfoundland (Tierra de los Baccallos): 'The land of codfish discovered by the Cortereals and where they were lost. Up to this time nothing of value has been found there, except the fishing of codfish, and these do not amount to much.'[35]

Ruysch's 1507/08 map provided a C. de Portogesi at the tip of 'Terra Nova', south of the 'Baccalauras' or Codfish Islands, but it does not show a 'Labrador' anywhere along the 'Bay of Greenland'. The Bristol fishermen from whom Ruysch received his North Atlantic briefings probably saw no reason to credit a foreigner like João Fernandes either with 'discovering' a Greenland whose existence and location they had taken for granted all their working lives or with claims to any stretch of the new coasts where they assumed they had prior rights. Nevertheless, it seems that after about 1502, Iberian and Italian cartographers credited João Fernandes both with having discovered a northern territory and with knowing Greenland's location. Soon, there were also maps asserting that Englishmen from Bristol had been the first to know about 'his' territory, but it is impossible to know what distinction the creators of these maps made between Greenland and Labrador. Both were shown as northern promontories on a continuous shoreline edging a Davis Strait closed off at the northern end.[36]

JOÃO'S BRISTOL CONTACTS

João's 1499 charter and his cartographic credits for discoveries suggest that he did not seek a shortcut to the riches of the Orient, unlike Cabot and son or the Corte Real brothers. João was a mariner experienced in northern navigation, a trader in non-glamorous commodities, a landowner whose fellow Terceirans had retained and exploited their own early discoveries in the new northern territories. He was also ambitious enough to obtain his own royal charter for exploration and colonisation. There is no record of the use he made of his charter, but it seems likely that in the spring or summer of 1500, he returned to the general region he had explored with De Barcelos. It is certain that late in that same year he was in Bristol – a natural stopover after a northwestern venture – together with two other Azoreans. By the following spring, the three men had formed a partnership with three Bristol merchants.

Together with João Fernandes, Francisco Fernandes and João Gonsalves, 'Squyers borne in the Isle of Surrys [Azores] under the obeisaunce of the kyng of Portingale', Richard Warde, Thomas Ashehurst and John Thomas of Bristol petitioned Henry VII on 19 March 1501 for a patent which the king granted that same day to his 'well-beloved subjects' and his 'well-beloved' Azoreans. Under a trade monopoly lasting ten years, the six men would have complete authority to sail to and exploit 'any town, city, castle, island or mainland by them thus newly found ... and as our vassals and governors, lieutenants and deputies to occupy, possess and subdue these, the property, title, dignity and suzerainty of the same being always reserved to us'.[37] Nowhere is there a specific mention of a fishery, but instead a strong suggestion that the syndicate's aim was a prospering colony with trade controlled by the six of them under English overlordship.

The charter nevertheless has a strong xenophobic subtext. João Fernandes and his Azorean companions apparently understood this, which raises the question of why they went along with an English undertaking that might eventually discriminate against them, when they already had their own ship and João's valid charter from the Portuguese king. However, João's agenda provided good reasons for a joint venture with Bristolians wanting to pursue plebeian profits along newly discovered coasts, rather than the phantom luxuries of the Far East. Joining with the three Bristol men also meant that Richard Warde and the two other Englishmen could petition Henry VII. João's likely inducements to his Bristol partners would have been previous experience with navigating to those coasts and an established legal claim to a particular area under his Portuguese charter. There are reasons to believe that especially Richard Warde, whose name appears first on the 1501 charter, may have wanted to compete with Bristol colleagues now clustering around Sebastian Cabot, whose father John's patent was still valid.[38]

Immediately after John Cabot's 1497 voyage, the expression 'the Isle' became synonymous with his discoveries across the Atlantic. Subsequent voyages using Cabot's original charter were also to 'the new Isle', 'The new Ilande' or 'the new Ile', until names such as 'the newe founde launde' and 'the Newfound Island' appear in stipulations for royal rewards. A short entry (datable to 2–7 January 1502) in the royal Household Book, 'Item to men of Bristol that found thisle C s.', should therefore not be interpreted as referring to a 1501 voyage by the new Anglo-Azorean syndicate soon after they obtained their 1501 charter. João and his companions had assured Henry VII that they would *not* interfere with the territory already being exploited by other Bristol men, and nothing in the Household Book entry suggests exploration of a different part of the new coast. The names of João Fernandez, Richard Warde and John Thomas are absent from this and any other subsequent English record until a royal charter dated 9 December 1502 specifically excludes them from western ventures. Victims of the rivalry between the Azorean João Fernandes and the Bristol merchant establishment, they had been upstaged by the men who had supported John Cabot and now grouped around his son Sebastian.[39]

Richard Warde disappeared completely from all known records, and so did João Fernandes, but their partner John Thomas was back in the Bristol merchants' good graces by 1504. Documents also show that, together with the 'merchants aliens' Francisco Fernandes and João Gonsalves, Thomas Asshehurst (the third Bristol partner in the 1501 Anglo-Azorean undertaking) was involved in Bristol-based Newfoundland enterprises from at least September 1502 until October 1506, by which time Francisco Fernandes had also run afoul of his Bristol bosses.[40]

The December 1502 charter leaves no doubt that a deep split had occurred within the original Anglo-Azorean syndicate of 1501. It shows the fissure clearly when it refers specifically to the 1501 charter and continues:

> nevertheless we are unwilling that the same Richard Warde, John Thomas and John Fernandez or any one of them…should in any way enter or go near any of the countries, islands, lands, places or provinces found, recovered or discovered anew in the future under the authority and licence of any of these our present letters, unless they shall have first obtained leave from the aforesaid Hugh, Thomas Asshehurst, John Gonzales and Francis…. And in case the said Richard Warde, John Thomas and John Fernandez, or any one of them…may wish…to make their way to these islands, countries, regions and other places aforesaid…they…shall be obliged from time to time to pay, furnish and sustain all and every the costs and charges to be arranged at each voyage with the aforesaid Hugh, Thomas Asshehurst, John Gonzales and Francis.[41]

In a stipulation that may have been aimed at their former association with João Fernandes, the charter also notes that João Gonsalves and Francisco Fernandes are to be treated as English subjects, also concerning customs and subsidies, provided they do not act as cover for foreign merchants.

The three men excluded from the new charter had not simply gone missing, as demonstrated by the fact that John Thomas was back in the good graces of his Bristol merchant colleagues by 1504. Instead, the lack of subsequent news about João Fernandes and Nicholas Warde may indicate that in 1501, they had pursued a project that had briefly involved John Thomas and that had been deeply offensive to powerful Bristol merchants.

TRACING JOÃO FERNANDES AND RICHARD WARDE

Before their first arrival together in Bristol, João Fernandes, Francisco Fernandes and João Gonsalves had likely spent the summer of 1500 exploring along the North American east coast on the strength of João's 1499 patent from the Portuguese king. Because João had already spent about three years investigating an area on which Pedro de Barcelos and other Azoreans had already set their sights, it is also likely that João had by this time decided where he wanted to concentrate his own efforts. Such a place would by definition have been within the Portuguese Tordesillas sphere and offering the natural resources common to the Labrador Newfoundland region.

João Fernandes's plans may have attracted Richard Warde, John Thomas and Thomas Asshehurst precisely because he did not focus on finding new markets for cloth, pots, pans and other European manufactured goods, but on exploiting major overseas resources for the European market. The Anglo-Azorean syndicate of 1501 made perfect sense, because many Bristol merchants also had their eye on the overseas cod fisheries, and many Portuguese wanted both to expand their own fisheries and to 'encourage English searches for alternative sources of fish in the western Atlantic, since the Icelandic fish trade had provided such an appreciable part of Portuguese imports'.[42] Vast American forests also beckoned.

Many areas along the Labrador-Newfoundland coasts had resources which Europe needed, but systematic exploitation depended on permanent settlements with skilled workers. European colonisers were certainly not reluctant to avail themselves of native slave labour, but the Azorean economy had depended on European immigrant labour until the 1460s, and João may well have rejected slave labour as unsuitable for an enterprise that called for European fishermen, farmers, whalers or lumberjacks. Protecting himself against indigenous New World people would have taken precedence over enslaving them. However, finding European settlers with the right skills for a northern undertaking would have been a challenge in the early sixteenth century, the first period for which there are moderately reliable population figures. Although Portugal had a population of barely one and a quarter million (Spain had about seven million and France fourteen), the country's expanding sea empire was already draining off people to Asia and Africa. Nor was England, with four million inhabitants, in a position to provide colonists for overseas ventures. Its population had barely started to recover from repeated famines and from epidemics in which the port cities of Bristol, Exeter and Norwich had proved especially vulnerable to infection from London or the Continent.[43]

All six associates in the 1501 Anglo-Azorean syndicate would have known that in the fishing business, permanent shore stations would enable people to fish from early spring until very late in the season and to supervise lengthy curing. Thus far, salting the fish caught away from home had been the only available method of preservation to either Iberian or English fishermen, and they did not have a suitable climate back home for wind-drying the fish. The drier climate north of Newfoundland might be suitable for stockfish drying, however. Control over a stretch of shoreline and people with the right skills were all that was needed besides the plentiful codfish.

Ruthlessness and ingenuity in the search for settlers and workers is such a recurrent theme in the history of fifteenth- and sixteenth-century exploration and colonisation that there is no reason to suppose that João Fernandes and his associates were different in their methods, or that others could not have undertaken similar enterprises in that general region during those years around 1500 for which the lack of documents is most pronounced. Given what we do know, the six syndicate members may well have decided that the Norse colony in Greenland, long known to some in Bristol's inner circle, might solve their recruitment problem – or something similar may have been suggested by another enterprise that left no records at all. It is in any case important to remember that the Norse Greenlanders disappeared when the wave of European expansion was lapping hard against their outer shores.

Emigration is particularly likely to appeal to the younger and most able-bodied members of a population, who are the ones a society can least afford to lose. João Fernandes with his Azorean and Bristol associates may have been the catalyst for the Eastern Settlement to lose the strongest and most fertile segment of their population around 1500. The Norse Greenlanders had all the necessary skills to exploit game on land and at sea, to fish in fresh and salt water, to prepare stockfish and other fish products, and to survive tough conditions. Their domestic animals were equally sturdy and would have been a desirable addition to any new settlement, and shipping both animals and people across the Davis Strait would involve a relatively short distance. To include the company of three Bristolians privy to Greenland information would have taken care of one major obstacle for João, namely that some of the Bristol merchants who regarded Greenland as 'theirs' had also maintained their own fishing interests along a stretch of Labrador even before John Cabot's 1497 voyage.

That would still have left the problem of persuading the Norse Greenlanders to join such an overseas scheme willingly. The Greenlanders would have known about Vínland, Markland and Helluland, but in order to pull up stakes and move westwards they would have had to be persuaded by someone with the leadership and organisational abilities of Eirik the Red – qualities that had also enabled John Cabot, the Corte Real brothers and João Fernandes to arrange their enterprises.[44] In addition, the Greenlanders would have had to be convinced that they were going to something better than what they would leave behind.

If the Norse Greenlanders had adjusted both their domestic and export economy to English demands for stockfish and other fish products that had now dwindled to the point where the Greenlanders were facing complete isolation, they would primarily have required assurance about transportation and help to get started with a new life, just as their ancestors had done when opportunity called. Conditions in the Eastern Settlement would not have had to be unspeakable for a new colonising venture to appeal; the first Greenland colonisers had certainly not been the most desperate people in Iceland.

Those who probed the Labrador coast for new economic opportunities could not foresee the disasters that became the invariable lot of Europeans when first trying to settle year-round on shores they had experienced only during non-winter conditions. They did not know that the isotherm dips way south in that region, with winter temperatures substantially lower than at a corresponding latitude in Greenland. If the Norse Greenlanders migrated west to a stretch of Labrador chosen by others, as it appears likely that they did, they may have ended up on the bottom of the Davis Strait before ever reaching the other shore, or they may have perished during their first winter in the new land from new diseases, from starvation or simply from the bitter cold. For them and for any who had stayed behind in Greenland, it would have been the beginning of a rapid decline – and of the end.

11

WHO WENT LOOKING
FOR THEM?

Having observed the vast quantities of ice 'conducted along the east shore of Old Greenland, as far as Cape Farewell', the English navigator and whaling expert William Scoresby the Younger noted in 1820 that nobody knew the fate of the poor Norse Greenlanders, who had been marooned since 1406 when all that ice churning off their coast had become a problem. Somewhat condescendingly, he added: 'Various attempts have been made by order of the Danish Government, for the recovery of this country, and for ascertaining the fate of the unfortunate colonists, but most of them were spiritless, and all of them failed in their object.'[1]

The saga of post-medieval efforts to reconnect with the Norse Greenlanders is indeed one of disappointments and could hardly have been otherwise, because changing notions of Greenland geography had contaminated earlier sources of information to such a degree that all former knowledge about where the Norse had settled was lost. To Scoresby and his fellow whalers, 'New Greenland' signified the archipelago that included the island of Spitzbergen, discovered by Willem Barentsz in 1596. 'Old Greenland' referred to Greenland's east coast from Cape Farewell north to about Scoresby Sound – a stretch of shore which no whaler worth his rum ration wanted to approach on account of the ice belt and other known dangers (Fig. 15), but which was believed to have been where the Norsemen settled.

On a map Scoresby drew in 1820, Greenland is called 'Old or West Greenland' to distinguish it from the Svalbard archipelago, which many

Fig. 15 Icebergs off the southeast Greenland coast in late August, the time of least ice

English whalers persisted in simply calling 'Greenland'. Greenland's east coast on Scoresby's map is delineated southwards from Gael Hamkes Land. Past 'Hold with Hope' is the notation 'Coast traced by William Scoresby 1819'; there are no place names until Öllumlengri some way above a promontory named Herjolfsness. Running south from there to Cape Farewell come several names with a distinct Norse flavour: St Olaus, Erics fiord, Dyrnæs Church, Whale I (Hvalsey) and so on, but Scoresby did not invent this practice. The earliest map that provides detailed Norse-style place names along the East Greenland shore is the map which the Dutchman Joris Carolus drew in 1626 at the urging of Christian IV of Denmark, and which was published in 1634.[2] The ideas behind this graphic representation of 'old' Greenland went much further back in time, however.

Aside from the Greenlanders themselves and others with experience in sailing to Greenland, meaningful knowledge about the country was already scarce in the two decades that led up to the 1408 Hvalsey wedding, as we see from the relative ease with which several people in Bergen accepted the 'drifting off' stories told there during that period. The work done around 1424–30 by the Danish map maker Claudius Clavus (Chapter

185

Ten) shows quite clearly that a geographical haze had begun to envelop Norse Greenland not only before Scoresby's time and before the first Danish 'rescue' expedition was thought of, but even before the Norse had closed down both of their communities.

Clavus's work amply illustrates the risks of visualising Greenland by the use of reason only, without recourse to practical sailing experience or to later geographical knowledge about the Arctic regions, but it does not prove that he was the very first person to imagine the Norse colony as located in southeastern Greenland. We know only that he was far from the last to do so. European information about the Norse Greenlanders was confused beyond help well before Ptolemaïc maps of the late fifteenth century dealt with Clavus's concepts of Greenland.

ERIK VALKENDORF'S GREENLAND PLANS

Reports of New World riches reached Dano-Norwegian authorities quickly in the post-Columbian period, and during the years 1514–16, the Danish-born Archbishop Erik Valkendorf of Norway (in office 1510–22) wanted to organise an expedition to Greenland in order to hug that province to the Dano-Norwegian bosom once more. He was in no doubt that descendants of the Norse settlers were still living out there and had, as far as he was concerned, never officially disassociated themselves from Denmark-Norway. Even so, he did not expect a particularly warm welcome for his 'rescue' attempt, because his expedition guidelines specified that when the ship reached Greenland, two men only should be sent ashore to see if they might make a safe landing, and all the sailors were warned against being gulled by the Norse Greenlanders. If they found the country unoccupied, they should build large bonfires, construct many large cairns and raise crosses as tokens of taking full possession.[3]

Valkendorf, a deeply educated man who spent much time abroad both as a student and on later travels, conceived his Greenland idea just before he spent thirty-seven weeks on the Continent negotiating the marriage between the Princess Elizabeth of Burgundy and the newly crowned Danish king, Christian II. The thirteen-year-old princess was married by proxy in Brussels in July of 1514, and Valkendorf brought the young queen from the Netherlands in 1515 for an August wedding in Copenhagen, where she would also be crowned queen of Denmark-Norway.[4] The archbishop no doubt returned home troubled in mind, because the king had showed no sign of shedding his mistress Dyveke, but also full of exciting ideas nourished among people who took a personal interest in the European exploitation of America.

Like most of his contemporaries, Valkendorf was convinced that western Greenland continued directly into the unexplored northern land mass that formed a part of the New World's link to Asia. It should come as no surprise, therefore, that his notes for the Greenland enterprise reveal a belief that this direct connection guaranteed the right to reclaim the Norse Greenland settlers for the Crown and the Roman Church and to obtain for Denmark-Norway a slice of that excellent American pie. In Greenland he expected to find not only profitable fur animals such as marten, lynx, white bears and wolverines, but more fish than in any other country, white falcons, hide and ivory of walrus, large quantities of soapstone and, best of all, precious metals, including silver mountains. Moreover, the country was less cold than Iceland and Norway, and the people there raised the best wheat anywhere.[5]

To Valkendorf's way of thinking, none of the recent European claimants had a better right to New World acreage than the Norse, who had showed up at the feast centuries before John Cabot sailed to those new shores on behalf of England. The archbishop's chief worry was how to access the heirs to those Norse pioneers by learning the old sailing route and overcoming the ice known to await mariners in altogether dangerous waters. To that end, he pursued early works that might tell him more about what to expect in the alien and hostile northern environment the Norse had made their own. It is to those efforts we owe the survival, in some form, of Ívar Bárdsson's 'Description of Greenland', which is so central to ruminations about the final phase of the Norse Greenland colony. As a key to why efforts to succour the Norse Greenlanders were doomed from the start, the 'Description' is equally significant because of the assumptions which Valkendorf, and people after him, brought to bear on Ívar's story.

ERIK VALKENDORF AND ÍVAR BÁRDSSON

The earliest extant version of the report Ívar gave in Bergen in 1364 is a seventeenth-century copy of a transcription in Danish made for Archbishop Valkendorf (Chapter Five). In Finnur Jónsson's 1930 critical edition of Ívar's 'Description', Jónsson expressed confidence in the sixteenth-century origins of that transcription, which he believed had been a part of the information Valkendorf collected about Greenland, and he chose that version to work from. He nevertheless observed that various addenda in the form of sailing descriptions were from a much later period, stemming from Jakob Rasch – a man passionately interested in rediscovering the Old Greenland. Jónsson did not pause, however, at statements to the effect that the old sailing route was no longer usable because of all the ice coming down from the north – a remark most likely inserted by a seventeenth-century copyist informed by whalers' reports about the Greenland Sea. Nor did it occur to Jónsson that a sequence of Greenland landmarks on a sailing route ascribed to Ívar's report locates the main Norse settlement on the east coast, very much in a manner of maps made after about 1600.

According to this naming sequence, a westbound mariner approaching Greenland on the old route and encountering the 'Gunnbjarnarskerries', midway between Iceland and Greenland, would now risk deadly peril from all the ice coming down from the north. Whether leaving from Bergen and bypassing Iceland altogether or departing from Iceland, a ship should head directly west until sighting the high Hvarf promontory, after which one must look for the tall mountain named 'Hvitserk', near which Herjolfsness is located. East of Herjolfsness, in Skagafjord, one would find the sizable Eastern Settlement, and far to the east of that again a large fjord, 'Berufjord', with no settlements and with a large reef blocking large ships from entering. Here the current runs hard, and there are whales and fish in abundance. The region belongs to the Greenlanders' cathedral, and whaling takes place with the bishop's permission. Sailing still farther east (i.e. northeast) leads to the fjord Allumlengri/ Öllumlengri ('the Longest of All'), the end of which nobody has seen. Next come quantities of ice and a harbour named 'Fimbudir', followed by an island east of the ice named 'Kaarsö'/Korsö' ('Cross Island'). This island, also the property of the cathedral, features white bears which may be hunted with the bishop's permission. Beyond lies a wasteland of snow and ice. Heading west from Herjolfsness, one reaches Ketilsfjord, where a proper settlement includes the 'Auros' church, which owns everything all the way into the fjord. Past Ketilsfjord are 'Rampnessfjord' and Einarsfjord as well as a large royal farm and a splendid church dedicated to Saint Nicholas; the region also contains a nunnery and a monastery. One may then continue to Hvalseyfjord, Eiriksfjord and Breidafjord. All this and more 'was told to us by Ívar Bárdsson, Greenlander, who was our manager at the bishop's farm at Gardar in Greenland for many years'.[6]

This confused (and confusing) sequence owes much to sources such as a 1608 doggerel poem, the *Danish Chronicle*, by Claus Christoffersen Lyschander (1558–1624), the *Groenlandia* written 1597–1602 by Arngrimur

Jónsson (1568–1648), and the *Greenland Annals* by Björn Jónsson from Skarðsá, who had copied much of his material around 1643 from a slightly earlier, anonymous compilation, rather freely adding notions of his own that included influence from the 1558 Zeno map (see 'Postscript' and below).[7]

Valkendorf obtained a papal indulgence for his expedition in 1514, but the voyage itself failed to materialise, in large part for lack of funds on the archbishop's part and also because he and his headstrong king had a falling out. Before that happened, however, Valkendorf had been instrumental in securing the 1514 publication, in Paris, of the *Gesta Danorum*, a highly idiosyncratic history of the Danes which Saxo Grammaticus had completed sometime between 1204 and 1216, after which time his manuscript had reposed for three centuries in the Sorø monastery library, although used by Claudius Clavus among others.[8] Once in print, the work fed the curiosity of every writer and cartographer interested in the Far North. It sold so well that it was republished in Basel in 1536 and appeared in a rather bowdlerised Danish translation in 1575. Valkendorf would naturally have been familiar with the work's narrative about a man named Thorkild, serving King Gorm the Old. Thorkild sailed far north of Hålogaland in Norway, where his crew disobeyed him and slaughtered a large number of sheep grazing without supervision. However, the animals turned out to belong to some trolls who were not best pleased.[9] There is but a short step from this passage to the story in Ívar's 'Description', handed down by Valkendorf and his copyist(s), of unsupervised animals being slaughtered in a Western Settlement spookily devoid of humans.

ÍVAR'S WIDER SPHERE OF INFLUENCE

Ívar's 'Description' exists in several translations, including Dutch, German, Latin and English. The English version was done by Master William Steere in 1608 and published in Samuel Purchas's 1625 compendium *Purchas his Pilgrimes*.[10] Purchas notes that this treatise by 'Iver Boty a Gronlander' had been translated into 'High Dutch' (i.e. German) in 1560 and subsequently into Low Dutch by the Dutch pilot and explorer Willem Barentsz (c. 1550–97), who worked from a text evidently supplied by a well-travelled merchant and politician named Daniel van der Meulen. That Barentsz version, which Purchas had borrowed from the cartographer Peter Plancius (1552–1622), was the one Master Steere borrowed from Purchas in order to translate the account of 'Iver Boty' for the English explorer

Henry Hudson. This circuit speaks volumes of how eagerly people at that time traded information about the Arctic region and its hoped-for shortcuts to Asian riches. Plancius, who became a founder of the Dutch East India Company, made a world map in 1594 showing the northeastern passage to Asia which he wanted the Dutch to explore.[11]

Barentsz had completed his translation of Ívar's report shortly before he set out in 1594 on the first of his three voyages to discover a northeast route to Asia – a vain quest that ended with his death in Novaya Zemlya. However, neither he nor Hudson a few years later would have had much help from the sailing directions associated with their version of Ívar's 'Description' while they felt their way through hostile Arctic waters. Besides reflecting ideas from the time when Björn Jónsson of Skarðsá penned his *Greenland Annals*, those directions bear the unmistakable imprint of the map of the North Atlantic which the Venetian Nicolò Zeno the Younger had published in 1558, claiming that it was based on fourteenth-century information from Venetian ancestors familiar with those northern waters. It was exposed as a fake only a little over a century ago. On Zeno's map, a large, peninsular Greenland runs diagonally from the southwest and arches above Iceland towards an undefined northeast link that dips down to northern Norway. Zeno also included a number of fictitious islands to the south and west with names such as Estotilant, Frislandia and Iscaria. Besides feeding the imaginations of Richard Henry Major and others in the nineteenth century, who were eager to link Zeno's work with Ívar Bárdsson as well as with 'Prince' Henry Sinclair of Orkney, the map also caused much more immediate damage, both with and without the help of Ívar's 'Description'.

THE 'NEW' GREENLAND EMERGES

After his 1596 Spitzbergen discovery, Barentsz drew a marvellous map of the Arctic (Fig. 3), published posthumously in the Hague in 1598, in the *Itinerario* of Jan Huyghen van Linschoten who had been along on Barentsz's first two voyages. As might be expected, given the long-standing Dutch role in shipping Norwegian stockfish for other nations, Barentsz's depiction of Norway and the White Sea region was amazing for its time.[12] He also showed his newly gained knowledge of the Novaya Zemlya region and demonstrated his belief that Spitzbergen was part of northeastern Greenland – a notion that pleased Christian IV of Denmark no end as soon as English, Dutch and Danish whaling began at Spitzbergen.

Bisected by 'Martin Frobishers Straytes', Barentsz's Greenland reaches far to the northeast in the Zeno manner and ends without further definition just south of 'Het nieuwe land' or Spitzbergen. Novaya Zemlya and northern Russia (also incomplete) likewise suggest a continuous Polar continent. Far up along the East Greenland coast lies St Thomas Cenobium (the Saint Thomas Monastery), which Zeno invented and which is yet another example of the general European conviction that the Norse had settled on Greenland's east coast.

The Saint Thomas Monastery and many other Zeno inventions were embraced by the innovative 1569 world map of Gerhard Mercator (1512–94) and had become cartographic dogma by the time Barentsz drew his map. Perceptions of Greenland grew even more complicated after Martin Frobisher's voyages to Baffin Island in 1576, 1577 and 1578. He and his navigators tried to fit Greenland – where they actually stepped ashore in 1578 – into Mercator's image of the North Atlantic and the Arctic, and southern Greenland became endowed with a brand new passage, Frobisher Strait, which connected the east and west coasts. Once born, that child had a long and lusty life both under its own name and amalgamated with the passage which the Norse Greenlanders supposedly called 'Öllumlengri'. The Zeno map does not show any kind of east-west passage through Greenland, because that notion first entered continental European minds with the Dutch and English translations of Ívar's 'Description' and the sailing route described above. In reality, the only through passage between Greenland's east and the west coasts is a narrow, fifty-five-miles long passage just above Cape Farewell, called Prince Christian's Sound or Ikerassuaq.

While explorers and map makers struggled to make sense of the Arctic and the sub-Arctic, the lack of knowledge throughout Europe about those regions was a boon to other charlatans offering 'information' about Greenland, a good example being 'Dithmar Blefkens his Voyages and Historie of Island and Groenland'. In a book published in 1607, the Dutchman Dithmar Blefken claimed that two Hamburg merchants sailing to Iceland in 1563 had taken him along as their chaplain, and many wonders did he there hear and behold. Drawing freely upon contemporary notions and his own fertile mind, he retailed highlights supposedly drawn from his own observations as well as from Icelandic monks, including one who had visited the Saint Thomas Monastery in Greenland. Blefken had been particularly keen to learn that the monk visiting Greenland had seen Pygmies, described as hairy to the outermost finger joints (the males with beards to their knees) and substituting hissing for human speech while they lived out their lives in utter darkness.[13]

With his remarks about the Pygmies, Blefken revealed a mental map of the Arctic where Greenland ran into northeasternmost Asia, to which the monstrous race of Pygmies had by then been relegated (Chapter Five).

MISPLACED, BUT NOT FORGOTTEN

While in Rome in 1522 to consult the pope about Christian II's increasingly disturbing behaviour, Valkendorf died without having had the chance to put his Greenland plans to the test, but Danish and Norwegian hopes of reconnecting with the Norse Greenlanders did not die with him. In December 1520, Christian II had evidently contemplated sending a fleet to Greenland, because he told his well-tested buccaneer Søren Norby to ready his ships for the task, to which Norby replied in February that he could not be ready until after Easter. However, when that time came, he found himself obliged to deal with rebellion in eastern Sweden, and soon he became so heavily embroiled in Baltic economic politics that he found himself as a most unwilling guest of the Grand Duke of Moscow. By 1528 he had finally managed to make his way to Vilnius in Lithuania and could send two messages to Christian II, with a follow-up letter from Breslau in Poland, in all of which he offered to help the now beleaguered king reclaim Greenland from the Grand Duke, said to be lording it over two bishoprics in Greenland as well as over a piece of Norway.[14]

It is quite clear from Norby's missives that he imagined Greenland located north of Norway in accordance with the B-redaction of sixteenth-century Claudius Clavus-derivative maps. It is no surprise, therefore, that growing geographical confusion about the country and its Norse inhabitants helped neither later attempts to reach the Norse settlements nor northern travellers who, through no fault of their own, found themselves beyond their ken. In the latter category one finds a couple of stories so often used as putative evidence for post-1500 Norse occupation of Greenland that they need a quick look here.

Bishop Ögmund Pálsson, the last Catholic bishop of Skálholt, left Iceland in 1520 to be consecrated by Archbishop Valkendorf, but was driven off towards Greenland by bad weather and high seas and made it home to Iceland only after many dangers. The next year he went to Trondheim again, only to find that Valkendorf had gone into exile. Finally consecrated in Copenhagen, Ögmund stayed in Iceland from 1522 until he had to flee in 1541. An eventful enough story, and true – unless one reads Björn Jónsson from Skárðsá's version predicated on the Eastern Settlement's being on the Greenland east coast. Björn has Ögmund and his people believing that they had seen Herjolfsness with people and sheep – except it was late in the day and the light had not been too good...[15]

Björn Jónsson is also the source of a story 'told within men's memory' about Jón 'Greenlander', a mariner who for many years had been in the service of Hanse stockfish merchants in Hamburg, and who earned his cognomen by drifting off to Greenland several times. On one of those occasions, his ship had entered a very large and wide and calm bay with many islands. The sailors stayed away from the populated islands, of which there were several, as well as from farms on the mainland, and anchored on an island with no people. Using their ship's boat, they went ashore on a small island where they found fishing huts and boat houses and fish-drying racks just like in Iceland, and there they saw a dead man lying face down on the ground. He had a well-made hood on his head, while the rest of his clothes were made partly of wool cloth, partly of sealskin. Next to him lay a bent knife, worn down by repeated sharpening, and this the sailors brought back home with them to go with their story. Björn adds that even in his own time, many sensible people thought there still were some Norse colonists in Greenland.[16] Several details in the tale suggest an actual voyage, but there is no telling when exactly it may have taken place (Finnur Jónsson estimated around 1540), nor may one assume that Jón's experience actually involved Greenland and not some part of Iceland's ragged, lonely coast, given the geographical notions that prevailed throughout the sixteenth century.

EARLY POST-VALKENDORF ATTEMPTS TO REACH THE NORSE

Valkendorf left Norway when his relationship with the increasingly volatile and despotic Christian II became untenable. A couple of years later, the king was in such bad odour with most of his subjects that in 1523 he, too, was forced into exile while his uncle, Duke Frederik of Holstein, was offered the Danish crown and subsequently that of Norway as well. When Christian II returned to Denmark after many years of exile, his uncle – now Frederik I of Denmark-Norway – promptly imprisoned him and kept him captive until Christian died in 1559, having outlived both Frederik I and Frederik's son and successor, Christian III. Connecting with the Norse Greenlanders did not appear on any royal agenda during all those turbulent years in between, although Christian III bethought himself sufficiently of the colony's presumed needs to cancel the long-standing royal prohibition against direct trade with Greenland.

A more active phase began with the accession of Christian III's son Frederik II (1559–88). Unlike Valkendorf, who had wanted to reclaim the Greenlanders for the Church of Rome, Frederik II saw the Norse Greenlanders as candidates for conversion to Lutheranism. Affirming Danish hegemony and improving the royal coffers with profitable merchandise would, as before, have taken precedence over pious locutions, however. The argument for Denmark's claim to Greenland was that the 1397 Kalmar Union had legitimised Danish hegemony over Norway and its colonies. Frederik II's personal interest would also have been fanned by the renewed focus on the North Atlantic generated by Zeno's startling publications.

A bizarre royal proclamation, written in Icelandic and dated 12 April 1568, was to be delivered to the Norse Greenlanders by the royal naval captain Christian Aalborg, who would have at his command a ship full of goods for distribution among the colonists. In return, the Norse were expected to confirm their allegiance to the Dano-Norwegian Crown. This proclamation was the letter Finn Gad identified as the sole 'evidence' for Norse Greenland's submission to the Norwegian Crown around 1265 (Chapter Six). There is no reason to think that Captain Aalborg had much luck with his expedition, if indeed the attempt was ever made. Other documents reveal that in 1579, Frederik II sent the Scot James Allday to Greenland. Leaving Copenhagen in the spring with two ships, Allday returned that same autumn to report that an ice belt had prevented their landing on Greenland's east coast when they sighted it. A 1581 adventure proposed by the Faeroese navigator and freebooter Mogens Heinesøn may be discounted altogether.[17]

Long a thorn in the side of English merchants engaged in Russian trade, the Dutch merchant Oliver Brunel had several years of experience with the Kola Peninsula and Siberia when he and a Norwegian partner signed a 1583 agreement with Frederik II to undertake an exploratory voyage to Greenland at their own cost. It is evident from the correspondence that both they and the king assumed a land connection between northeastern Greenland and Russia similar to that envisioned by Søren Norby and Christian II, and that any exploration would take place in conjunction with an eastbound Arctic voyage they were contemplating for themselves. We do not know if they profited personally from their undertaking; the Danish king certainly did not. It is nevertheless unlikely that this or any of the other failed enterprises dampened his wish to reach that cold and distant country he regarded as his by rights. His interest in other nations' activities in the Arctic was so strong that in 1582 he praised Frobisher in a letter to Elizabeth I, written to thank her for the Order of the Garter presented to him in Copenhagen by a delegation that included Frobisher. On that occasion Frederik had discussed his own ambitions with Frobisher, and he had evidently kept up the connection by correspondence, because in 1587 Frobisher wrote to the king to thank him for his kindnesses and declared himself ready to serve him.[18]

CONCERTED EFFORTS BY CHRISTIAN IV

Frederik II's son and successor, Christian IV (1588–1648), was a forceful personality with many interests, strong opinions, excellent foreign connections (he was the brother-in-law of James I) and a decided fondness for trade. Before he concentrated on laying the foundations of a wider Danish empire, he organised three royal expeditions to reclaim the Norse Greenland settlements, all of which failed because, as before, nobody knew where to look.

Responding to an increased interest in Icelandic sources regarding Greenland, the Icelandic clergyman Arngrímur Jónsson (1568–1648) spent the years 1597–1602 gathering all he could learn into a small book, *Grönlandia*. He borrowed willingly from Björn Jónsson's *Greenland Annals*, and among his non-Icelandic sources he listed Saxo Grammaticus and Mercator's maps, whose geographical views he clearly shared when describing Greenland as a huge land stretching from 'Biarmeland' (White Russia) to the New World. He also assured his readers that at the time the Norse settled in Greenland, the country had been completely habitable from 'Hvitserk' on the east coast all the way to the southwestern part, and that there were still forests there.[19]

As convinced as his predecessors that the Norse Greenlanders were still around and just needed to be tracked down, King Christian IV in 1605 sent three navy ships to Greenland to assert Danish sovereignty. The expedition was under the command of the Scot John Cunningham aboard the *Trost*, which was captained by the expedition's chief pilot, the Englishman James Hall. Another Englishman, John Knight, was captain of the *Katten*, and the Danish nobleman Godske Lindenow was in charge of the third ship, *Løven*.

Upon reaching Cape Farewell, the expedition split up. Hall wrote in his report to the king that Lindenow then returned home aboard the *Løven* because of fear of the ice, while Christian IV's cheerleader Claus Christoffersen Lyschander (see further below) claimed in his 1608 *Danish Chronicle* that those aboard the *Løven* were convinced that Hall was mistaken in the course he set. Very likely, both explanations apply to

Lindenow's early return to Copenhagen with two Inuit captives and with furs and other trade goods. The ice was real enough, and it is also clear that the Danish captain and his crew were convinced that they should search the east coast for Norse Greenland farms, while the Englishmen were determined to explore up along Greenland's west coast. The latter approach is what one would expect from people who had been commissioned because of previous exposure to the seas around southern Greenland. Their experience had likely been acquired by sailing with Queen Elizabeth I's explorer John Davis during his three attempts (1585, 1586 and 1587) to find a northwest passage and may also have included a stint with Martin Frobisher a decade earlier.[20]

Davis had been ashore in western Greenland several times without identifying anything he saw as 'old' Greenland, but the mariners who had sailed with him would at least know that the western shore was far more hospitable than the eastern side. The four maps which Hall drew on his own voyage, and which are still at The British Library, show the west coast as far as to Disko Bay and feature a number of names given by Hall. On trips ashore, he believed he had found silver and took samples home with him, while Cunningham, who had followed his own route up along the west coast meanwhile, captured four natives to take back to Denmark. He shot one of them for violent resistance, after which he had to use a cannon blast to scatter a large group of enraged natives. The Norse proved as elusive as ever, but Christian IV was undaunted and sent five ships on a second expedition the following year, with Lindenow in command aboard the *Trost* and with Hall as the first mate and pilot to the fleet. *Løven* was captained by John Cunningham. Only two of the ships reached Greenland, where their men spent much of their time on the west coast collecting silver ore which, along with five or six more captive Inuit, they brought back to Denmark, where the ore was declared worthless.[21]

Still with his chief focus on reaching the old Norse settlements, Christian IV sent out a third expedition to Greenland in 1607, this time with specific instructions to land on the east coast and to show great care and politeness if encountering the Norse. Predictably, the churning ice belt off that coast prevented any landing, which did nothing to discourage the notion that this was where one must continue to look. Three quite dissimilar maps owe their existence to Danish efforts at reconnecting with the Greenland Norse up to that time: the map drawn around 1590 by the young Icelander Sigurður Stefánsson, the 1605 work of the Danish theologian Hans Poulsen Resen (1561–1638) and the 1606 map by the Icelandic Bishop Guðbrandur Thorláksson.[22] This is not the place for a detailed analysis of these works, but it may safely be said that each one exemplified the conviction that the east coast was where Eirik the Red had led his settlers, and that Greenland's perceived location and land connections, combined with the Vínland voyages, entitled Denmark to a prime stake in the New World.

CLAUS CHRISTOFFERSEN LYSCHANDER (1558–1624)

The *Danish Chronicle*, a mindnumbingly long, doggerel poem published in 1608 by Claus Christoffersen Lyschander, puts to rest any lingering doubts about Danish ambitions in the sixteenth and seventeenth centuries. Purporting to tell the history of Norse Greenland, from the introduction of Christianity up to and including the 1607 expedition to reconnect with the settlement, Lyschander's poem is salted with apocrypha – regurgitated in pseudo-historical works to this day – that reflect contemporary ideas and affirm the moral and political imperative for Danish endeavours to assert their rights in Greenland and the New World. In addition to considerations discussed earlier, Lyschander demonstrates awareness of the chief requirement for claiming a portion of America, namely primary possession by a Christian prince – never mind pagan natives. According to Lyschander, the Greenland colony and its Vínland appendage had been Christian from the very beginning: 'And Eirik [the Red] laid his hand on Greenland and planted both people and the Faith in Vínland, present there to this day.' Deserving Christians all, the Norse prospered in their rich new land, built towns and constructed a monastery dedicated to Saint Thomas 'east of Greenland's wildest shore'.[23]

CHANGING PRIORITIES

Christian IV sponsored no more expeditions to search for the Norse Greenlanders after 1607. He focused instead on exploiting the resources of his perceived Arctic possessions and their strategic locations for exploring both a northeast and the northwest passage to India. In 1614, an agreement was reached for the 'Noordsche Compagnie' regarding fishing, whaling and trade 'on or to the coasts between Novaya Zemlya and the Davis Strait, including Spitzbergen and Bear Island', on which occasion Christian IV claimed the right to Spitzbergen as a part of the Norwegian tribute country of Greenland.[24]

Although subsequent sailings were focused on Spitzbergen or the Davis Strait, private enterprise had not turned its back on Greenland's west coast. There are no records accounting for Captain James Hall's activities in the years immediately following 1607, but in 1612 he returned to Greenland in charge of an expedition with two ships, sponsored by several Merchant Adventurers of London, whose purpose was to trade with the Inuit and to fetch home silver ore from the mine Hall thought he had discovered in 1605. With the Englishman William Baffin (circa 1584 –1622) as chief pilot, the expedition came in at Cape Farewell and then followed the west coast up beyond Nuuk. While in Amerdlok fjord, Hall was killed by an Inuk's dart and died within hours. His companions buried him on a nearby island and later returned to England, where their 'silver' ore once again proved useless.[25]

Mercantile interests were also behind the three voyages to Greenland which the Dutch-born David Danell undertook for the Danish Customs Department in 1652, 1653 and 1654. They resulted in lacklustre trade with the Inuit along the west coast and included failed attempts to land on the southeast coast, which as usual was blocked by ice. West coast expeditions by explorers and traders up to that point had not involved forays far enough inland to produce confrontations with Norse farm ruins in either of the two former settlements, and the general conviction that the main Norse settlement had been on Greenland's east coast remained undented.

That conviction was also brought along by the energetic Norwegian missionary Hans Egede, who arrived in the outer Nuuk area in 1721 with an ardent wish to convert the Norse Greenlanders to the Lutheran faith and with hard-won support from the Greenland Company in Bergen and Danish authorities for his undertaking. The merchants and secular authorities involved shared an earnest desire to establish a lucrative trade with the Inuit who thus far had engaged in barter with Dutch whalers in the area.

HANS EGEDE (1686–1758)

When the thirty-five-year-old Hans Egede stepped ashore from the good ship *Haabet* ('Hope') on the island Igdluerunerit in the outer Godthaabsfjord, he was accompanied by his wife and children as well as by a number of Norwegian men and women to help with the work of establishing a mission station in a rough new land. 'Wild people' who, in their boats, had escorted *Haabet* the last distance, seemed friendly enough ashore, at least at first, and helped the Norwegians construct their house. As it turned out, the Inuit assumed that the visitors would leave in the autumn, just like the Dutch whalers, and then the house would be theirs.[26]

The Norwegians at 'Haabets Havn' (Hope Harbour) had no intention of leaving Greenland, but Egede worried greatly over their food supplies and over the Inuit's lack of interest in bartering fresh game and fish for the trade goods chosen by the Greenland Company in Bergen. As the first winter wore on, scurvy added to the troubles encountered by the Norwegians huddling together in the one house, but they made it through somehow until June, when not just one, but two ships arrived from home with supplies and letters. With restored energy and optimism, Egede decided to explore farther inland, in part to find a more benign location for his people (the mission moved inland to Nuuk in 1728, where Egede's house still stands). In the spring of 1723, he also travelled south along the west coast to look at some old ruins which Inuit familiar with the region had seen with their own eyes, and which Egede was convinced must be the remains of the Western Settlement, whose denizens clearly were no more, but who Egede thought must to some degree have intermarried with the 'wild people'.

Neither Egede nor anyone else at the time had any idea of the immense distance and other obstacles involved in going overland to the east coast, where Egede was fully convinced that the main Norse settlement had been. He hoped on his journey south to find a possible overland route from there and to learn more meanwhile about the Norse in the 'Western Settlement'. While travelling in the southwest, he was much taken with the evidence he saw of Norse farmsteads and was particularly interested in the roofless shell of the Hvalsey church, which his Inuit guides told him had been destroyed by the Norse themselves before they left. Like many people after him, he took a shovel to the church floor in the hope of finding objects of interest, but all he succeeded in doing was to disturb the medieval strata.

He was never to know that he had located the heart of the Eastern Settlement, which so many frustrated explorers had hoped to find. He returned to Nuuk and, while he waited to bring the Eastern Settlement inhabitants into an appropriate religious frame of mind, he pressed on with his efforts to convert the 'wild people' to Christianity, as he had done almost since his arrival in 1721. He became known as the Apostle of Greenland, and the second European colonisation of Greenland began with him.

LAST EFFORTS

By royal order, two ships under the command of Captain Løvenørn of the Danish Navy were sent to East Greenland in 1786 to look for the Eastern

Settlement, deserted or otherwise. The expedition found no way to land inside the formidable barrier of ice, but a fresh attempt was made the following year. Again, the results were so disappointing that there were no further attempts for a number of years, until William Scoresby proved in 1822 that it was possible to make one's way inside the ice belt and land on the coast at 70° 31'N.

Scoresby's success made the Danish authorities worry that he would eventually claim a large slice of Greenland for England, and a special Danish commission determined that an expedition should use umiaks ('women's boats') to manoeuver inside the ice belt from Cape Farewell to Scoresby Sound and to ascertain, if possible, former Norse occupancy. W. A. Graah, a lieutenant in the Danish Navy, was put in charge of the enterprise and left Copenhagen in 1828. After wintering in Nanortalik in southernmost Greenland, he spent two exhausting years exploring up and down a long stretch of the eastern shore without seeing any evidence of Norse farms past or present. During a sojourn in the southwest, where Graah and his men brought the inevitable shovels, they dug the Hvalsey church floor to a depth of two or three feet, without finding much except for evidence of Egede's excavations. It nevertheless convinced Graah that this, and not on the east coast, was where one should seek the Old Norse settlement.[27]

The belief in an east coast Eastern Settlement was finally put to rest by the 1883–85 expedition to southeastern Greenland in which the two Danish naval officers Gustav Holm and V. Garde, using umiaks, travelled north *inside* the ice belt as far as to Ammassalik and found no signs anywhere of Norse habitation.[28]

CONFRONTING A HARSH WORLD

Every one of the explorers' reports mentioned this far is a testimony to human fortitude in the face of Arctic conditions and with little protection against the effects of extreme cold and desperately inadequate nourishment. Scoresby, who did all his Arctic travels by ship, had some advice for those who wanted to explore farther into the Polar regions. They should travel overland, and

> the principal articles provided by the experienced traveller for his subsistence, consist of tea, oatmeal, bacon, bread…but no spirits; and whenever he finds it necessary to use artificial stimuli for accelerating the circulation of the blood, and promoting the heat of the system, instead of resorting to spirituous liquors, knowing them to be injurious, he

drinks freely of warm tea…His relish, with his tea, consists of a bit of broiled bacon, and perhaps a little oatmeal porridge.[29]

That said, Scoresby had no illusions about the impact of the Arctic environment on the human psyche.

An Arctic winter consists of the accumulation of almost everything atmospheric phenomena that is disagreeable to the feelings, together with the privation of those bounties of heaven, with which other parts of the earth, in happier climates, are so plentifully endowed. Here, during the whole of the winter months, the cheering rays of the sun are neither seen nor felt, but considerable darkness perpetually prevails; this, with occasional storms of wind and snow, and a degree of cold calculated to benumb the faculties of man, give a character to those regions most repugnant to human feeling.[30]

NO FINAL CHAPTER YET

That the Norse Greenlanders disappeared, seemingly without a trace, still has a powerful hold on our imaginations. At least one reason for this is the human reluctance to accept such utter oblivion – it is downright frightening to think that an entire group of people not unlike ourselves can vanish without any explanation for what happened. Consequently, many scholars have applied themselves over the years to unravelling the Norse Greenlanders' fate, and fiction writers have found fertile soil in that myth-shrouded medieval society.

When Scoresby wrote down his impressions of Greenland and the Arctic, knowledge of Greenland's geography was still incomplete, to say the least, but it had come a long way since the works of Sigurður Stefánsson (about 1590) and Hans Poulsen Resen (1605) and their efforts to envision Greenland's position relative to the New World.[31] Both men had scrupulously tried to account for all three of the major American locations to which Leif Eiriksson had reportedly assigned the names Helluland, Markland and Vínland, but when realistic information about North American resources and topography started to accumulate, a profound change in focus occurred in both European and North American thinking. An obsession with Vínland began in the nineteenth century, at the same time as an offshoot of a growing romantic preoccupation with 'lost' peoples, tribes and languages replaced unfocused economic greed, and it became fashionable to ponder not only the fate of the Norse Greenlanders, but their experience of North America during a supposedly short, but intense, period of exploration followed by a lasting retreat to Greenland and an unknown fate.

Nobody knows for certain how many Norse Greenlanders there were at any given time, but modern scholars estimate the joint population of the two settlements to have been somewhere between three thousand and five thousand individuals at the peak of the curve – far fewer than the numbers envisioned by nineteenth- and early twentieth-century enthusiasts whose intellectual footprints are still with us. Some investigators have expected to find surviving traces of the Norse Greenlanders among the Inuit of Greenland and/or eastern Canada – the explorers Fridtjof Nansen and Vilhjalmur Stefánsson, for example, believed that the Greenland Norse are still with us genetically in 'blonde Eskimos'.[32] Hoping to examine this claim, the Icelandic anthropologists Gísli Pálsson and Agnar Helgason went to Greenland and to the Cambridge Bay region in Northern Canada in 2002 in order to test the DNA of three hundred and fifty present-day Inuit living in those two areas. Their aim was to compare the results with genetic markers from modern Icelanders, but no match turned up, nor did a subsequent comparison with DNA from modern Greenland Inuit suggest that a discernible genetic mingling of Norse and Inuit had taken place during the Middle Ages.

While we wait to learn where the Norse went after they closed down their Greenland colony, we may reasonably believe that during their society's existence, some of their number went to other Nordic countries and to the British Isles and stayed there, quietly blending in with their surroundings and adding to both the local population and their new family's lore. Had even one such story been written down, we would have been infinitely richer.

Postscript

THE FICTIONAL NORSE IN NORTH AMERICA

Medieval Norse activities in Greenland and North America have long been a magnet to some who, for a variety of reasons, prefer a homemade story to the far more fascinating reality gradually revealed by research.[1]

Far from putting an end to fanciful notions about the Norse in North America, twentieth-century evidence for Norse voyages westwards from Greenland only gave further encouragement to alternative histories festooned with 'Norse' objects found in America, untroubled by the fact that the L'Anse aux Meadows ruins so far constitute the only known Norse housing site in North America and by the reality that few Norse Greenlanders would have been available for travel at the best of times. Much as in other discussions about who reached America before Christopher Columbus, chauvinism nurtured by 'Norse roots' accounts for several of the cult notions that have sprung up around the Greenland Norse. Basement-inventor stubbornness, anti-intellectualism, overblown egos, indiscriminate competitiveness and even racism may also enter the picture, but common to all these stories is their origin in post-Columbian myths.

Two myths that spawned cult notions about early British voyages to North America, and that are closely tangential to fantasies involving the Norse, may be traced to their beginnings and perfectly illustrate how a speck of misrepresentation may become a sizable chunk of alternative history.

PRINCE MADOC OF WALES

The first myth concerns what Richard Hakluyt in 1589 called 'The most ancient Discovery of the West Indies by Madoc the sonne of Owen Guynneth Prince of North-wales, in the yere 1170, taken out of the history of Wales, lately published by M. David Powel, Doctor of Divinity.' Prince Madoc, who had left his brothers in Wales to quarrel among themselves, reportedly set sail westwards from Wales and headed so far north after leaving the Irish coast that he came to an unknown land that 'must needs be some part of that countrey of which the Spanyards affirme themselves to be the first finders since Hannos time. Whereupon it is manifest that that countrey was by Britaines discovered, long before Columbus led any Spanyards thither.' Madoc sailed home to Wales and later returned to the fair country he had visited, this time accompanied by a number of emigrants. 'I am of opinion that the land whereunto he came was some part of the West Indies,' Hakluyt wrote – an opinion with which his literary heir Samuel Purchas concurred. Dr John Dee – Queen Elizabeth's adviser, Hakluyt's friend and the man with whom the Madoc claim originated – was more precise. On the back of Dee's remarkable map of part of the northern hemisphere, dating from about 1580, there is a list of Queen Elizabeth's claims to the New World. The first entry reads: 'Circa Anno 1170. The Lord Madoc, Sonne to Owen Gwynnedd Prynce of Northwales, led a colonie and inhabited in Terr Florid, or thereaboute.'[2]

The second myth about British pre-Columbian sailings to America is rather more elaborate and tenacious than the one concerning Prince Madoc, which is such a transparent fabrication that the preface to John Seller's 1671 book *The English Pilot* stated that Seller himself did not believe the Welsh tale.[3]

EARL HENRY SINCLAIR OF ORKNEY

When first planted, the seeds to the still-flourishing tale about 'Prince' Henry Sinclair of Orkney were not British and did not mention any sort of Henry. Instead, our hero was named Zichmni and first saw public light in 1558, when the Venetian nobleman Nicolò Zeno the Younger published a map of the North Atlantic which he claimed was based on a late fourteenth-century map he had found in his attic, and accompanied the map with a combined narration-and-correspondence text, supposedly also from the same period and, like the map, directly involving earlier members of the Zeno family: Nicolò, Antonio and Carlo.

The elder Nicolò Zeno had reportedly set off on a voyage northwards from Venice in 1380 and been shipwrecked during his trip home on an island called Frislanda. It was 'much larger than Ireland' and ruled by the king of Norway, who was presently at war with a doughty neighbouring prince named Zichmni. Nicolò, an exemplary mariner, became Zichmni's pilot and served him so well that he was knighted, whereupon he decided to send for his brother Antonio. There is no need here to go into the events and locations involved over the subsequent fourteen years; suffice it to say that neither the texts nor the map have any place names or descriptions remotely pointing to Orkney.

As the current Shetland archivist, Brian Smith, noted in his clever debunking of the Earl-Henry-in-America fantasy, the first tentative equation of Zichmni with the first Sinclair earl of Orkney was made in the 1780s, when the English travel writer John Reinhold Forster decided to interpret the Zeno map and texts, both of which were generally accepted as genuine until the English scholar Frederic W. Lucas proved them otherwise at the end of the nineteenth century.[4] A century more was to pass, however, before Forster's embryo grew into a lusty child just a couple of decades before Lucas's revelations about Zeno's work.

Richard Henry Major, curator of the British Museum's Map Room from 1844 until his retirement in 1880, first published his own elaborations on the Zeno map and texts in 1873. His wide experience with old maps unfortunately did not exclude flights of fancy. With all the authority of his Establishment position he firmly equated Zeno's purely fictitious islands and place names with actual North Atlantic locations, and a year later, he assured a Massachusetts audience:

> In the detection of these various realities, I had made a considerable advance towards the perception of the truth with respect to this venerable and old document; but I might never have succeeded, had it not been that Johann Reinhold Forster, the distinguished companion of Captain Cook, had already, in 1784, made the valuable suggestion that 'Zichmni' was the Southerner's mode of writing 'Sinclair,' Henry Sinclair being at the time in question Earl of Orkney and Caithness, and every circumstance, geographical, political, and historical, which close critical observation and research have enabled me to develop out of the story, has shown beyond all doubt that he was right.

Major's information about the Norse Greenlanders and their North American activities came chiefly from the *Antiquitates Americanae*. He evidently considered that sufficient background for combining Forster's theories with his own comparison of the Zeno texts and Ívar Bárdsson's report on Greenland, which he found in agreement on all major points and constituting proof, if any was still needed, that Zeno's ancestors had been visiting the Norse colonies in the North Atlantic more than a century before the time of Columbus.[5]

THE WESTFORD STONE

Henry Sinclair had not yet been credited with going to North America, but a proud member of the Sinclair clan became one of the early promoters of that twist to an already convoluted Zeno story, and another enthusiast, Frederick Pohl, took the legend to its final absurdity by finding solid North American evidence for Henry Sinclair's expedition to the New World, an event Pohl declared had taken place on 2 June 1398. There was even a monument to a member of Henry's band, a Knight Templar who had died on American soil, Pohl claimed, namely the image on a stone first found in Westford, Massachusetts in the 1880s. At the time, it had been identified as an Indian carving, but Pohl and successive embroiderers on the Sinclair story knew better. This fattened-up version of the Sinclair myth claims that the carving showed a medieval knight in full armour, with his sword and shield, and that it clearly corroborated the mention in Zeno's text that a cousin of Zichmni/Henry Sinclair had died while on the new continent. Despite having been thoroughly debunked by scholars, the story still shows regular signs of life, but it may be put to rest by the judgment recently made by David K. Schafer, curatorial assistant for Archaeology at Harvard University's Peabody Museum of Archaeology and Ethnology. The Westford stone's image, says Schafer, is not Indian, nor does it represent a fourteenth-century knight. It shows a T-shaped engraving – possibly scratched by two young boys in the late 1800s – which is surrounded by weathering marks and glacial scratches.[6]

THE NEWPORT TOWER

In the 1930s, William Goodwin (chiefly remembered as the creator of an 'American Stonehenge' region) identified the sword on the Westford stone as Norse, thus adding grist to the mill of cult historians eager to link the stone with the Newport Tower in Rhode Island, the 'Norse' origins of which were first vouched for by the authors of the *Antiquitates Americanae*. The tower's origin is scarcely a secret, because there is now ample archaeological and documentary evidence that it was built in the mid to late seventeenth century as a windmill on Governor Benedict Arnold's estate and that it is similar to the seventeenth-century Chesterton windmill in Warwickshire, which is still standing.[7] The Newport structure has nevertheless kept its hold on imaginations that prefer to be untrammelled by historical and archaeological evidence about the tower, about the known record of the medieval Norse in Greenland and North America or about other contenders for a pre-Columbian European presence in New England. While the 'Norse church' thesis still dominates in cult history versions of the Newport Tower's origin and purpose, there have been other contenders over the years, such as that the tower's architecture incorporates an astronomical alignment; that it had been constructed as a lighthouse for sixteenth-century European mariners; and, of course, that Henry Sinclair had ordered its construction. Taking a quite different tack, the English author Gavin Menzies claimed that the twenty-eight-feet-tall tower had been built in 1421 by Chinese mariners from a fleet which Admiral Zheng He had charged with circumnavigating and exploring the whole world. Arguing that the tower served the Chinese as a lighthouse and astronomical observatory, Menzies dismissed the notion that the medieval Norse would even have been able to erect such a stone structure. He also assigned Chinese workmanship to the Dighton Rock in Massachusetts; a stone carved by Algonkian natives but variously claimed over the years to be Welsh, Norse, Phoenician, Hebrew and Portuguese.[8]

In their 1837 book, Rafn and Magnusen had embraced a Norse pedigree also for the Dighton Rock because it fit so well with their notions of where Vínland must have been located. Over the years, other American rocks, big and little, have been given similar medieval Norse associations, along with 'Norse mooring holes' in Minnesota and an assortment of swords, drinking horns and even ruin sites which have proved to be neither medieval nor Norse. The list of hoaxes is long and growing, but only a couple of more 'Norse' rocks central to Vínland fantasies warrant discussion here.

THE KENSINGTON RUNE STONE

A sturdy slab of greywacke unearthed by a Swedish-American farmer in Kensington, Minnesota in 1898 is commonly known as the Kensington Rune Stone. At first, nobody was impressed by its dramatic tale carved in runes and carefully dated to 1362. The main text (on the stone's front) reports that a group of Norwegians and Swedes exploring far westwards from Vínland had returned to their camp from a day of fishing and found ten of their men 'dead and red with blood', and an inscription following the stone's edge adds that they had left ten men by their ships, which were fourteen days' journey away, and it gives the date as 1362. No whisper of archaeological evidence for a Norse presence in the area has been found to this day, and experts called in to evaluate the stone right after its discovery took a dim view indeed of its authenticity. In 1908, however, the self-styled historian Hjalmar Holand made the Kensington Rune Stone the centrepiece of his own version of the Norse-in-America story, in which he argued that both the stone and the Newport Tower were evidence of a royal Norwegian expedition datable to 1355–64 and featuring Paul Knutsson, one of King Magnus's trusted men.

Holand's claim is still alive and well today, although the king's order to Paul Knutsson, dated late in 1354, is known only from a sixteenth-century copy and mentions Greenland only; there is nothing that may be construed as an order to continue west to North America. There is no reason to think that the voyage ever took place or that the poverty-stricken King Magnus could even have assembled and paid for such an expedition. In truth, his and his advisers' grasp on reality appears to have been tenuous, for in June 1350, less than a year after the Black Death had struck Norway, a summons written in the king's name and issued in hard-hit Bergen ordered eight prominent North Iceland farmers, who had complained about the bishop of Hólar, to take 'the first ship leaving Iceland after they have heard or seen the letter'.[9]

In 1354, when the original Paul Knutsson authorisation was supposedly written, both Denmark and Norway were still reeling after the Black Death, and shipping had suffered so badly that Ívar Bárdsson was unable to return home to Bergen from Greenland until 1364. If genuine, the Paul Knutsson letter would have been but one of several fourteenth-century documents pretending royal concern with salvaging the Faith. An explanation for either copying or inventing the letter in the sixteenth century would lie in the fact that the letter is not an expression of solicitude for the Greenlanders' Christian faith, but bears the unmistakable imprint of Danish post-Columbian efforts to re-establish claims to Norse Greenland – an issue which the preceding chapter took up.

As noted earlier, modern archaeological evidence for continued Norse travels from Greenland across to North America argues very strongly for locations well to the north of Newfoundland. Had there been so many mid-fourteenth-century Norse travellers farther south that they would leave inscribed rocks for one of their own people to find, we should expect at least some archaeological signs of their activities wherever 'Norse' objects of any size have been found, in locations that have certainly been well scrutinised. There is absolutely no such corroboration, or at least none that has passed professional muster.

For over a century, seasoned experts in runology, archaeology, linguistics and history have judged the Kensington Rune Stone to be a deliberate hoax provoked by the 1892 Columbus celebrations. It is notable that the current defenders of the stone's authenticity do not come from the disciplines necessary to evaluating the stone and Holand's claims. The last of the stone's academic defenders, Professor Henrik Williams at Uppsala, firmly withdrew his support when a 2003 discovery made in Sweden proved that the disputed runes on the Kensington Rune Stone were used in the nineteenth century in Dalarne, Sweden – the native turf of one of the suspected hoaxers.[10]

So far, all the archaeological evidence for continued Norse crossings to America suggests that the voyagers kept to the coasts while preferring the northern stretches of the American coasts, where they could find the lumber and iron they needed and top up their profits with hunting before a comparatively short return voyage to Greenland. Common sense also tells us that with Norse Greenland manpower scarce and the daily struggle for subsistence constant, the Greenlanders would not have sent their small North American working parties far into the interior, away from the safety of shore and ships. The risks would have been too great and the prospect for a commensurate economic return nonexistent. Equally irrational is the idea that any group of people supposedly fleeing from hostile North American natives would have wasted precious time carving an elaborate story into a stone slab! A story, furthermore, that carefully divided the party into Swedes and Norwegians – the composition of the hoaxers' own Minnesota community – and that was careful to mention Vínland, the uncontested focus of nineteenth-century interest in Norse voyages to North America. It was the very place to which the Greenland Norse had not returned during their subsequent exploitation of North American resources.

THE SPIRIT POND STONES

A demonstrable preoccupation with Vínland to the exclusion of Helluland and Markland is an excellent indicator that an object with 'Norse' associations is a modern fake. Another case in point is Maine's contribution to this fertile field: four small stones discovered on two occasions (1971 and 1972) by the Spirit Pond near Popham Beach. They featured inscriptions in runes obviously borrowed from the Kensington

Rune Stone and had a map and other illustrations intended to evoke details found in the two Vínland sagas. The American historian Erik Wahlgren saw the collective message of the crudely distorted Icelandic texts and the illustrations as a 'quadruple satire on the Vinland voyages', but several Norse-in-America believers have taken issue with this sensible assessment.[11]

Nobody knows who carved these rocks and placed them by the Spirit Pond, but my guess is that the artificer was a graduate student and practical joker with a knowledge of Old Norse and runes, not unlike the five University of Minnesota graduate students who chiselled 'AVM' and the year 1363 into a partially exposed boulder in the Kensington Rune Stone Park in 1985. After the event had taken place, a few scholars working on the Norse in America, myself included, were informed of the deed, lest the joke be carried too far when the runic inscription came to light, as it was bound to do. That happened in 2001, when the stone was discovered by Kensington Rune Stone enthusiasts. They were especially struck by the stone's date of 1363 – just a year later than the one inscribed on the Kensington Rune Stone. In the midst of the ensuing intense activity among those who believed that crucial new evidence for medieval Norse activities in the Kensington Rune Stone's immediate vicinity had now been found, the creators of the 'Ave Maria stone' informed the Minnesota Historical Society of the inscription's origins and of the motivation for their own actions, namely that the stone's discovery might give rise to a public discussion and demonstrate the part which gullibility and ignorance had played in making a 'Norse' icon of the Kensington Rune Stone. This hope was fulfilled, and although those who had fallen publicly for the bait were not best pleased, the excitement over the new discovery eventually died of its own accord.[12]

In contrast to the makers of the 'Ave Maria stone', the author of the Spirit Pond rock inscriptions never came forward, and the stones' status as 'Norse' objects has continued although their historical authenticity is highly suspect on a number of grounds. Not the least of the problems is a crude map of the immediate find area, accompanied by an inscription claiming that the Spirit Pond location is Hóp in Vínland, a two days' journey south from Canada. An apparent date of 1011 is also given.[13] Furthermore, even if the name 'Canada' (first used by Jacques Cartier in 1535) had existed in the eleventh century, the Norse would not have employed it – they invariably gave Norse names to the North American regions they saw: Helluland, Markland and Vínland. But while the Spirit Pond rocks' use of 'Canada' several centuries before the name's first written appearance is troubling, the map and its unblushing association with

Vínland shown on one of the four rocks is even more so. The fixation on Vínland is by its very nature modern.

Just like other travellers in both Antiquity and the Middle Ages, the Norse would no doubt have sketched sea marks and provided verbal information to guide someone to a specific location, much like the pre-Christian Greeks with their periploi (rutters or sailing directions). But the Norse did not even have a word for map or chart, and they never made a graphic record for outsiders of their familiarity with the northern world and of its location relative to countries farther south and east. Medieval Icelandic and Norwegian literature demonstrates that otherwise, the general Norse concept of the world was no different from that of their contemporaries elsewhere in Europe, with a spherical world taken for granted and Asia, Africa and Europe envisaged as interconnected and accounting for the world's entire land mass.[14]

By the nineteenth century, the general public was considerably better informed, although not necessarily about the Norse Greenlanders' geographical knowledge. When addressing the question of Norse voyages, both scholars and non-scholars were in any case focused on Vínland as representing the Norse 'discovery' of America. That mindset permeates the *Vinland Map*, another map for which a 'Norse' connection has been claimed, with consequences considerably greater than from the carvings on the Spirit Pond rocks.[15] This artefact's public career illustrates Norse myth making in our own time so well that it warrants a closer look here.

THE *VINLAND MAP*

In 1965, Yale University Library in New Haven, Connecticut, announced that it had acquired a mid-fifteenth-century volume with a manuscript map showing the Norse discovery of North America around AD 1000. At the same time, Yale University Press released *The Vinland Map and Tartar Relation*, authored by two British scholars and one American. R. A. Skelton was the superintendent of maps in the British Museum; George D. Painter was an expert on incunabula and an assistant keeper in the British Museum's Department of Printed Books; while Thomas E. Marston was the curator of Medieval and Renaissance Manuscripts at Yale University Library. The three men's primary aim was to assure the public that the unique Yale map dated from about 1440 and was a credible representation of Norse experience in North America, showing information passed down through several centuries. Their secondary purpose was to analyse the text manuscript *Hystoria Tartarorum* (*Tartar*

Relation) with which the map had been bound at the time of purchase in 1957. In addition, the map and the *Tartar Relation* had soon become associated with a mid-fifteenth-century binding containing parts of the *Speculum Historiale* by Vincent of Beauvais, but that acquisition was of interest to the three authors only because of the binding involved.

The map became known as the *Vinland Map* because, in the extreme northwest, it features a large island with two deep inlets, identified by two Latin legends as Vinilanda Insula. The shorter of the two map legends says: 'Island of Vínland discovered by Bjarni and Leif in company.' The Yale book's translation of the longer legend reads:

> By God's will, after a long voyage from the island of Greenland to the south toward the most distant remaining parts of the western ocean sea, sailing southward amidst the ice, the companions Bjarni [byarnus] and Leif Eiriksson [leiphus erissonius] discovered a new land, extremely fertile and even having vines, the which island they named Vínland. Eric [Henricus] legate of the Apostolic See and bishop of Greenland and the neighboring regions, arrived in this truly vast and very rich land, in the name of Almighty God, in the last year of our most blessed father Pascal, remained a long time in both summer and winter, and later returned northeastward toward Greenland and then proceeded in most humble obedience to the will of his superiors.[16]

Some scholars familiar with Norse sailings in the North Atlantic were understandably baffled, not the least because the Vínland sagas describe the voyages of Bjarni Herjolfsson and Leif Eiriksson as separate ventures, but for the defenders of the Kensington Rune Stone, the Newport Tower and other objects supporting an alternative history of the Norse in America, the new Yale acquisition quickly became a bonanza.

Many reputable scholars in non-Norse fields also hailed Yale's new map as authentic, however, and their views dominated until 1974, when a symposium took place in London that included both defenders and detractors of the map's claim to authenticity. The event was chaired by Helen Wallis, Skelton's successor as superintendent of the Map Room at The British Library, and it was sponsored by the Royal Geographical Society. Among the number of scholarly issues addressed on that occasion, the symposium brought the chemical composition of the map's ink into the debate.[17]

The British scientist A.D. Baynes-Cope was now finally at liberty to disclose the discoveries which he and A.E. Werner had made during a brief examination of the *Vinland Map* and its 'sister' manuscripts at The British Museum Research Laboratory in 1967, by which time the purported authenticity of Yale's new treasure had already burrowed into the public consciousness. This first specialist investigation of the three manuscripts had resulted in several significant observations that have stood the test of time, but which are little known even today because the two Museum scientists were prevented by Yale's confidentiality requirement from reporting publicly on the results of their examination. That changed when the American scientists Walter and Lucy McCrone presented their own ink report at the 1974 symposium and corroborated the 1967 British Museum Research Laboratory findings. The McCrones' investigations, done at Yale's request, had shown that the map's ink was not a conventional medieval iron-gall mixture and that it contained microscopic spherules of anatase titanium oxide of a uniform size developed for the paint industry after 1917.[18]

Taken together with Baynes-Cope's evidence, the McCrones' analysis strongly suggested that the map was a post-World War I product. Scientists at the University of California at Davis later disputed the McCrones' analysis, as did others, but the ink issue was generally considered settled shortly before Walter McCrone's death in 2002, when two British scientists, Robin J. H. Clark and Katherine L. Brown at the Christopher Ingold Laboratories, University College, London, published a study supporting every major point made by Werner, Baynes-Cope, McCrone and Kenneth Towe, another leading American scientist convinced of the *Vinland Map*'s fake nature. Using Raman microprobe spectroscopy on the map and one of its sister manuscripts, Brown and Clark had discovered that the ink on the map is carbon based and has nothing in common with the ink in the *Tartar Relation*, which is a conventional iron-gall ink. Anatase – a relatively rare form of titanium dioxide – was found only in the yellowish line that remains where the black pigment has fallen off, and those anatase crystals were without exception of the industrially modified sort commercially available only after about 1923.[19]

The discussion about the *Vinland Map* will not be over until the map's last defender falls silent – an event one might have thought assured by the quality of the scientific evidence about the ink alone, not to mention by the map's cartographic peculiarities and its glaring misinformation about the Norse. Unfortunately, even when high-level scientific evidence repeatedly demonstrates that a cult object is not as advertised, arguments in the object's favour can still continue. Non-expert hair splitting is easy and common and has also been brought to bear on the map's cartographic and historical conundrums. Those characteristics are visible to the naked eye and demonstrate beyond any doubt that the map is a modern fake produced by someone with an excellent knowledge of mid-fifteenth-century mapping and geography and taking a strong interest in the medieval Norse forays to North America, but suffering from a considerable information gap.

Twelve years of archival, cartographic and historical research convinced me that the map in all likelihood was made in the 1930s by the German Jesuit priest Father Josef Fischer, SJ (1858–1944), in order to tease anti-Catholic German Nazi 'scholars' touting supposedly Norse history, and I have found no reason to change my mind after publishing *Maps, Myths, and Men: The Story of the Vinland Map* in 2004. I found evidence that the *Vinland Map* could not possibly be a product of the 1440s, because the very first time Leif and Bjarni found Vínland together was in 1765, in the *Historie von Grönland* by the German Herrnhüter David Crantz, who briefly summarised medieval Norse activities in Greenland and noted that after Bjarni Herjolfsson had reported seeing unknown lands in the west, Leif Eiriksson 'fitted out a ship with 35 men, and went to sea with Biærn'.[20] Crantz attributed his information to Paul Henry Mallet's *Introduction à l'histoire de Dannemarc* (1755–56) and Bishop Erik Pontoppidan's *Natural History of Norway* (1752, English tr. 1755), both of whom had relied on Arngrímur Jónsson (ca. 1600) and Thormodus Torfæus (1636–1719), who in turn had confirmed their information with Adam of Bremen.[21]

Mallet had indeed acknowledged his reliance on the works of Arngrímur Jónsson and Thormodus Torfæus, but with results quite different from those Crantz claimed. After recapitulating the story of Bjarni's drifting off, Mallet wrote: 'The following summer, viz. in the year 1002', Bjarni went to Norway to see 'count [Earl] Eric' and told about his sighting of the unknown land in the west. Stung from being chided about his lack of curiosity, Bjarni on his return to Greenland 'began to think seriously of exploring those lands with more attention. Leif, the son of that same Eric rufus who had discovered Greenland ... being desirous of rendering himself illustrious like his father, formed the design of going thither himself; and prevailing on his father Eric to accompany him they fitted out a vessel with five and thirty hands.' Mallet added that when Eirik fell off his horse on the way to the ship, Leif had decided to set sail without his father.[22] Mallet had correctly understood both Arngrímur Jónsson and Torfæus, who had conveyed the saga information just as we know it today.[23]

The German Crantz had simply misread Mallet's French and created a new version of the Norse sailing to Vínland, but the author's respectability as a churchman, coupled with widespread continental ignorance about the medieval Norse, gave the myth a substantial boost, and Crantz's book gained a wide readership among non-Scandinavian readers interested in the recently (1721) recolonised Greenland. The work was still considered current in 1864 when Charles Francis Hall provided his own account of the medieval Norse in *Life with the Esquimaux*, where he cited Crantz, and Crantz's book was also familiar to Father Fischer when he wrote *The Discoveries of the Norsemen in America* in 1902 and claimed to have found a number of early maps indicating knowledge of the Norse voyages to North America.[24]

The conviction that the medieval Norse had left a cartographic record of their brief *Vínland* experience stayed with Fischer until the end of his days, and he remained passionately interested in the topic even after his Nordic mentors had died and he turned to other cartographic subjects because he no longer had the necessary access to the relevant sources. He never mastered any of the Nordic languages or patronymic traditions (hence the absurd leiphus erissonius for Leif Eiriksson), and his ideas about the medieval Norse Greenlanders left much to be desired at the best of times. The evidence points to Fischer's having made the *Vinland Map* shortly after Hitler came to power in 1933 and the Nazis invented their own bogus history of 'Norse' ancestors to bolster their claims to Aryan supremacy and a Greater Germany. That would have been enough to inspire an aging, decent, scholarly priest to draw a map which he thought might at one time have existed in some form, and to fill it with cartographic and historical riddles guaranteed to vex any Nazi 'scholar' faced with pronouncing on the map if it became public property upon its author's death.

The story obviously turned out quite differently, but the notions arising about the Norse in the North Atlantic, after the 1965 Yale launch of the map and the accompanying book, were not of Fischer's making. They were the consequence of the three Yale authors' failure to spot several revealing mistakes about the medieval Norse Greenlanders in the longer Vínilanda Insula legend and their failure to grasp the point of the map altogether. They did not understand that when the Greenland bishop Eirik Gnúpsson (Henricus) went to Vínland, his voyage would have constituted the last link in an early and successful worldwide missionary outreach by the Roman Church.

NORUMBEGA

A second cartographic myth involving the Norse took shape in Northern Europe towards the end of the sixteenth century with the claim that the name 'Norumbega', then appearing on several maps of North America, was a variant of 'Norway' and indicated that this was where one should look for descendants of the Norse in Greenland as well as for some of the northwestern Atlantic locations described by Zeno.[25]

Norumbega, or variants of that name, reached full-blown cartographic status when Giacomo Gastaldi placed 'Nurumberg' in New France on his 1548 map of North America. It was also made much of – sometimes with alluring associations of wealth and urban splendours – on the beautiful mid-sixteenth-century manuscript maps of the Dieppe school. These maps, which illustrated French discoveries in the 'Norumbega' region, suggested the area around the St Lawrence River rather than the Penobscot in Maine, with which Norumbega has also been associated. Travellers' reports were sought-after sources of information among the Dieppe cartographers, and the fanciful stories which Jean Alfonce de Saintonge told when he returned to Dieppe, after piloting the Sieur de Roberval's colonising fleet to the St Lawrence in 1542, gained considerable influence. Claiming that on his excursion up the Noronbegue river, he had reached the 'city of Noronbegue', Jean Alfonce gave his imagination full rein when he described its citizens, who were dressed in furs, wore sable cloaks and worshipped the sun, and who used many words that sounded like Latin. Last, but certainly not least, he said that these people were tall and fair.

Very likely, Jean Alfonce had read one of the circulating copies of the letter which Giovanni da Verrazzano wrote to François I of France after returning to Dieppe from his 1524 exploration along the North America east coast, where he had made his first landfall at Cape Fear and continued northwards to Angoulême (New York Harbour) and Refugio (Narragansett Bay). He described the Refugio natives as tall and fair and provided the seed to urban fantasies when he wrote that 'if [the people of Refugio] had the skilled workmen we have, they would erect great buildings, for the whole maritime coast is full of various blue rocks, crystals, and alabaster, and for such a purpose it has an abundance of ports and shelter for ships'.[26]

Giovanni's brother, Girolamo da Verrazzano, in 1529 made two world maps in which he illustrated Giovanni's discoveries in Nova Gallia, and there we find the beginnings of the Norumbega name, written variously as as oranbega and oranbegha and applied to an inlet more or less in the Penobscot region. Nobody to this day knows what the name signified to the Verrazzano brothers, but through the conflation of a series of cosmographical, literary and cartographical works, the land and city of Norumbega arose, taking its name from the glorious Renaissance city of Nuremberg, whose Latin name was Noremberga/Norimberga. Verrazzano's glowing description of Refugio had become evidence for an embryonic New World version of Nuremberg, much as the Aztec capital of Temixtitan was seen as a startup version of Venice.

The explorations of Samuel de Champlain deflated the Norumbega balloon; his 1612–13 map of the St Lawrence region shows norembegue as just a minor settlement on the outer Penobscot shore. Europeans were nevertheless drawn to that mythical land for about a century after Gastaldi had placed Nurumberg on his 1548 North American map, and to this day, some people remain convinced that a part of New England and southern Canada had been settled by Norse Greenlanders – tall and fair-skinned like the natives described by Jean Alfonce and Verrazzano and as shown on some mid-sixteenth-century maps.

The 'Norse' myth began in 1570 with the map of North America which Abraham Ortelius drew for his famous atlas *Theatrum Orbis Terrarum*, which shows Norombega as a large territory just south of the St Lawrence, with Terra de Baccalaos (Newfoundland-Labrador) directly east of it. Continuing north on the mainland, the river R. de Tormenta marks the southern limit of Niccolò Zeno's Estotilant. Again reminiscent of Zeno, there is an elongated Greenland as well as a smaller Groclant, clearly borrowed from Gerhard Mercator, who a year earlier had demonstrated his general acceptance of Zeno's ideas.[27] Hans Poulsen Resen's 1605 map of the North Atlantic shows how thoroughly both Zeno's ideas and the notion of Norumbega as a Norse preserve had taken hold in the Danes' American ambitions. The map has Estotilanda as a peninsula between a peninsular Greenland and an equally peninsular Markland, and it locates Vínland relatively far south, just north of the supposed land of Norumbega.

When Zeno's map and texts were eventually proved fake, it was no longer possible to argue that the people whom the enterprising Zeno brothers had supposedly encountered in the northwestern Atlantic were Norsemen just a hop, skip and jump from Norumbega. However, because the Norse Greenlanders remained unaccounted for and Norumbega must surely be where they had ended up, the myth survived and tied in neatly with other fantasies about the Norse in North America.

Reference Notes

DI – *Diplomatarium Islandicum*
DN – *Diplomatarium Norvegicum*
MoG – *Meddelelser om Grønland*

NOTE ON SOURCES

1   DN 17: 849.
2   [Adamus Bremensis] Francis J. Tschahn, tr. and ed., *History of the Archbishops of Hamburg-Bremen*, New York, 1959, pp. 193, 196, 200, 206–11, 213–15, 218–19.
3   (Adamus Bremensis), *History*, pp. 134, 183, 193, 216–19.

CHAPTER 1

1   The Greenland Ice Cap was first crossed overland, from east to west, by Fridtjof Nansen in 1888.
2   'Saga of Eirik the Red,' in Magnus Magnusson, and Hermann Pálsson, trs., *The Vinland Sagas: The Norse Discovery of America*, Penguin Classics (first pub. 1965), pp. 76–77. The Icelandic scholar Ólafur Halldórsson argues that Eirik may have grown up in western Iceland (Halldórsson, Ólafur, *Grænland í miðaldaritum*, Reykjavík: Sögufélag, 1978, pp. 319–21).
3   Jóhannesson, Jón, *Íslendinga Saga: A History of the Old Icelandic Commonwealth*, Haraldur Bessason, tr., Winnipeg, 1974, p. 99.
4   Magnusson and Pálsson, *Vinland Sagas*; Hreinsson, Víðar, gen. ed., *The Complete Sagas of the Icelanders*, Reykjavík, 1997, vol. I.
5   Liestøl, Aslak, 'Runes,' in Alexander Fenton, and Hermann Pálsson, eds, *The Northern and Western Isles in the Viking World*, Edinburgh, 1984, pp. 232–33; Seaver, Kirsten A., *The Frozen Echo: Greenland and the Exploration of North America ca. A.D. 1000–1500*, Stanford, California, 1996, p. 16.
6   Rafn, Carl Christian, and Finn Magnusen, comps. and eds, *Antiquitates Americanae*, Hafniæ: Regia Antiquarium Septentrionalium, 1837 (Newport Tower, pp. 400–05).

7 Nørlund, Poul, 'Buried Norsemen at Herjolfsnes,' MoG 67 (1), Copenhagen: 1924, pp. 14–19; Seaver, *Frozen Echo*, p. 10.

8 Storm, Gustav, *Monumenta historica norvegiæ latine conscripta*, Kristiania [Oslo]: A.W. Brøgger, 1880, pp. 72–76.

9 Keyser, R., P.A. Munch, and C.R. Unger, eds, *Speculum Regale. Konungs-skuggsjá. Konge-Speilet*, Christiania [Oslo]: Werner & Co., 1848, pp. 5–47. English tr. by Laurence Marcellus Larson, *The King's Mirror [Speculum regale]*, New York, 1917.

10 'Saga of the Greenlanders,' ch. 1; 'Saga of Eirik the Red,' ch. 2, in Magnusson and Pálsson, *Vinland Sagas*; Pálsson, Hermann, and Paul Edwards, *Landnámabók*, Winnipeg: University of Manitoba Press, 1972, chs. 91–92; Andreasen, Claus, 'Nordbosager fra Vesterbygden på Grønland,' pp. 135–46 in *Hikuin* 6 (1980), pp. 135–36; Sørensen, Ingrid, 'Pollenundersøgelser i møddingen på Niaqussat,' pp. 296–304 in *Grønland* 30 (1982); Seaver, *Frozen Echo*, pp. 21–22.

11 Diamond, Jared, *Collapse: How Societies Choose to Fail or Succeed*, New York: Viking, 2005; quotes pp. 2, 6, 7.

12 Diamond, *Collapse*, p. 11.

13 See, e.g., Edwards, Kevin J., J. Edward Schofield, and Dmitri Mauquoy, 'High resolution paleoenvironmental and chronological investigations of Norse landnám at Tasiusaq, Eastern Settlement, Greenland,' pp. 1–15 in *Quaternary Research* 69 (2008).

CHAPTER 2

1 [Adamus Bremensis], *History*, pp. 193, 196, 200, 206–11, 213–15, 218–19.

2 Greenland turned out to be an island, but map makers had for many years believed it to be connected to North America in the Far North.

3 Harley, J. B., and David Woodward, eds, *The History of Cartography*, vol. 1: *Cartography in Prehistoric, Ancient, and Medieval Europe and the Mediterranean*, Chicago and London, 1987, p. 263; Russell, Jeffrey, *Inventing a Flat Earth: Columbus and Modern Historians*, New York: Praeger, 1991.

4 These boards were apparently carved panels decorating the front of the pallets on which people sat and slept.

5 'Saga of the Greenlanders,' ch. 1; 'Saga of Eirik the Red,' ch. 2; Pálsson and Edwards, *Landnámabók*, chs. 89, 158.

6 Pálsson and Edwards, *Landnámabók*, chs. 150 (Gunnbjörn), 151–52 (Snæbjörn).

7 Pálsson and Edwards, *Landnámabók*, ch. 3 (Nadd-Odd).

8 Lehn, Waldemar H., 'Skerrylike mirages and the discovery of Greenland,' pp. 3612–19 in *Applied Optics* 39: 21 (2000), quote p. 3612.

9 Foote, Peter G., 'Icelandic sólarsteinn and the medieval background,' pp. 140–54 in Michael Baranes, Hans Bekker-Nielsen, and Gerd Wolfgang Weber, eds, *Aurvandilstá*, Odense, 1984.

10 DI 3: 419–98 (1394 and later).

11 Nicolet, C., *Space, Geography, and Politics in the Early Roman Empire*, Ann Arbor (Michigan), 1991, p. 105; Edson, Evelyn, *The World Map 1300–1492: The Persistence of Tradition and Transformation*, Baltimore, 2007 (Fra Mauro quote p. 160, citing Tullia Gasparini Leporace, Il Mappamondo di Fra Mauro, Rome: 1956, tav. 35); Foote, Peter G., ed., *Olaus Magnus: A Description of the Northern Peoples, 1555*, 3 vols, London, 1996–98, Book 21, ch. 1; Seaver, Kirsten A., 'Olaus Magnus and the "compass"on Hvitsark,' pp. 235–54 in *The Journal of Navigation* (London), May 2001; Seaver, *Frozen Echo*, pp. 16–19.

12 Vebæk, Christen Leif, 'The church topography of the Eastern Settlement and the excavation of the Benedictine convent at Narsarsuaq in the Uunartoq fjord,' *MoG: Man & Society* 14, Copenhagen: 1991, pp. 65–71; Thirslund, Vebæk, Christen Leif, and Søren Thirslund, *The Viking Compass Guided Norsemen First to America*, Skjern (Denmark), 1992; Thirslund, Søren, 'Sailing directions of the North Atlantic Viking Age (from about the year 860 to 1400),' pp. 55–64 in *The Journal of Navigation* 50: 1 (1997); Thirslund, Søren, *Viking Navigation: Sun-compass Guided Norsemen first to America*. Foreword by Sir Robin Knox-Johnston, Skjern (Denmark), 1997; Busch, Jørgen, 'Norrøn navigation over Nordatlanten,' Polarfronten (Copenhagen): 2005: 4, back page.

13 Vigfússon, Guðbrandr, and Theodor Möbius, eds, *Fornsögur: Vatnsdælasaga, Hallfreðarsaga, Flóamannasaga*, Leipzig, 1860.

14 Hermannsson, Halldor, ed., *The Book of Icelanders*, Ithaca: Cornell University Library, 1930, chs. 1, 6; Seaver, Kirsten A., *Maps, Myths, and Men: The Story of the Vinland Map*, Stanford (California): Stanford University Press, 2004, pp. 33–35.

15 Pálsson and Edwards, *Landnámabók*, ch. 5 (naming Iceland); 'Saga of the Greenlanders,' ch. 1, 'Saga of Eirik the Red,' ch. 2 (naming Greenland).

16 I owe that voyage to the New York Yacht Club's invitation to lecture aboard the *Professor Molchanov* on an expedition cruise in August–September 2007.

17 'Saga of the Greenlanders,' chs. 1–2; Pálsson and Edwards, *Landnámabók*, chs. 91–92.

18 'Saga of the Greenlanders,' chs. 2–3.

19 'Saga of the Greenlanders,' ch. 1; Pálsson and Edwards, *Landnámabók*, chs. 92–93.

20 Kellogg, Robert, 'Introduction,' in Hreinsson, ed., *Complete Sagas*, vol. I, p. xli.

21 'Saga of the Greenlanders,' ch. 2.

22 Seaver, Kirsten A., 'Thralls and queens: Aspects of female slavery among the medieval Norse,' in vol. 1, pp. 147–67, Gwyn Campbell, Suzanne Miers, and Joseph C. Miller, eds, *Women and Slavery*, Athens (Ohio) Ohio University Press, 2007.

23 Lynnerup, Niels, 'Life and death in Norse Greenland,' pp. 285–94 in William W. Fitzhugh, and Elisabeth I. Ward, eds, *Vikings: The North Atlantic Saga*, Washington and London, 2000, esp. p. 291.

24 E.g., Buckland, Paul C., 'The North Atlantic environment,' pp. 146–53 in Fitzhugh and Ward, Vikings, esp. pp. 147–48.

25 E.g., Roussell, Aage, 'Farms and churches in the mediaeval Norse settlements of Greenland,' MoG 89(1), 1941, p. 24; Diamond, Collapse, p. 250; Schofield, J. Edward, Kevin J. Edwards, and Charlie Christensen, 'Environmental impacts around the time of Norse landnám in the Qorlortoq valley, Eastern Settlement, Greenland,' pp. 1643–57 in Journal of Archeological Science 35 (2008); Seaver, Frozen Echo, pp. 49–50.

26 Gulløv, Hans Christian, ed., Grønlands forhistorie (Greenland's Pre-History), Copenhagen, 2004, pp. 235–38.

27 Arneborg, Jette, 'Greenland and Europe,' pp. 304–17 in Fitzhugh and Ward, Vikings, esp. pp. 310–11; Lynnerup, 'Life,' pp. 286–89.

28 E.g., Bruun, Daniel, 'Arkaeologiske Undersøgelser i Julianehaab Distrikt,' MoG16, Copenhagen, 1917; Nörlund, Poul, and Mårten Stenberger, 'Brattahlid,' Meddelelser om Grönland 88 (1), Copenhagen, 1934; Krogh, Knud, Viking Greenland, Copenhagen,1967; Seaver, Frozen Echo, ch. 1, esp. p. 20.

29 For preliminary reports on this large project, see Arneborg, Jette, and Hans Christian Gulløv, Man, Culture and Environment in Ancient Greenland: Report on a Research Programme, Copenhagen, 1998; Gulløv, Grønlands, pp. 238–40.

CHAPTER 3

1 Gunnarsson, Gísli, 'Given good time, legs get shorter in cold weather,' pp. 184–93 in Sigurðsson and Skaptason, Aspects.

2 Berthelsen, Christian, Inger Holbech Mortensen, and Ebbe Mortensen, eds, Kalaallit Nunaat/Greenland Atlas, Piersuiffik, 1990, pp. 32, 112; Diamond, in Collapse, p. 226, argues that it would have taken the Norse generations to figure out which farm sites were suitable and unsuitable.

3 Seaver, Frozen Echo, pp. 102–03.

4 Seaver, Frozen Echo, p. 50.

5 Seaver, Frozen Echo, pp. 21, 48–58 passim, 74, 120, 127, 162, 220–21, 241–42, 253.

6 Philbert, Poul-Erik, 'Man er hvad man spiser,' pp. 12–13 in Polarfronten 2 (2002).

7 Holm Olsen, Inger Marie, 'The Helgøy Project: Evidence from farm mounds: Economy and settlement pattern AD 1350–1600,' in Norwegian Archeological Review 14 (1981). 96; Vollan, Odd, 'Torskefiske,' Kulturhistorisk leksikon for nordisk middelalder 18 (1974), cols. 506–10; Kurlansky, Mark, Cod: A Biography of the Fish that Changed the World, Penguin Books: 1997, pp. 19, 35, 243, 251.

8 Seaver, Maps, Myths, pp. 60–63.

9   Mattox, William G., 'Fishing in West Greenland 1910–1966: The development of a new native industry,' *MoG* 197:1 (1973): 18–20, 28–29, 32–33; Kurlansky, *Cod*, pp. 38, 41–43; Drever, Charles, *Cod Fishing at Greenland: The White Fish Authority*, typescript, ca. 1972 (British Library x.313/380), pp. 1–32.

10   E.g., McGovern, Thomas, 'Bones, buildings, and boundaries: Palæoeconomic approaches to Norse Greenland,' pp. 193–230 in Christopher D. Morris, and D. James Rackham, eds, *Norse and Later Settlement and Subsistence in the North Atlantic*, Glasgow, 1992, esp. pp. 195–96; McGovern, Thomas, and G.F. Bigelow, 'Archaeozoology of the Norse site Ø17a Narssaq District, Southwest Greenland,' pp. 85–101 in *Acta Borealia* 1 (1984), esp. pp. 96–97; Polarfronten 2 (2002), pp. 12–13; Bødker Enghoff, Inge, 'Hunting, fishing and animal husbandry at The Farm Beneath the Sand, Western Greenland: An archaeozoological analysis of a Norse farm in the Western Settlement,' *MoG: Man and Society* 28 (2003), pp. 47–50. See also Seaver, *Frozen Echo*, pp. 54–60.

11   Norris, Kenneth S., and Flip Nicklin, 'Beluga: White whale of the North,' pp. 2–31 in *National Geographic* 185: 6 (1994); McGovern, Thomas H., Gerald F. Bigelow, Thomas Amorosi, James Woollett, and Sophia Perdikaris, 'The zooarchaeology of Ø17a,' pp. 58–74 in C.L. Vebæk, 'Narsaq – a Norse landnáma farm,' MoG: Man & Society 18, Copenhagen, 1993; Diamond, *Collapse*, pp. 229–30 (arguing that the Greenland Norse had a taboo against eating fish).

12   Lynnerup, Niels, 'The Norse settlers in Greenland: The physical anthropological perspective,' *Acta Borealia* 1 (1991), pp. 93–96; Lynnerup, 'The Greenland Norse: A biological-anthropological study,' *MoG: Man & Society* 24 (1998); Scott, G. Richard, Carrin M. Halffmann, and P.O. Pedersen, 'Dental conditions of Medieval Norsemen in the North Atlantic,' pp. 183–207 in *Acta Archaeologica* 62 (1991/1992), esp. p. 199; McGovern, Thomas, 'Economics of Extinction in Norse Greenland,' pp. 404–34 in T.M. Wrigley, M.J. Ingram, and G. Farmer, eds, *Climate and History: Studies in Past Climates and Their Impact on Man*, Cambridge (England), 1980, pp. 404–25.

13   McGovern, 'Economics,' pp. 404–29.

14   Jared Diamond comes down especially hard on the Norse Greenlanders, observing, for example: 'Greenland provides us with our closest approximation to a controlled experiment in collapses: two societies (Norse and Inuit) sharing the same island, but with very different cultures, such that one of those societies survived while the other one was dying.' Diamond, *Collapse*, p. 21.

15   According to Diamond, the Norse had a 'bad attitude' from the start toward the native peoples they met and called Skrælings or 'wretches', yet he faults the colonists for not adopting Inuit clothing more 'appropriate to Greenland's cold climate'. Diamond, *Collapse*, pp. 220–24, 246–47, 258, 265, 272; see also Seaver, *Frozen Echo*, pp. 239–42.

16 Veale, Elspeth M., *The English Fur Trade in the Later Middle Age*, Oxford: Clarendon Press, 1968, p. 29.

17 Kristínsson, Axel, 'Productivity and population in pre-Industrial Iceland,' in Sigurðsson and Skaptason, *Aspects*, pp. 258–63; Seaver, *Frozen Echo*, pp. 81–82.

18 Bowman, Sheridan, *Radiocarbon Dating: Interpreting the Past*, London: British Museum Publications, 1990, p. 22.

19 Diamond, *Collapse*, p. 250.

20 Holm, Poul, 'Ireland, Norse in,' pp. 323–25 in Pulsiano, Phillip, ed., *Medieval Scandinavia*, New York: Garland Publishing, 1993; Sawyer, Birgit and Peter, *Medieval Scandinavia: From Conversion to Reformation circa 800–1500*, Minneapolis (Minnesota), 1993, pp. 101–03; Seaver, 'Thralls and queens,' pp. 147–67.

21 Seaver, *Frozen Echo*, ch. 7, esp. pp. 179–80; Foote, Peter G., and David M. Wilson, *The Viking Achievement*, London and New York, 1970, p. 67; Sutherland, Patricia D., 'The Norse and Native Norse Americans,' pp. 238–47 in Fitzhugh and Ward, *Vikings*, esp. p. 241; Sutherland, Patricia D., 'Strands of culture contact: Dorset-Norse interactions in the Eastern Canadian Arctic,' pp.159–69 in M. Appelt, J. Berglund, and H.C. Gulløv, eds, *Identities and Cultural Contacts in the Arctic*, Copenhagen, 2000, pp. 159–69.

22 Seaver, *Frozen Echo*, pp. 6, 239–41; Diamond, *Collapse*, pp. 190, 235–36.

23 McCullough, Karen, and Peter Schledermann, 'Mystery cairns on Washington Irving Island,' pp. 289–98 in *Polar Record* 35 (1999); Rask, Rasmus, and Finn Magnusen, 'Efterretning om en i Grønland funden Runesteen med dens Forklaring, forfattet af Professor Rask, og nogle dertil hørende Oplysninger ved Professor F. Magnusen' pp. 309–43 in *Antikvariske Annaler* (Copenhagen) 4: 2 (1827), with an addendum (pp. 367–79) by P. Kragh; Seaver, *Maps, Myths*, pp. 29, 31–32, 35.

24 Seaver, *Maps, Myths*, pp. 71–75; Seaver, Kirsten A., 'Ettertraktete tenner: Middelalderens handel med hvalrosstann og afrikansk elfenbein,' pp. 231–50 in *Historisk Tidsskrift* (Oslo), 2006, no. 2.

25 Andersen, Erik, and Claus Malmros, 'Ship's parts found in the Viking settlements in Greenland. Preliminary assessments and wood-diagnoses,' pp. 118–22 in Clausen, *Viking Voyages*; Seaver, *Frozen Echo*, p. 28; Seaver, *Maps, Myths*, p. 36.

26 Willerslev, Eske, et al., report 7 July 2007, accessed 10 July 2007, at http://news.nationalgeographic.com/news/2007/07/070705-oldest-dna.html

27 Andreasen, Claus, and Jette Arneborg, 'Gården under sandet. Nye nordboundersøgelser i Vesterbygden,' *Grønlandsk kultur-og samfundsforskning*, 1992, pp. 39–40; Nielsen, Niels, 'Evidence on the extraction of iron in Greenland by the Norsemen', *Meddelelser om Grønland* 76 (1930), pp. 193–213; Seaver, *Frozen Echo*, p. 31; Seaver, *Maps, Myths*, pp. 50–52. *Author's note*: Norwegian medieval iron exports were never in the form of crude blooms, but in the form of spatulate rods, ready for shaping.

28 I am indebted to the Danish geologist Karsten Secher for the information
    that bog iron is scarcely observed in the context of iron-rich weathering
    products in Greenland. Although hydrated iron oxide (limonite), the
    primary iron-enriched weathering product, is fairly common in Greenland,
    sufficient deposits of similar highgrade iron ore (brown iron ore) are not
    known. Secher's references: Boggild, O.B., 'The mineralogy of Greenland,'
    MoG149: 3, 1953; Petersen, O.V., and K. Secher, 'The minerals of Greenland,'
    The Mineralogical Record 24: 2 (1993); Secher, K., and H. Stendal,
    'Weathering products of sulfides in the Arctic – with a case history on a Cu-
    Ni-sulphide occurrence in West Greenland,' pp. 499–522 in S.S. Augusthis,
    ed., Weathering: Its Products and Deposits, Athens, (Greece), 1989, vol. 2.
29 Wallace, Birgitta, 'L'Anse aux Meadows, the western outpost,' in Clausen,
    Viking Voyages, pp. 35–37.

CHAPTER 4

1   Ingstad, Helge, Land under the Pole Star, London,1966, p. 116.
2   E.g., Jones, Gwyn, Norse Atlantic Saga, Oxford, 1986 (2nd ed.), p. 277. See
    also Seaver, Frozen Echo, p. 38.
3   'Saga of Eirik the Red,' ch. 5. For a further discussion of Gunnlaug's biography
    of Olaf Tryggvason (d. 999), see Seaver, Frozen Echo, pp. 15, 60–61.
4   Helluland would also have included Cape Chidley and other treeless areas
    immediately south of the Hudson Strait.
5   Sigurðsson, Gísli, 'The quest for Vínland in saga scholarship,' pp. 232–37 in
    Fitzhugh and Ward, Vikings, pp. 233–34; Professor Kari Ellen Gade, Indiana
    University, personal communications 16 May and 4 July 1998.
6   Wallace, Birgitta L., 'The Vikings in North America: Myth and reality,' pp.
    206–12 in Ross Samson, ed., Social Approaches to Viking Studies, Glasgow,
    1991; Wallace, Birgitta L., 'The Norse in the North Atlantic: The L'Anse aux
    Meadows settlement in Newfoundland,' pp. 486–500 in Sigurðsson and
    Skaptason, Aspects.
7   Ingstad, Helge, 'Vinland ruins prove Vikings found the New World,' pp.
    708–35 in National Geographic Magazine 126 (Nov. 1964). Author's note:
    Spindle whorls weighted the end of the yarn during spinning.
8   Wallace, 'L'Anse aux Meadows,' pp. 2009–13; Smith, Kevin P., e-mails to
    author, September–October 1999; Smith, Kevin P. , 'Who lived at L'Anse aux
    Meadows?' in Fitzhugh and Ward, Vikings, p. 217.
9   Concerning 'yet another island of the many found in that ocean,' Adam
    wrote: 'It is called Vinland because vines producing excellent wine grow wild
    there. That unsown crops also abound on that island we have ascertained
    not from fabulous reports but from the trustworthy relations of the Danes.'
    Adam of Bremen, History, Book IV, chs. 38–39, p. 219.
10 DI 11: 131.

11 Tyrkir's name is generally seen as a copyist's mistake for 'Tyskir' (German).

12 The Beothuk and other natives the Norse encountered are discussed in Chapter Six.

13 Seaver, Kirsten A., 'Land of wine and forests: The Norse in North America,' *Mercator's World* 5: 1 (2000), pp.18–24; Seaver, Kirsten A., 'Far and yet near: North America and Norse Greenland,' pp. 3–5, 23 in *Viking Heritage Newsletter* 1: 1 (2000), Visby (Sweden); Seaver, *Maps, Myths*, p. 37.

14 Plumet, Patrick, 'Les maisons longues dorsétiennes de l'Ungava,' pp. 253–89 in *Géographie Physique et Quaternaire* 36: 3 (1982).

15 Storm, Gustav, ed., *Islandske Annaler Indtil 1578*, Oslo, 1977 (repr. of 1888 ed.), pp. 19, 59, 112, 213, 252, 320, 353, 403, 473; Pálsson and Edwards, *Landnámabók*, ch. 17.

16 Andersen, Erik, and Claus Malmros, 'Ship's parts found in the Viking settlements in Greenland,' pp. 118–22 in Clausen, *Viking*; Nørlund, 'Buried,' pp. 60–71, 251. See also Seaver, *Frozen Echo*, pp. 28, 100; Seaver, *Maps, Myths*, pp. 47–50.

17 Arneborg and Gulløv, *Man, Culture*; News release re Patricia Sutherland, Canadian Museum of Civilization, Hull, Quebec, 1 December 1999; Patricia Sutherland, personal e-mail 12 December 1999; Sutherland, 'The Norse,' p. 241; Sutherland, 'Strands,' pp. 159–69.

18 Skaare, Kolbjørn, 'En norsk penning fra 11. årh. funnet på kysten av Maine, U.S.A.,' pp. 2–17 in *Meddelelser fra Norsk Numismatisk Forening*, May 1979; McGhee, Robert, 'Contact between Native North Americans and the medieval Norse: A review of the evidence,' *American Antiquity* 49 (1984), p. 28; McGhee, Robert, 'The Skraellings of Vínland' in Clausen, *Viking*, pp. 49–50; McGhee, Robert, 'A new view of the Norse in the Arctic,' *Scientific American: Discovering Archaeology* 2: 4 (2000), p. 58; Carpenter, Edmund, *Norse Penny*, New York: The Rock Foundation, 2003.

19 Lebel, Serge, and Patrick Plumet, 'Étude Technologique de l'Exploitation des Blocs et des Galets en Métabasalte par les Dorsétiens au Site Tuvaaluk (DIA.4, JfEI-4),' pp. 143–70 in *Journal canadien d'archéologie* 15 (1991); McGhee, 'Contact,' p. 13; Roussell, Aage, 'Sandnes and the neighbouring Farms,' *MoG* 88: 2 (1936), pp. 106–8; Arneborg, Jette, personal communication 21 March and 26 April 1993; Fitzhugh, William W., 'A Review of Paleo-Eskimo Culture History in Southern Quebec, Labrador and Newfoundland,' *Inuit Studies* 4: 1–2 (1980), pp. 29–30; Fitzhugh, William W., personal communication 25 May 1996; Seaver, *Frozen Echo*, p. 26.

20 Fitzhugh, 'Review,' p. 30; Harp, Elmer, 'A Late Dorset Copper Amulet from Southeastern Hudson Bay,' pp. 33–44 in *Folk* 16/17(1975); Plumet, Patrick, 'Le Site de la Pointe aux Bélougas (Qilalugarsiuvik) et les maisons longues dorsétiennes,' *Archéologie de l'Ungava* (Montréal) 18 (1985), pp. 188–90, 195 (Plate 32; photos 79, 81–82), 357–58; Plumet, Patrick, personal communication 29 March 2001.

21 Sabo, George and Deborah, 'A possible Thule carving of a Viking from Baffin Island N.W.T.,' pp. 33–42 in *Canadian Journal of Archaeology* 2 (1978); Seaver, *Frozen Echo*, pp. 39–40; Seaver, *Maps, Myths*, p. 50, illustr. p. 51.

22 Fitzhugh, William W., and Jacqueline Olin, eds, *Archeology of the Frobisher Voyages*, Washington, D.C., 1993. Nobody has yet tested these blooms for chemical compatibility with the Labrador Iron Trough, which runs north to Ungava Bay, or compared them with samples of worked iron from Norse Greenland farmsteads, where slag from reworked blooms is common. A recent study on medieval iron samples from Greenland did not compare either the iron or the slag samples analysed with compositional information from the American side, despite results as anomalous to the study's data base as those obtained on a corroded iron nail from a Western Settlement farm at Nipaatsoq. See Fitzhugh and Olin, *Archeology*; Fitzhugh, William W., 'Iron blooms, Elizabethans, and politics: The Frobisher Project 1974–1995,' pp. 12–21 in *The Review of Archaeology* 17: 2 (1997); Buchwald, Vagn Fabritius, 'Ancient iron and slags in Greenland,' MoG: Man & Society 26 (2001), pp. 44–47; Seaver, Kirsten A., 'Baffin Island mandibles and iron blooms,' in Symons, *Meta Incognita*, vol. 2, pp. 563–74; Seaver, *Maps, Myths*, pp. 50–52.

CHAPTER 5

1 Plumet, Patrick, 'L'Esquimau: Essai de synthèse de la préhistoire de l'arctique esquimau,' *Revista de Arqueología Americana* 10 (1996), pp. 12–13; Seaver, *Maps, Myths*, pp. 33–34.

2 Gulløv, *Grønlands*, pp. 177–79; Andreasen, Claus, Joel Berglund, Niels Frandsen, and Ane Marie B. Pedersen, eds, *Traces: 4400 Years of Man in Greenland* (James Manley, tr.), Nuuk (Greenland): Greenland National Museum and Archives, 2004, pp. 16–17, 46.

3 For details and analyses, see Seaver, 'Pygmies.'

4 Russell, *Inventing*, pp. 4, 27–36, 41, 51–53, 59–64.

5 Storm, Gustav, 'Ginnungagap i Mytologien og i Geografien,' in Axel Koch, ed., *Arkiv för nordisk Filologi* 6 : 2 (1890), pp. 340, 342–43.

6 Bjørnbo, Axel Anton, and Carl S. Petersen, *Fyenboen Claudius Claussøn Swart (Claudius Clavus): Nordens ældste Kartograf*, Copenhagen, 1904, pp. 47, 49, 98, 101–02, 132 (map p. 91).

7 From Karjala, the Finnish name for Karelia.

8 Bjørnbo and Petersen, *Fynboen*, p. 179.

9 Bjørnbo and Petersen, *Fynboen*, pp. 178–79; Pliny, *Natural History*, H. Rackham, tr., Cambridge (Massachusetts), 1999 (reprint of 1942 ed. in Latin and English), vol. 2: 521 (Book VII: 2). Only the Skálholtbók version of the 'Saga of Eirik the Red' mentions Unipeds.

10 Storm, Gustav, 'Den danske Geograf Claudius Clavus eller Nicolaus Niger,' pp. 129–46 in *Ymer* 9: 1–2 (Stockholm, 1889), esp. p. 140.

11 Bjørnbo, *Fynboen*, pp. 177–79, 236–37; Storm, *Monumenta*, pp. 72–76.

12 Jones, *Norse Atlantic*, pp. 92–93. *Author's note*: Modern Norwegian has no such word as skræla. Jones seems to have conflated the Old Norse skrækja with the modern Norwegian skråle, both of which imply a raucous voice); Hans Christian Gulløv, 'Natives and Norse in Greenland,' in Fitzhugh and Ward, *Vikings*, p. 319, citing Dirmid Ronán F. Collis, '"Kalaaleq" < (skinn) Klædast? (Does "Kalaaleq" derive from "klaedast" (dressed in skins)?' *Études Inuit Studies* 12: 1–2, p. 259. However, klædast means 'dressed/dressed in cloth' in both Old Norse and modern Icelandic. It has nothing to do with skins or with any known terms for Inuit/Eskimo.

13 Seaver, *Frozen Echo*, p. 21; Seaver, *Maps, Myths*, p. 33.

14 Lattimore, Richard, tr., *The Iliad of Homer*, Chicago, 1951, p. 100; Pliny, *Natural History*, vol. 2, pp. 151, 303, 391, 479, 519, 523–25.

15 Taylor, Eva G. R., 'A letter dated 1577 from Mercator to John Dee,' pp. 56–68 in *Imago Mundi* 13 (1956); Seaver, Kirsten A., 'How strange is a stranger? A survey of opportunities for Inuit-European contact in the Davis Strait before 1576,' pp. 523–52 in Symons, *Meta Incognita*, vol. 2; DN 5: 152, 17: 1260, 1263; Jónsson, Finnur, 'Grønlands gamle Topografi efter Kilderne, Østerbygden og Vesterbygden, *Meddelelser om Grønland* 20 (1899); Jónsson, Finnur, ed., Ívar Bárðarson, *Det gamle Grønlands Beskrivelse udgiven efter Haandskrifterne*, Copenhagen, 1930.

16 Taylor, 'Letter,' pp. 57–58; Seaver, *Frozen Echo*, pp. 122–26, 132–36.

17 Descelier World Map, 1550, British Library Add MS 24065.

18 Jónsson, 'Det gamle,' pp. 29–30. Quote tr. by K. A. Seaver.

19 Arneborg, Jette, *Kulturmødet mellem nordboer og eskimoer* [*The cultural encounter between Norsemen and Eskimos*], PhD dissertation, Copenhagen University, 1991, esp. p. 150; Gulløv, *Grønlands*, p. 278.

20 For an overview of the Thule migration, see McGhee, Robert, 'Radiocarbon dating and the timing of the Thule migration,' pp. 181–91 in Martin Appelt, Joel Berglund, and Hans Christian Gulløv, eds, *Identities and Cultural Contacts in the Arctic*, Copenhagen, 2000.

21 *DI* 3: 59.

22 Schledermann, Peter, 'Nordbogenstande fra Arktisk Canada,' pp. 222–25 in Clausen, *Viking*; Schledermann, Peter, 'Preliminary results of archeological investigations in the Bache Peninsula region, Ellesmere Island, NTW,' pp. 459–74 in *Arctic* 31(1978); Schledermann, Peter, 'Ellesmere Island: Eskimo and Viking Finds in the High Arctic,' pp. 574–601 in *National Geographic* 159: 5 (1981), esp. pp. 594, 600; Schledermann, Peter, 'Ellesmere: Vikings in the Far North,' pp. 238–56 in Fitzhugh and Ward, *Vikings*; Schledermann, Peter, and Karen McCullough, 'Western Elements in the Early Thule Culture of the Eastern High Arctic,' *Arctic* 33: 4 (1980), pp. 833–34; Schledermann, Peter, and Karen McCullough, *Late Thule Culture Developments on the Central East Coast of Ellesmere Island*, Copenhagen, 2003, pp. 9–19; Seaver, *Frozen Echo*, pp. 39–43.

23 Sutherland, Patricia D., and Robert McGhee, 'Arktisk kontakt,' pp. 12–15 in *Skalk* 3 (1983); Sutherland, 'The Norse.'

24 Schledermann, Peter, 'A.D. 1000: East meets west,' pp. 189–92 in Fitzhugh and Ward, *Vikings*; Cox, Steven L., 'A Norse penny from Maine,' pp. 206–07 in Fitzhugh and Ward, *Vikings*; Rogers, Penelope Walton, 'The raw materials of textiles from GUS – with a note on fragments of fleece and animal pelts from the same site,' pp. 66–73 in Arneborg and Gulløv, *Man, Culture.*

25 Sutherland, 'Strands,' p. 163.

26 Sutherland, 'Strands,' pp. 164–65.

27 Seaver, *Frozen Echo*, pp. 39–42, 124–26, 227–29.

CHAPTER 6

1 Pálsson and Edwards, *Landnámabók*, chs. 95–108. Aud was called 'Unn' in the *Laxdæla Saga.*

2 'Kristni saga,' in B. Kahle, ed., *Kristnisaga, Tháttr Thorvalds ens Vidförla, Tháttr Ísleifs Biskups Gissurarsonar, Hungrvaka* (Altnordische Saga-Bibliothek 11), Haller, 1905, pp. v, xvi, 1–13.

3 For more about these three kings, see the 'Saga of Hákon the Good,' the 'Saga of Olaf Tryggvason' and the 'Saga of Saint Olaf.' All three sagas may be found in any edition of Snorri Sturluson's history of the Norwegian kings, often entitled *Heimskringla.*

4 *Nytt fra Norge* (Oslo) 44: 3 (1998), p. 14; Gelsinger, Bruce, *Icelandic Enterprise: Commerce and Economy in the Middle Ages*, Columbia (South Carolina), 1981, pp. 124–25.

5 Logan, F. Donald, *The Church in the Middle Ages*, London and New York, 2002, pp. 52–65.

6 (Adam of Bremen), *History*, p. 218.

7 Berglund, Joel, *Hvalsø: The Church and the Magnate's Farm*, Qaqortoq (Greenland), 1982, p. 22.

8 Gulløv, *Grønlands*, p. 252.

9 Helgason, Agnar, Sigrun Sigurdardóttir, Jeffrey R. Gulcher, Ryk Ward, and Kari Stefánsson, 'mtDNA and the origin of the Icelanders: Deciphering signals of recent population history,' pp. 999–1016 in *American Journal of Human Genetics* 66 (2000). For a Norse primer on the Icelanders' cultural heritage, see Pálsson and Edwards, *Landnámabók.*

10 Pálsson and Edwards, *Landnámabók*, ch. 17; Storm, *Islandske*, pp. 19, 59, 112, 251–52, 320, 473; Seaver, *Frozen Echo*, pp. 32–33; Seaver, *Maps, Myths*, pp. 4–8 passim, 33, 20, 43, 53–56 passim, 254–63 passim, 289–93, 309, 320–22; Skelton et al., *Vinland Map*, pp. 225–26, 255–60.

11 'Saga of the sworn brothers,' in Hreinsson, *Complete Sagas*, vol. 2, p. 376; Jónsson, 'Grønlands gamle,' p. 327.

12 Byock, Jesse L., *Medieval Iceland*, Berkeley (California), 1988, pp. 91–95; Skovgaard-Petersen, Inge, 'Islandsk egenkirkevæsen,' pp. 230–96 in *Scandia* 26 (1960).

13 'Tale of the Greenlanders,' in Hreinsson, *Complete Sagas*, pp. 372–82.

14 *DN* 17B, pp. 199–200, 281; Storm, *Islandske*, pp. 20–21, 59–60, 112–13, 119, 180, 252, 320–22, 474; Keyser, R., and P. A. Munch, eds, *Norges gamle Love*, 5 vols, Oslo, 1846–95, vol. 1, pp. 439–41.

15 Skaaning Høegsberg, Mogens, 'A reassessment of the development of the cathedral at Garðar, Greenland,' pp. 74–96 in *Archaeologica Islandica* 6 (2007).

16 *DN* 17B, p. 281; Helgason, Jón, *Islands Kirke fra dens Grundlæggelse til Reformationen*, Copenhagen, 1925, pp. 106–12; Nørlund and Roussell, 'Norse Ruins,' pp. 16–17; Storm, *Islandske*, pp. 22, 60–62, 114, 119–23, 180–82, 254, 322, 324–25, 474, 476–77.

17 Bröste, K., and K. Fischer-Møller, 'Medieval Norsemen at Gardar: Anthropological investigation,' *MoG* 89 (3), 1944, pp. 4–9; Nørlund, Poul, and Aage Roussell, 'Norse ruins at Gardar, the episcopal seat of mediaeval Greenland,' *MoG* 76 (1), 1929, pp. 26–28, 32–55; Roussell, Aage, 'Farms', pp. 46, 131–35; Gulløv, *Grønlands*, pp. 248–52; Seaver, *Frozen Echo*, pp. 65–68, Storm, *Islandske*, pp. 123, 182.

18 Nørlund and Roussell, 'Norse Ruins,' p. 137; Seaver, 'Baffin Island,' pp. 563–74. A report on the Icelandic ox skulls was given by Orri Vésteinsson in his address 'Settlement in Light of Recent Archeological Investigations,' on 16 September 2000, at the Viking Millennium International Symposium in St John's, Newfoundland.

19 Roussell, 'Farms,' pp. 48, 107, 135, figs. 27, 28, 74, 75; Vebæk, 'Church topography,' pp. 21–27.

20 Krogh, Knud, 'Om Grønlands middelalderlige kirkebygninger,' pp. 294–310 in *Minjar og Menntir: Festskrift til Kristján Eldjarn*, Reykjavík, 1976, pp. 294–310; Vebæk, 'Church topography,' pp. 5–20; *DN* 6: 10.

21 Helgason, *Islands Kirke*, pp. 102–05, 115–18.

22 *Regesta Norvegica*, Oslo: Norsk Historisk Kjeldeskriftfond, 1889–1979, vol. 1: 173, 199; Helgason, *Islands Kirke*, pp. 133–39.

23 *DI* 3: 15, 16 (Biskupatál); *DN* 17B, p. 282; Storm, *Islandske*, pp. 128–29, 187–89, 327–28, 480–81.

24 The church at Sandnes was judged to have had a Gothic chancel with a nave added later. Vebæk, 'Church topography,' pp. 5–20. See also list of churches in Henrik M. Jansen, 'Critical account of the written and archeological sources' evidence concerning the Norse settlements in Greenland,' *MoG* 182 (4), 1972.

25 In 1253, for example, Innocent IV had to give the Norwegian archbishop dispensation for 100 ecclesiastics in the Nidaros archdiocese, allowing their promotion to all positions in the Church even if born out of wedlock. *DN* 6: 27.

26 Helgason, *Islands Kirke*, pp. 145–52; *Regesta Norvegica* 1: 468–69.

27 Hødnebø, Finn, and Hallvard Magerøy, eds, *Norges kongesagaer,* 4 vols, Oslo, 1979, vol. 4, pp. 7–14, 253–54; Helgason, *Islands Kirke,* pp. 152–54; *DN* 15: 29; 17B, pp. 197, 282; Storm, *Islandske,* pp. 26f, 50, 65, 67, 70, 131f, 134f, 139, 141, 190, 193ff., 258, 260, 328, 330, 337, 480, 482ff; *DI* 1: 152, 9: 2.

28 Gad, Finn, 'Grønlands tilslutning til Norgesvældet 1261,' pp. 259–72 in *Grønland* 12 (1964).

29 Hødnebø and Magerøy, *Norges,* vol. 4, pp. 253, 311.

30 *DN* 17 B, p. 282; Storm, *Islandske,* pp. 50, 337.

31 Storm, *Islandske Annaler,* p. 330; Rafn and Magnusen, *Grønlands Historiske,* vol. 3, pp. 238–47; Halldórsson, *Grænland,* pp. 53–55, 147; Hødnebø and Magerøy, *Norske kongesagaer,* vol. 4, p. 311.

32 Authén Blom, Grethe, *Kongemakt og privilegier i Norge inntil 1387,* Oslo, 1967, p. 137.

33 *DN* 15: 29, 18: 33.

34 *DN* 6: 9; 19: 281.

35 Helgason, *Islands Kirke,* p. 173; *DN* 6: 35–39, 42–66; *Regesta* 2: 206–14.

36 Authén Blom, *Kongemakt,* pp. 172–76; Keyser and Munch, *Norges gamle Love* 2, pp. 354, 462, 481.

37 *Regesta* 2: 292–98, 340, 342, 347; *DN* 17: 871–77, 17B, pp. 205, 282, 19: 310; Storm, *Islandske,* pp. 50, 70–72, 338, Rafn and Magnusen, *Grønlands Historiske,* pp. 90–93.

38 *DN* 10: 9; 17B: p. 221.

39 *DN* 3: 73, 76–80, 99, 101; 4: 97–103; 6: 71; 7: 54, 59–62, 63, 72–73; 8: 26–35; 9: 84; 10: 10; 17B, pp. 282–83, 289; Rafn and Magnusen, *Grønlands Historiske,* vol. 3, pp. 15–19, 94; Storm, *Islandske,* pp. 151, 203, 341–43.

40 *DN* 7: 103–04; Munch, Peter Andreas, *Pavelige Nuntiers Regnskabe,* Christiania, 1864, pp. 25, 29; Seaver, *Frozen Echo,* pp. 80–82.

41 In 1328, the Norwegian archbishop forbade the collectors of papal tithes from taking more than half of those tithes, because Pope John XXII had given the other half to the Norwegian king for fighting the heathen Russians – and those funds were to be supervised by the archbishop. *DN* 2: 210, 4: 182, 9: 100; *Kulturhistorisk* 4: col. 210, 13: cols. 250–55.

42 *DN* 5: 152, 8: 128–35, 17B: p. 206; *Kulturhistorisk* 12: col. 539; Gad, 'Grønlands,' pp. 259–72.

43 Jónsson, *Det gamle,* pp. 24–27.

44 *DN* 5: 152, 17B: pp. 282–83; Storm, *Islandske,* pp. 210, 212; Rafn and Magnusen, *Grønlands Historiske,* vol. 3, p. 463.

45 *DN* 4: 293; 17: 61.

46 Storm, *Islandske,* pp. 212–13, 353.

47 Storm, *Islandske,* pp. 275–76, 353–55, 396, 404.

48 Skovgaard-Petersen, 'Islandsk,' pp. 230–96.

49 Jónsson, *Det gamle,* pp. 8–9; McGovern, 'Economics,' pp. 406, 414–16; Diamond, *Collapse,* pp. 192, 245.

50 *DN* 12: 103; 17B: p. 283; Storm, *Islandske*, pp. 227–28, 282, 364, 414.

51 *DN* 5: 268.

52 *DN* 17: 177, 180, 183; 17B: pp. 209, 283; Storm, *Islandske*, pp. 282, 365–66, 414; Rafn and Magnusen, *Grønlands Historiske*, vol. 3, pp. 129–30.

53 Nørlund, 'Buried,' p. 54; Roussell, 'Farms,' pp. 190–96.

54 *DN* 6: 527; 17: 759.

55 Magnusson, Magnus, and Werner Forman, *Viking: Hammer of the North*, London, 1976, p. 41; Nørlund, 'Buried,' pp. 60–67.

56 Nørlund, 'Buried,' pp. 60–71, 251; Nørlund and Roussell, 'Norse Ruins,' p. 137.

CHAPTER 7

1 Larson, *King's Mirror*, p. 142; Keyser et al., *Konge-speilet*, p. 42.

2 On the usefulness of luxury commodities, see Hedeager, Lotte, 'Centerdannelse i et langtidspersektiv: Danmarks jernalder,' pp. 89–95 in Egil Mikkelsen, and Jan Henning Larsen, eds, *Økonomiske og politiske sentra i Norden ca. 400–1000 e. Kr.*, Oslo, 1992.

3 Hildebrand, Bror, ed., *Diplomatarium Suecanum*, vol. 5 (1341–1347), Stockholm, 1856: nos. 4226, 42313; Stefánsson, Vilhjalmur, and Eloise McCaskill, *The Three Voyages of Martin Frobisher*, 2 vols, London: Argonaut Press, 1938, vol. 1, pp. xliii–xliv.

4 *DN* 8: 96, 135; 10: 30; 19: 293, 493.

5 Seaver, 'Ettertraktete.'

6 McGovern et al., 'The zooarchaeology,' pp. 66–67; *DI* 5: 562, 652 and p. 1086; 6: 101, 147, 159, 164, 208, 273, 467.

7 Taylor, Michael, *The Lewis Chessmen*, London, 1978.

8 Andersen, Haakon A., *Kunsthåndverket i middelalderen: Fra Trondheims skattkammer* [Trondheim]: 1997, p. 40; Blindheim, Martin, *Middelalderkunst fra Norge i andre land – Norwegian Medieval Art Abroad*, Oslo, 1972, pp. 9, 17.

9 Bødker Enghoff, 'Hunting,' pp. 15, 30, 91.

10 'Egil's Saga' in Hreinsson, *Complete Sagas*, vol. 1, pp. 50–51; Bately, Janet, ed., *The Old English Orosius*, London, 1980, pp. 14–16.

11 Blindheim, Charlotte, and Roar L. Tollnes, *Kaupang: Vikingenes handelsplass*, Oslo, 1972.

12 Blindheim, Charlotte, 'Kaupang i relasjon til andre nordiske sentra: Et diskusjonsinnlegg,' pp. 137–49 in Egil Mikkelsen, and Jan Henning Larsen, eds, *Økonomiske og politiske sentra i Norden ca 400–1000 e. Kr.*, Oslo, 1992, esp. pp. 138–48; Skre, Dagfinn, ed., *Kaupang in Skiringssal*, Aarhus (Denmark) and Oslo, 2007.

13 Helle, Knut, *Kongssete og Kjøpstad, Fra opphavet til 1536. Bergen bys historie*, vol. 1, Bergen/Oslo/Tromsø, 1982, pp. 114–15; Mikkelsen, Egil,

Fangstprodukter i vikingtidens og middelalderens økonomi: Organiseringen av massefangst av villrein i Dovre, Oslo, 1994, ch. 6.

14 Keyser and Munch, *Norges gamle* 2: 170; 3: 134–35.

15 Authén Blom, *Kongemakt*, p. 172.

16 *DN* 2: 258; 8: 127–28.

17 Hansson, Pär, ed., *Novgorod-Örebro-Lübeck after 700 years 1295–1995*, Örebro (Sweden), 1995, pp. 30–31; Mikkelsen, *Fangstprodukter*, pp. 164–67.

18 Höhlbaum, Konstantin, ed., *Hansisches Urkundenbuch*, Halle, 1879–1886, vol . 2, pp. 117–19; Keyser and Munch, *Norges gamle*, vol. 3: 47.

19 Authén Blom, Grethe, *St. Olavs by, Trondheim bys historie*, Trondheim, 1956, pp. 829–31.

20 Seaver, *Frozen Echo*, pp. 95, 153–54, 170–72, 250.

21 *Kulturhistorisk leksikon* 14, cols. 507–10.

22 *Kulturhistorisk leksikon* 14, pp.120–22.

23 *Kulturhistorisk leksikon* 14, pp.120–22.

24 Authén Blom, *Kongemakt*, p. 201; Keyser and Munch, *Norges gamle* 2: 258; *DI* 9: 6; *DN* 11: 110.

25 *DI* 3: 315, 451; 18: 33; Storm, *Islandske*, pp. 282, 364, 413–14.

26 *DI* 3: 367; *DN* 1: 345, 458; 2: 515–20; 18: 33; 21: 133; Storm, *Islandske*, pp. 365–66.

27 Authén Blom, *Kongemakt*, p. 48; *DN* 11: 61; *Kulturhistorisk leksikon*, vol. 4, cols. 210–11; vol. 17, cols. 651–55; vol. 20, col. 446; Keyser and Munch, *Norges gamle* 3: 74.

28 Storm, *Islandske*, pp. 282, 364–65, 414; Jóhannesson, Jón, 'Reisubók Bjarnar Jorsalafara,' pp. 68–96 in *Skirnir* 119 (1945).

CHAPTER 8

1 Storm, *Islandske*, pp. 213, 290, 353.

2 Henschen, Folke, *The History of Diseases*, London, 1966, p. 64.

3 Storm, *Islandske Annaler*, pp. 285, 367–68.

4 (Adam of Bremen), *History* (Tschan tr.), p. 217.

5 White, Paul A., *Non-Native Sources for the Scandinavian Kings' Sagas*, New York, 2005, pp. 14–15.

6 White, *Non-Native*, pp. 16–19.

7 Helgason, *Islands Kirke*, p. 152; Hødnebø and Magerøy, *Norges*, vol. 1, pp. xiv–xvii.

8 Karlsson, Gunnar, *The History of Iceland*, Minneapolis (Minnesota), 2000, pp. 72–76.

9 Karlsson, *History*, pp. 79–80.

10 Karlsson, *History*, pp. 80–82.

11 Karlsson, *History*, pp. 90–91.

12 Keyser and Munch, *Norges gamle*, vol. 3: 134–35; *DI* 2: 176–77; Storm, *Islandske*, pp. 146, 199, 388.

13 Karlsson, *History*, pp. 100–02.

14 *DI* 3: note p. 439; 5: Register: 'Kristín Björnsdóttir Jorsalafare.'

15 *DI* 5, p. 1088; Espólin, Jón, *Íslands Árbækur*, Copenhagen, 1821–55, part 1, pp. 82–84, 91–98, 102–05, 110; Storm, *Islandske*, pp. 225–28, 277–79, 281, 284, 296, 357–62, 364, 366, 407–11, 413, 416; Seaver, *Frozen Echo*, Appendix A.

16 Espólin, *Árbækur*, part 1, p. 112; *DI* 3: 333, 411; 8: 11; 9: 13 (etc.).

17 *DI* 3: 226, 263, 305, 359, 360, 376, 383–86, 398; 4: 10, 16, 348, 567, 568; 5: 586, 582, 587; 12: 10, 11; Espólin, *Árbækur*, part 1: pp. 104–06, part 2: p. 4; Seaver, *Frozen Echo*, Appendix B.

18 *DI* 3: nos. 408, 511, 582; 6: 5.

19 *DI* 9: 5.

20 Storm, *Islandske*, p. 275; Seaver, *Frozen Echo*, pp. 88–89; Karlsson, *History*, pp. 111–17.

21 Espólin, *Árbækur* 2: Preface.

22 *Annálar 1400–1800*, 5 vols, Copenhagen, 1922–61, vol. 1, pp. 13–20; *DI* 3: 578, 580, 632; 4: 341, 372, 376, 638; 12: 13.

23 *DN* 11: 110.

24 Espólin, *Árbækur*, vol. 2, p. 8; Storm, *Islandske*, pp. 289–90; *DN* 18: 33; 19: 535–55, 657–60, 667–706.

25 Bjarnason, Einar, 'Auðbrekku bréf ok Vatnsfjarðarerfdir,' pp. 370–411 in *Saga* 37 (1962), pp. 304–08; Storm, *Islandske*, p.288; *Kulturhistorisk leksikon* 14: col. 28

26 Storm, *Islandske*, p. 288–89, 296; *DI* 4: 638.

27 Bishop Egil Andresen, acting Archbishop of Nidaros, explained the order of these two ceremonies while standing in Hvalsey church during the 600th anniversary for the wedding.

28 Storm, *Islandske*, pp. 281, 364, 413, 416. On Thorstein's literacy, see Karlsson, Stefán, *Islandske originaldiplomer indtil 1450*, Copenhagen, 1963, p. liv and document 171.

29 *DI* 3: 597 (1409), 630–32 (1414); 4: 376 (1424). According to Finn Magnusen, Bishop Odd Einarsson of Skálholt made verified transcripts of all three documents.

30 Storm, *Islandske*, p. 289; *Annálar 1400–1800*, vol. 1, pp. 13, 16; Thorsteinsson, Björn, *Enska öldin í sögu íslendinga*, Reykjavík, 1970, pp. 46–49.

31 *DI* 3: 599–602; Seaver, *Frozen Echo*, pp. 165–68.

32 Bjarnason, 'Audbrekku,' p. 407; Storm, *Islandske*, pp. 289–90.

33 *DI* 4: 50, 5: 126; 6: 578, 633.

34 *DI* 4: 506; 5: 550 and p. 1086; *DN* 20: 789; *Kulturhistorisk leksikon* 20: cols. 151–52 (Björn Thorsteinsson); Storm, *Islandske*, p. 370; Thorsteinsson, *Enska*, pp. 111–19; Seaver, *Frozen Echo*, ch. 7.

CHAPTER 9

1   Pálsson and Edwards, *Landnámabók*, chs. 5, 24.

2   *Kulturhistorisk leksikon*, vol. 9, col. 666 (Lars Hamre).

3   This small manuscript map belongs to The British Library: Cotton MS Tiberius B.V., 56v.

4   Carus-Wilson, Eleanora Mary, 'Iceland Trade,' pp. 155–82 in E. Power and M. M. Postan, eds, *Studies in English Trade in the Fifteenth Century*, London, 1933, pp. 159–60; Williamson, James A., *Cabot Voyages and Bristol Discovery under Henry VII*, Cambridge (England), 1962, p. 4; *Kulturhistorisk leksikon*, vol. 22 (1976): cols. 151–52 (Björn Thorsteinsson).

5   Storm, *Islandske*, p. 293.

6   Storm, *Islandske* , pp. 290, 369; *Annálar*, pp. 8–9; DI 16: 80; Thorsteinsson, *Enska*, pp. 25, 27; Thorsteinsson, Björn, 'Henry VIII and Iceland,' pp. 67–101 in *Bulletin of the Institute for Historical Research* 151(1957–59), pp. 67ff.

7   Storm, *Islandske*, pp. 290, 292; Seaver, *Frozen Echo*, pp. 160–61.

8   Bjarnason, 'Audbrekku,' p. 407; Storm, *Islandske*, pp. 290–91.

9   Thorsteinsson, *Enska*, pp. 29–30, 38, 48–49; *Annálar*, pp. 19–20. Storm, *Islandske*, pp. 290–91; *Annálar*, pp. 19–20; Thorsteinsson, Björn, 'Íslands- og Grænlandssiglingar Englendinga á 15. öld of fundur Norður-Ameríku,' pp. 3–71 in *Saga* 4–5 (1965–67), pp. 28–30.

10   DI 3: 597, 632; Thorsteinsson, *Enska*, pp. 33–34, 76–77; Halldórsson, *Grænland*, p. 297; Karlsson, *Islandske*, pp. xxxii–iii, xxxviii, li.

11   *Annálar*, pp. 20–21; Storm, *Islandske*, pp. 291–92; *DI* 3: 640.

12   *Kulturhistorisk leksikon* 12, col. 392 (Jakob Benediksson); Thorsteinsson, *Enska*, pp. 46–49.

13   DI 3: 642, 644, 16: 77, 80 and pp. 220–25; DN 20B: 733, 738–39, 742 and p. 5. The Duke's reply and King Henry's letter are in The British Library: Cotton MSS, Nero B. III, ff. 30–31.

14   Storm, *Islandske*, p. 291; *Kulturhistorisk leksikon*, vol. 20, cols. 151–52 (Björn Thorsteinsson); Thorsteinsson, 'Íslands- og Grænlandssiglingar,' pp. 19–20; Thorsteinsson, 'Henry VIII,' pp. 68–69, 72–72.

15   DI 4: 376.

16   *Annálar*, p. 22; DI 4: 313, 330–31, 333, 352, 355; Espólin, *Árbækur*, vol. 2p. 16; Thorsteinsson, *Enska*, pp. 52–53, 56.

17   English merchant vessels carried salt, flour, malt, honey, pots, pans, shears, locks, cloth, and articles of clothing such as shawls and hats. (Carus-Wilson, Eleanora Mary, *The Merchant Adventurers of Bristol*, Bristol, 1962, p. 6.)

18   Nørlund, 'Buried,' pp.122–25, 149–51; Arneborg, Jette, Hans Christian Gulløv, and Jens P. Hart Hansen, 'Menneske og miljø i fortidens Grønland,' pp. 39–47 in *Forskning i Grønland/tusaat* 1 (1988), p. 43; Seaver, *Frozen Echo*, pp. 170–72.

19   Vebæk, Christen Leif, 'Vatnahverfi: An Inland District of the Eastern Settlement in Greenland,' *MoG: Man & Society* 17 (1992), pp. 85–86 (including fig. 119), 120; Carus-Wilson, Eleanora Mary, *The Overseas Trade*

of Bristol, London, 1967, pp. 171, 180; Vagn Fabritius Buchwald, 'Ancient Iron and Slags in Greenland,' *MoG: M&S* 26 (2001), p. 35; Seaver, *Frozen Echo,* pp. 172–74, 227–53; Seaver, *Maps, Myths,* pp. 44–47.

20 Seaver, *Frozen Echo,* pp. 167–68, 176.

21 *DI* 9: 20; Seaver, *Frozen Echo,* pp. 167–68.

22 *DI* 4: 381; Thorsteinsson, *Enska,* pp. 65–66; Thorsteinsson, 'Íslands- og Grænlandssiglingar,' pp. 33–34.

23 *Annálar,* pp. 22–23; *DI* 4: 333, 343; *DN* 20: 749.

24 *DI* 4: 331, 336, 341 and p. 331; *DN* 1: 670, 756; *Annálar,* p. 23; Storm, *Islandske,* p. 293; *Kulturhistorisk leksikon* 20, cols. 151–52 (Björn Thorsteinsson); Thorsteinsson, *Enska,* pp. 262–64.

25 *Annálar,* pp. 23–25; *DI* 4: 348, 380–81, 16: nos. 81–84; Storm, *Islandske,* p. 293; Carus-Wilson, 'Iceland,' pp. 165–66.

26 *DI* 4: 558, 16: 81, 88; Thorsteinsson, *Enska,* pp. 101–03.

27 *DI* 4: 328; Thorsteinsson, *Enska,* pp. 101–03 Carus-Wilson, 'Iceland,' p. 167; Ravenstein, E.G., *Martin Behaim: His Life and His Globe,* London, 1908, p. 74.

28 Carus-Wilson, 'Iceland,' pp. 163–65; Carus-Wilson, *Overseas,* pp. 56–58; Carus-Wilson, *Merchant,* p. 6.

29 *DI* 16: 86, 87, 90, 20; 47–48, 771; Thorsteinsson, *Enska,* pp. 90–93, 99.

30 Quinn, David Beers, *England and the Discovery of America,* London, 1974, p. 48; Thorsteinsson, *Enska,* pp. 262–63, 274–76. Carus-Wilson, *Overseas,* pp. 5–9.

31 *Annálar,* pp. 25–27; *DI* 4: 352, 355, 401, 408, 501, 8: 18, 9: 23, 16: 85; Storm, *Islandske,* p. 294.

32 *Annálar,* pp. 26–27; *DI* 4: 506; *DN* 20: 789; *Kulturhistorisk leksikon* 20: cols. 151–52 (Björn Thorsteinsson); Thorsteinsson, *Enska,* pp. 96, 116–18, 138.

33 *DI* 16: 149; *DN* 17: 556–60, 566, 17B: pp. 267, 284–85; Thorsteinsson, *Enska,* p. 112, 147–53; Storm, *Islandske,* p. 370; Carus-Wilson, 'Iceland,' p. 170.

34 E. g., *DI* 16: 8; Carus-Wilson, *Overseas,* pp. 252–53.

35 *DI* 5: 443.

36 *DI* 3: pp. 493–96; 5: 5, 57, 175. pp. 819, 837, 199, 201, 225, 227, 322.

37 *DI* 5: 138, p. 848; 10: 22, 23, 28, 11: 12–15; 16: 215, 217, 219, 230; Thorsteinsson, *Enska,* pp. 186–87, 207–13; Pastor, Ludwig, *The History of the Popes,* 2 vols, London, 1891, vol. 2, p. 383; Carus-Wilson, 'Iceland,' pp. 179–80; Carus-Wilson, *Overseas,* pp. 136–37; Espólin, *Árbækur* 2, p. 66.

38 *DI* 6: 66–67, 101, 147, 159, 164, 208, 273, 467; 10: 23, 27, 11: 22, 5: 562, 652 and p. 1086; Thorsteinsson, *Enska,* pp. 22–28; Thorsteinsson, 'Íslands- og Grænlandssiglingar,' pp. 65–66; Seaver, *Frozen Echo,* pp. 202–04.

39 Thorsteinsson, *Enska,* pp. 242–43; Seaver, *Frozen Echo,* pp. 202–04.

40 *DI* 6: 617; 7: 499, 550; 8: 72, 73, 16: 230 and pp. 445–46; Thorsteinsson, 'Henry VIII,' pp. 71–72; Thorsteinsson, *Enska,* pp. 256–57.

41 *DI* 5: 446; 6: 633, 659; 7: 285.

42 Carus-Wilson, *Merchant Adventurers,* pp. 15–16.

43 Seaver, *Frozen Echo,* pp. 265–75, 284–94.

CHAPTER 10

1 Oddsson, Gísli, 'Annalium in Islandia farrago' (Halldór Hermannsson, ed.), in *Islandica* 10 (1917), pp. i–vii, 2; tr. in Jones, *Norse Atlantic*, p. 95.

2 Seaver, *Frozen Echo*, pp. 86, 96, 104–12.

3 Seaver, *Frozen Echo*, pp. 96, 174–79 passim, 189, 226, 237–38.

4 *DI* 1: 1; *DN* 17: 515–18, 1085.

5 E.g., *DI* 4: 744, 748–58, 760–61.

6 Translation used: Rey, Louis, 'Gardar, the "Diocese of Ice,"' pp. 324–33 in *Arctic* 37: 4 (1984), esp. pp. 331–32.

7 *DN* 6: 527, 17B, pp. 267–68; *DI* 4: 776; Thorsteinsson, *Enska*, pp. 65–66, 174–89.

8 Rey, 'Gardar,' pp. 332–33; Latin transcript in Bobé, Louis, ed., 'Diplomatarium Groenlandicum 1492–1814,' *MoG* 55 (3), 1936, pp. 3–4; Seaver, *Frozen Echo*, pp. 96, 237–38.

9 *DN* 17: 754, 758, 759, 761, 762, 1147, 17 B: p. 286.

10 Fredskild, Bent, 'Paleobotanical investigations of some peat bog deposits of Norse age at Quagssiarssuk, South Greenland,' pp. 1–41 in *MoG* 204: 5 (1978); Fredskild, Bent, 'Agriculture in a marginal area: South Greenland from the Norse landnam (AD 985) to the present (1985),' pp. 381–84 in Hilary H. Birks, H.J.B. Birks, Peter Emil Kaland, and Dagfinn Moe, eds, *The Cultural Landscape: Past, Present and Future*, Cambridge (England), 1988; Seaver, *Frozen Echo*, pp. 243–48; Seaver, *Maps, Myths*, pp. 81–82.

11 Edwards, Kevin J., and J. Ed Schofield, 'Land use history for Hvalsey and the Eastern Settlement of Greenland – the environmental record.' Address given at The Hvalsey Conference in South Greenland, 12–19 September 2008.

12 Thorsteinsson, Ingvi, 'The environmental effects of farming in South Greenland in the Middle Ages and the twentieth century,' pp. 258–63 in Sigurðsson and Skaptason, *Aspects*.

13 Kristínsson, 'Productivity.'

14 Arneborg, Jette, Jan Heinemeier, Niels Lynnerup, Henrik L. Nielsen, Niels Rud, Árny E. Sveinbjörnsdóttir, 'Change of diet of the Greenland Vikings determined from stable carbon isotope analysis and 14C dating of their bones,' *Radiocarbon* 41: 2 (1999), pp. 157–58; McGovern, Thomas, 'The economics of landnám. Animal bone evidence from Iceland and Greenland.' Report at conference on 'The North Atlantic Saga,' Reykjavík, 9–11 August 1999; Seaver, *Frozen Echo*, pp. 238–48.

15 See, e. g., Lynnerup, 'Greenland Norse,' pp. 126–28; Seaver, *Maps, Myths*, p. 67.

16 Valkendorf's aborted expedition received a papal indulgence on 17 June 1514 (*DN* 17: 1260, 1263); Seaver, *Maps, Myths*, pp. 67–68.

17 Carus-Wilson, *Overseas*, p. 125.

18 Carus-Wilson, *Overseas*, p. 125.

19 Quinn, *England*, pp. 47–48; Seaver, *Frozen Echo*, ch. 8.

20 Kisbye Møller, J., 'Isaac de la Peyrère: Relation du Groenlande,' pp. 168–84 in *Grønland* 29 (1981); Lintot, Henry, and John Osborn, eds, *A Collection of Voyages and Travels*, 2 vols, London, 1744, vol. 2, pp. 363–406; *Diplomatarium Islandicum* 6: 66, 67, Seaver, *Frozen Echo*, pp. 205–06, 251, 361 note 65; Seaver, *Maps, Myths*, pp. 83–84.

21 Harrisse, Henry, *The Discovery of North America*, 2 vols, London, 1882, vol. 1, p. 131 (citation from Francisco López de Gómara, Historia de las Indias Seville: 1553), Quinn, *North America*, p. 136.

22 Seaver, Kirsten A., '"A Very Common and Usuall Trade": The Relationship Between Cartographic Perceptions and Fishing in the Davis Strait c.1500–1550,' pp. 1–26 in Karen Severud Cook, ed., *Images and Icons of the New World: Essays on American Cartography*, London, 1996.

23 Lainema, Matti, and Juha Nurminen, *Ultima Thule: Arctic Explorations*, Helsinki, 2001, p. 27 has a colour illustration of the map; Bjørnbo and Petersen, *Fyenboen*, pp. 47, 49, 98, 101–02, 132.

24 Bjørnbo, Axel Anton, 'Cartographia Groenlandica,' *MoG* 48 (1912), pp. 101, 108.

25 Fischer, Josef, 'Die kartographische,' p. 35; Seaver, *Maps, Myths*, ch. 9.

26 Larsen, Sofus, *The Discovery of North America Twenty Years Before Columbus*, London, 1925; Seaver, 'Olaus Magnus,' pp. 239–46; Seaver, *Frozen Echo*, pp. 199–201, 256–60.

27 Seaver, *Frozen Echo*, pp. 260–63, 275.

28 Seaver, *Frozen Echo*, pp. 275–77.

29 Seaver, *Frozen Echo*, p. 277.

30 Seaver, *Frozen Echo*, pp. 263–64, 277–80. The Cantino map belongs to the Biblioteca Estense in Modena, Italy.

31 Seaver, *Frozen Echo*, pp. 214–18, 279.

32 Seaver, *Frozen Echo*, pp. 281–83.

33 Brown, G.W., Marcel Trudel, and André Vachon, eds, *Dictionary of Canadian Biographical*, Toronto, 1965, vol. 1, pp. 304–05; Carus-Wilson, *Overseas*, pp. 236, 286; Morison, Samuel Eliot, *The European Discovery of America: The Northern Voyages*, New York, 1971, vol. 1, p. 210; Quinn, *England*, pp. 55, 57; Williamson, *Cabot*, pp. 118, 235; Biggar, Henry Percival, *The Precursors of Cartier, 1497–1534*, Ottawa, 1911, pp. 31–32; Quinn, David Beers, Alison M. Quinn, and Susan Hillier, eds, *New American World: A Documentary History of North America to 1612*, 5 vols, New York, 1979, vol. 1, p. 145; Seaver, *Frozen Echo*, pp. 283–84.

34 Ruddock, Alwyn A., 'John Day of Bristol and the English voyages across the Atlantic before 1497,' pp. 177–89 in *The Geographical Journal* 132: 2 (1966), p. 232; Quinn, David Beers, *North America from Earliest Discoveries to First Settlements: The Norse Voyages to 1612*, London, 1977, p. 96.

35 Seaver, *Frozen Echo*, pp. 285–91; Ribeiro map – see http://www.henry-davis.com/MAPS/Ren/Ren1/346mono.html, also image #346B. Accessed 3 December 2008.

36 Seaver, *Frozen Echo*, pp. 287–92.

37 Biggar, *Precursors*, pp. 40–59; Quinn, Quinn and Hillier, *New*, vol. 1, pp. 103–09; Williamson, *Cabot*, pp. 235–47.

38 Quinn, Quinn and Hillier, *New*, vol. 1, p. 103; Quinn, *England*, pp. 114–15; Quinn, *North*, pp. 124–25; Seaver, *Frozen Echo*, pp. 292–93, 296.

39 Quinn, Quinn and Hillier, *New*, vol. 1, pp. 103, 109; Quinn, *England*, p. 121; Williamson, *Cabot*, pp. 127; 214–16 Seaver, *Frozen Echo*, pp. 193–96.

40 Ruddock, Alwyn A., 'The Reputation of Sebastian Cabot,' pp. 95–99 in *Bulletin of the Institute for Historical Research* 47 (1974), p. 98; Quinn, Quinn and Hillier, *New*, vol. 1, pp. 117–20; Seaver, *Frozen Echo*, pp. 297–302.

41 Quinn, Quinn and Hillier, *New*, vol. 1, pp. 111–16.

42 Quinn, *England*, pp. 49, 85.

43 Rahn Phillips, Carla, 'The growth and composition of trade in the Iberian empires, 1450–1750,' pp. 34–101 in James D. Tracy, ed., *The Rise of Merchant Empires*, New York, 1990, p. 48, note 21; Hatcher, John, *Plague, Population and the English Economy, 1348–1530*, London, 1977, pp. 27–30, 43, 55–58, 60–64; Slack, Paul, *The Impact of Plague in Tudor and Stuart England*, London, 1985, pp. 15–17, 56–68, 70–73 (esp. fig. 1, p. 71), 84–89, p. 169.

44 Seaver, *Frozen Echo*, pp. 304–28 and App. C.

CHAPTER 11

1 Scoresby, William, the Younger, *An Account of the Arctic Regions with a History and Description of the Northern Whale-Fishery*, 2 vols, Edinburgh, 1820, vol. 1, pp. 5, 66–67.

2 Scoresby, *Account*, vol. 2 (map); Ehrensvärd, Ulla, *The History of the Nordic Map from Myths to Reality*, Helsinki, 2006, p. 168.

3 *DN* 17: 1260, 1263; Rafn and Magnusen, *Grønlands historiske*, vol. 3, pp. 490–96.

4 Benedictov, Ole Jørgen, *Fra rike til provins, 1448–1536*, Oslo, 1977, pp. 290–97.

5 Jónsson, *Det gamle*, pp. 31–32; Seaver, *Frozen Echo*, p. 32; Hamre, Lars, *Erkebiskop Erik Valkendorf: Trekk av hans liv og virke*, Oslo, 1943, pp. 51–52.

6 Jónsson, *Det gamle*, pp. 17–30.

7 Jónsson, *Det gamle*, pp. 9–10, 14, 19; Halldórsson, *Grænland*, pp. 270, 444.

8 Bjørnbo and Petersen, *Fynboen*, p. 53.

9 (Saxo Grammaticus), *Saxonis Grammatici Danorvm Historiæ*, Paris, 1514 (copy used: British Library 6247); (Saxo Grammaticus), *Saxonis Grammatici Danorvm Historiæ*, Basel, 1536 (copy used: British Library 590.k.10.); Saxo Grammaticus, *Den danske Krønike* (Anders Sørensen Vedel, tr.), Copenhagen, 1851, pp. 1–22; Hamre, *Erkebiskop*, p. 67.

10 Purchas, *Hakluytus Posthumus*, vol. 13, pp. 163–68.

11 Burger, C. P., Jr., 'Een Werk van Willem Barents Teruggevonden,' pp. 225–40 in *Het Boek* 17, Den Haag (The Netherlands), 1928, p. 225; Parker, John,

ed., *Merchants and Scholars: Essays in the History of Exploration and Trade*, Minneapolis, 1965, pp. 6–7.

12 On this shipping process, see Qubs-Mrozewicz, Justyna, *Traders, Ties and Tensions: The Interaction of Lübeckers, Overrijsslers and Hollanders in Late Medieval Bergen*, Hilversum (The Netherlands), 2008.

13 Purchas, *Hakluytus Posthumus*, vol. 3, pp. 643–45, 651, vol. 13, pp. 492–519; *Allgemeine Deutsche Biographie* (Die Historische Kommission bei der Bayerischen Akademie der Wissenschaften), 56 vols, Leipzig, 1875–1912, vol. 47 (1903), p.17 ('Blefken, Dithmar').

14 *DN* 14: 626–27, 633, 638, 640; Bobé, Louis, 'Opdagelsesrejser til Grønland 1473–1806: Inledning til Diplomatarium Groenlandicum 1492–1814,' *MoG* 55 (1) (1936), pp. 5–6; Larsson, Lars J., 'Sören Norby, Moskva och Grönland,' pp. 67–81 in *Scandia* 45: 1 (1979).

15 Rafn and Magnusen, *Grønlands Historiske*, vol. 3, pp. 505–07.

16 Rafn and Magnusen, *Grønlands Historiske*, pp. 513–16.

17 Rafn and Magnusen, *Grønlands Historiske*, vol. 3, pp. 199–200, 639–50.

18 Spies, Marijke, *Arctic Routes to Fabled Lands: Oliver Brunel and the Passage to China and Cathay in the Sixteenth Century*, Amsterdam, 1997, pp. 15, 18; Bobé, 'Opdagelsesrejser,' pp. 7–9; Bobé, 'Diplomatarium,' nos. 13–16.

19 Jónsson, *Grönlandia*, pp. 1–12, 54; Halldórsson, *Grænland*, p. 444.

20 Rafn and Magnusen, *Grønlands Historiske*, vol. 3, p. 673; Gosch, C. C. A., ed., *Danish Arctic Expeditions 1605 to 1620*, 2 vols, London, 1887, vol. 1, pp. iii–iv, xi, xxv–xxviii, xxxvi, xli–xlv, 7–81.

21 Ehrensvärd, *History*, pp. 163, 165; Gosch, *Danish*, pp. lxxxiv, lxxxvii–xcvii.

22 Seaver, Kirsten A., 'Renewing the quest for Vínland: The Stefánsson, Resen and Thorláksson maps,' pp. 42–49 in *Mercator's World* 5: 5 (2000).

23 Lyschander, Claus Christopherse, *Den Grønlandske Chronica*, original 1608 ed. reprinted Copenhagen, 1726, esp. pp. 5, 14–16, 19–26 (quotes pp. 5 and 19 tr. by K.A. Seaver); Seaver, *Maps, Myths*, pp. 56–59.

24 Bobé, 'Oppdagelsesrejser,' p. 14.

25 Gosch, *Danish*, vol. 1, pp. c–cix, 82–137.

26 Here and in the following, information about Egede's mission builds on what the author learned during four visits to Greenland and on Egede, Hans, 'Relationer fra Grønland 1721–36 og Det Gamle Grønlands nye Perlustration, 1741,' (Louis Bobé, ed.), *Meddelelser om Grønland*, 54 (1925); Egede, Hans, *Det Gamle Grønlands Perlustration eller Naturel-Historie* (Didrik Arup Seip, ed., facsimile of original), Oslo, 1988.

27 Ryder, C., 'Tidligere expeditioner til Grønlands nordkyst nordfor 66° N. br.,' *Geografisk Tidsskrift* 11 (1891–92), pp. 70–74, 85–86; Scoresby, *Account*, vol. 1, p. 67; Graah, W. A., *Narrative of an Expedition to the East Coast of Greenland Sent by Order of the King of Denmark, in Search of the Lost Colonies*, London, 1837 (1976 reprint of the original used for this book).

28 Holm, Gustav F., and V. Garde, 'Den østgrønlandske expedition udført i aarene 1883–1885 under ledelse af G. Holm,' *Meddelelser om Grønland* 9, 10 (1888–89).

29 Scoresby, *Account*, vol. 1, pp. 30–35.

30 Scoresby, *Account*, p. 324.

31 Seaver, Kirsten A., 'Renewing the Quest for Vínland: The Stefánsson, Resen and Thorláksson maps,' pp. 42–49 in *Mercator's World* 5: 5 (2000) .

32 Nansen, Fridtjof, *In Northern Mists*, tr. by Arthur G. Chater, London: William Heinemann, 1911, 2 vols, vol. 2, pp. 101–03; Stefánsson, Vilhjalmur, and Eloise McCaskill, *The Three Voyages of Martin Frobisher*, London: Argonaut Press, 1938, p. lxviii.

POSTSCRIPT

1 Newcomers to this inventive literature will find it well represented by, e.g., Pohl, Frederick J., *The Vikings on Cape Cod: Evidence from Archeological Discovery*, Pictou, Nova Scotia, 1957; Landsverk, Ole G., *The Kensington Runestone: A Reappraisal of the Circumstances under which the Stone was Discovered*, Glendale (California), 1961.

2 Hakluyt, Richard, *The Principal Navigations Voyages Traffiques & Discoveries of the English Nation*, Glasgow: James MacLehose and Sons, 1904 (12 vols based on 1589 ed.), vol. 7, pp. 133–34; Purchas, Samuel, *Hakluytus Posthumus or Purchas his Pilgrimes*, Glasgow: James MacLehose and Sons, 1905 (20 vols based on original 1625 ed.), vol. 14, p. 298; Dee, John, 'Map of part of the northern hemisphere,' British Library, Cotton MS Augustus I.1.1. *Author's note*: Modern scholars often trace the story of Madoc to Dr. Dee's friend, Sir George Peckham, *A True Reporte*, 1583, also written in support of Queen Elizabeth I's claim to the New World.

3 Seller, John, *The English Pilot: The First Book*, Published by the Special Licence and Approbation of His Royal Highness the Duke of York. London: John Darby, 1671.

4 Smith, Brian, 'Earl Henry Sinclair's fictitious trip to America,' *New Orkney Antiquarian Journal* 2 (2000), read as prepublication typescript; Lucas, Frederic W., *The Annals of the Voyages of the Brothers Nicolo and Antonio Zeno in the North Atlantic… and the Claim Founded thereon to a Venetian Discovery of America*, London, 1898.

5 Major, Richard Henry, tr. and ed., *The Voyages of the Venetian Brothers, Niccolò & Antonio Zeno, to the Northern Seas, in the XIVth Century, Comprising the Latest Known Accounts of the Lost Colony of Greenland; and of the Northmen in America before Columbus*, London: Hakluyt Society, 1873; Major, Richard Henry, *The Voyages of the Venetian Brothers Zeno to the Northern Seas in the Fourteenth Century*, Boston: Massachusetts Historical Society, 1875, quote p. 7.

6 http://www.orkneyjar.com/history/historicalfigures/henrysinclair/west knight.htm, consulted 20 June 2008; http://en.wikipedia. org/wiki/ Westford_Knight, consulted 20 June 2008; Smith, 'Earl Henry.'

7 E.g., Hertz, Johannes, 'The Newport Tower,' p. 376 in Fitzhugh and Ward, *Vikings*; Seaver, *Maps, Myths*, p. 55.

8 Carlson, Suzanne, 'Loose Threads in a Tapestry of Stone: The Architecture of the Newport Tower,' on <www.neara.org/CARLSON/newporttower.htm> (NEARA accommodates the views of pre-Columbianists of various hues); Menzies, Gavin, *1421: The Year China Discovered America*, New York: HarperCollins, 2003, pp. 328–30 (2002 British edition entitled *1421: The Year China Discovered the World*); Wahlgren, Erik, *The Vikings and America*, London, 1986, p. 108; Seaver, Kirsten A., 'Walrus pitch and other novelties: Gavin Menzies and the Far North,' 2006, on <http://www.1421exposed.com>

9 *DN* 21: 83; *DI* 2: 529; Seaver, *Frozen Echo*, p. 103 and n. 41.

10 A useful overview: Blegen, Theodore C., *The Kensington Runestone: New Light on an Old Riddle*, St. Paul (Minnesota), 1968. For the 2003 Swedish discovery, see Sköld, Tryggve, articles on the Kensington Rune Stone and Edvard Larsson's runes in *DAUM-katta*, winter 2003, winter 2004, June 2005 and spring 2007, accessible at http://www.sofi.se/daum/

11 Wahlgren, *Vikings*, pp. 115–19.

12 http://www.usatoday.com/news/nation/2001/11/06/viking.html; http:// www.winonadailynews.com/articles/2001/08/12/stories/news/3stone.txt

13 Wahlgren, *Vikings*, p. 116.

14 Seaver, Kirsten A., 'Pygmies of the Far North,' pp. 63–87 in *Journal of World History* 19: 1 (2008).

15 See Seaver, *Maps, Myths*, for details about many aspects concerning this map.

16 Skelton, Raleigh A., Thomas E. Marston, and George D. Painter, *The Vinland Map and the Tartar Relation*, New Haven (Connecticut), Yale University Press, 1965, pp. 139–40.

17 Wallis, Helen, F.R. Maddison, G.D. Painter, D. B. Quinn, R. M. Perkins, G. R. Crone, A. D. Baynes-Cope, and Walter C. and Lucy B. McCrone, 'The strange case of the Vinland Map: A Symposium,' pp. 183–217 in *The Geographical Journal* 140: 2 (1974). *Author's note*: Wallis had her first misgivings about the map back in 1957, when it was offered to the British Museum and promptly rejected by the Department of Manuscripts.

18 For an interesting later light on this matter, see Baynes-Cope, Arthur David, and A.E. Werner, letter, p. 8 in *Mercator's World* 6 (1996).

19 Brown, Katherine L., and Robin J.H. Clark, 'Analysis of pigmentary materials on the Vinland Map and Tartar Relation by Raman Microprobe Spectroscopy,' pp. 3658–61 in *Analytical Chemistry* 74 (2002).

20 Crantz, David, *History of Greenland* (*Historie von Grönland*), 2 vols, London, 1765, vol. 1, pp. 254–55.

21 Pontoppidan, Erik, *Norges Naturlige Historie*, Copenhagen, 1752; *The Natural History of Norway*, London, 1755; Mallet, Paul Henry, Introduction à l'histoire de Dannemarc, Copenhagen: L.H. Lillie, 1755–56.

22 Mallet, Paul Henry, *Northern Antiquities. A Translation of 'Introduction à l'Histoire de Dannemarc' [1755–56, 2 vols]*, T. Percy, tr., London, 1770, pp. 279–83.

23 Jónsson, Arngrim, *Grönlandia: Eller Historie om Grønland af Islandske Haandskrevne Historie-Bøger....og først i det Latinske Sprog forfatted af Arngrim Jonsson*, tr. from Latin into Icelandic by Einar Eyjolfsson (1688), reprinted, Copenhagen 1732, pp. 43–45; Torfæus, Tormod, *Gronlandia antiqua*, tr. by the author as *Det gamle Grønland*, Copenhagen, 1706, reissued Oslo, 1947.

24 Hall, Charles Francis, *Life with the Esquimaux: The narrative of Captain Charles Francis Hall of the Whaling Barque 'George Henry' from 29 May 1860 to 13 September 1862*, London, 1864, pp. 39–41; Fischer, Josef, SJ, *Die Entdeckungen der Normannen in Amerika*, supplementary vol. 21 of *Stimmen aus Maria-Laach*, Freiburg in the Breisgau, 1902; Fischer, Josef, SJ, 'Die Kartographische Darstellung der Entdeckungen der Normannen in Amerika,' Proceedings, 14th International Congress of Americanists 1904, 2 vols, Stuttgart, 1906, vol. 1, pp. 31–39; Fischer, Josef, SJ, *The Discoveries of the Norsemen in America*, Basil Soulsby, tr., London, 1903.

25 Seaver, Kirsten A., 'Norumbega and Harmonia Mundi in Sixteenth-Century Cartography,' *Imago Mundi* 50 (1998), pp. 34–58; Seaver, *Maps, Myths*, p. 59.

26 Verrazzano's letter is reprinted in Wroth, Lawrence E., *The Voyages of Giovanni da Verrazzano 1524–28*, New Haven and London, 1970.

27 Ortelius, Abraham, *Theatrum Orbis Terrarum*, Antwerp, 1570. Copy used: British Library Maps C.2.c.1.

Works Cited

(Adam of Bremen) Francis J. Tschahn, tr. and ed., *History of the Archbishops of Hamburg-Bremen*, New York, 1959.

Allgemeine Deutsche Biographie (Die Historische Kommission bei der Bayerischen Akademie der Wissenschaften), 56 vols, Leipzig, 1875–1912, vol. 47 (1903).

Andersen, Erik, and Claus Malmros, 'Ship's parts found in the Viking settlements in Greenland,' pp. 118–22 in Clausen, Viking.

Andersen, Haakon A., *Kunsthåndverket i middelalderen: Fra Trondheims skattkammer*, [Trondheim]: 1997.

Andreasen, Claus, 'Nordbosager fra Vesterbygden på Grønland,' pp. 135–46 in *Hikuin* 6 (1980).

Andreasen, Claus, and Jette Arneborg, 'Gården under sandet. Nye nordboundersøgelser i Vesterbygden,' *Grønlandsk kultur- og samfundsforskning*, 1992.

Andreasen, Claus, Joel Berglund, Niels Frandsen and Ane Marie B. Pedersen, eds, *Traces: 4400 Years of Man in Greenland* (James Manley, tr.), Nuuk (Greenland): Greenland National Museum and Archives, 2004.

Annálar 1400–1800, 5 vols, Copenhagen, 1922–61.

Appelt, Martin, Joel Berglund and Hans Christian Gulløv, eds, *Identities and Cultural Contacts in the Arctic*, Copenhagen, 2000.

Arneborg, Jette, *Kulturmødet mellem nordboer og eskimoer* [The cultural encounter between Norsemen and Eskimos], Ph.D. dissertation, Copenhagen University, 1991.

Arneborg, Jette, 'Greenland and Europe,' pp. 304–17 in Fitzhugh and Ward, *Vikings*.

Arneborg, Jette, Hans Christian Gulløv and Jens P. Hart Hansen, 'Menneske og miljø i fortidens Grønland,' pp. 39–47 in *Forskning i Grønland/tusaat* 1 (1988).

Arneborg, Jette, and Hans Christian Gulløv, *Man, Culture and Environment in Ancient Greenland: Report on a Research Programme*, Copenhagen, 1998.

Arneborg, Jette, Jan Heinemeier, Niels Lynnerup, Henrik L. Nielsen, Niels Rud, Árny E. Sveinbjörnsdóttir, 'Change of diet of the Greenland Vikings determined from stable carbon isotope analysis and 14C dating of their bones,' *Radiocarbon* 41: 2 (1999).

Authén Blom, Grethe, *St. Olavs by, Trondheim bys historie*, Trondheim, 1956.

-------- *Kongemakt og privilegier i Norge inntil 1387*, Oslo, 1967.

Bately, Janet, ed., *The Old English Orosius*, London: 1980.

Baynes-Cope, Arthur David, and A.E. Werner, letter, p. 8 in *Mercator's World* 6 (1996).

Benedictov, Ole Jørgen, *Fra rike til provins, 1448–1536*, Oslo, 1977.

Berglund, Joel, Hvalsø: *The Church and the Magnate's Farm*, Qaqortoq (Greenland), 1982.

Berthelsen, Christian, Inger Holbech Mortensen and Ebbe Mortensen, eds, *Kalaallit Nunaat/Greenland Atlas*, Piersuiffik, 1990.

Biggar, Henry Percival, *The Precursors of Cartier, 1497–1534*, Ottawa, 1911.

Bjarnason, Einar, 'Auðbrekku bréf ok Vatnsfjarðarerfdir,' pp. 370–411 in *Saga* 37 (1962).

Bjørnbo, Axel Anton, 'Cartographia Groenlandica,,' *Meddelelser om Grønland* 48 (1912).

Bjørnbo, Axel Anton, and Carl S. Petersen, *Fyenboen Claudius Claussøn Swart (Claudius Clavus): Nordens ældste Kartograf*, Copenhagen, 1904.

Blegen, Theodore C., *The Kensington Runestone: New Light on an Old Riddle*, St. Paul (Minnesota), 1968.

Blindheim, Charlotte,' Kaupang i relasjon til andre nordiske sentra: Et diskusjonsinnlegg,' pp. 137–49 in Egil Mikkelsen and Jan Henning Larsen, eds , *Økonomiske og politiske sentra i Norden ca 400–1000 e. Kr.*, Oslo, 1992.

Blindheim, Charlotte, and Roar L. Tollnes, *Kaupang: Vikingenes handelsplass*, Oslo, 1972.

Blindheim, Martin, *Middelalderkunst fra Norge i andre land – Norwegian Medieval Art Abroad*, Oslo, 1972. Bobé, Louis, 'Opdagelsesrejser til Grønland 1473–1806: Inledning til Diplomatarium Groenlandicum 1492–1814,' *Meddelelser om Grønland* 55(1) (1936).

-------- ed., 'Diplomatarium Groenlandicum 1492–1814,' *Meddelelser om Grønland* 55 (3), 1936.

Bødker Enghoff, Inge, 'Hunting, fishing and animal husbandry at The Farm Beneath the Sand, Western Greenland: An archaezoological analysis of a Norse farm in the Western Settlement,' *Meddelelser om Grønland: Man and Society* 28 (2003).

Brown, Katherine L., and Robin J.H. Clark, 'Analysis of pigmentary materials on the Vinland Map and Tartar Relation by Raman Microprobe Spectroscopy,' pp. 3658–61 in *Analytical Chemistry* 74 (2002).

Bowman, Sheridan, *Radiocarbon Dating: Interpreting the Past*, London: British Museum Publications, 1990.

Bröste, K., and K. Fischer-Møller, 'Medieval Norsemen at Gardar: Anthropological investigation,' *Meddelelser om Grønland* 89(3), 1944.

Brown, G.W., Marcel Trudel and André Vachon, eds, *Dictionary of Canadian Biographical*, Toronto, 1965.

Bruun, Daniel, 'Arkaeologiske Undersøgelser i Julianehaab Distrikt,' *Meddelelser om Grönland* 16, Copenhagen, 1917.

Buchwald, Vagn Fabritius, 'Ancient iron and slags in Greenland, Meddelelser om Grønland': Man & Society 26 (2001).

Buckland, Paul C., 'The North Atlantic environment,' pp. 146–53 in Fitzhugh and Ward, *Vikings.*

Burger, C.P., Jr., 'Een Werk van Willem Barents Teruggevonden' pp. 225–40 in *Het Boek* 17, Den Haag (The Netherlands), 1928.

Busch, Jørgen, 'Norrøn navigation over Nordatlanten,' *Polarfronten* (Copenhagen), 2005: 4, back page.

Byock, Jesse L., *Medieval Iceland*, Berkeley (California), 1988.

Carlson, Suzanne,' Loose Threads in a Tapestry of Stone: The Architecture of the Newport Tower,' on <www.neara.org/CARLSON/newporttower.htm>

Carpenter, Edmund, *Norse Penny*, New York: The Rock Foundation, 2003.

Carus-Wilson, Eleanora Mary, 'Iceland Trade,' pp. 155–82 in E. Power and M. M. Postan, eds, *Studies in English trade in the fifteenth century*, London, 1933.

--------- *The Merchant Adventurers of Bristol*, Bristol, 1962.

--------- *The Overseas Trade of Bristol*, London, 1967.

Clausen, Birthe L., ed., *Viking Voyages to North America*, Roskilde (Denmark), 1993.

Cox, Steven L., 'A Norse penny from Maine,' pp. 206–07 in Fitzhugh and Ward, *Vikings.*

Crantz, David, *History of Greenland* (Historie von Grönland), 2 vols, London, 1765.

Dee, John, 'Map of part of the northern hemisphere,' British Library, Cotton MS Augustus I.1.1.

Descelier World Map, 1550, British Library Add MS 24065.

Diamond, Jared, *Collapse: How Societies Choose to Fail or Succeed*, New York: Viking, 2005.

Diplomatarium Islandicum, 16 vols, Copenhagen and Reykjavík: 1857–1959.

Diplomatarium Norvegicum, vols 1–21, Oslo, 1849–1970.

Drever, Charles, *Cod Fishing at Greenland: The White Fish Authority*, typescript, 32 pp., ca. 1972 (British Library x.313/380).

Edson, Evelyn, *The World Map 1300–1492: The Persistence of Tradition and Transformation*, Baltimore, 2007.

Edwards, Kevin J., J. Edward Schofield, and Dmitri Mauquoy, 'High resolution paleoenvironmental and chronological investigations of Norse *landnám* at Tasiusaq, Eastern Settlement, Greenland,' pp. 1–15 in *Quaternary Research* 69 (2008).

Edwards, Kevin J., and J. Ed Schofield, 'Land use history for Hvalsey and the Eastern Settlement of Greenland – the environmental record.' Address given at The Hvalsey Conference in South Greenland, 12–19 September 2008.

Egede, Hans, 'Relationer fra Grønland 1721–36 og Det Gamle Grønlands nye Perlustration, 1741,' (Louis Bobé, ed.), *Meddelelser om Grønland*, 54 (1925).

------- *Det Gamle Grønlands Perlustration eller Naturel-Historie* (Didrik Arup Seip, ed., facsimile of original), Oslo, 1988.

Ehrensvärd, Ulla, *The History of the Nordic Map from Myths to Reality*, Helsinki, 2006.

Espólin, Jón, *Íslands Árbækur*, 13 parts, Copenhagen, 1821–55.

Fischer, Josef, S. J., *Die Entdeckungen der Normannen in Amerika*, supplementary vol. 21 of *Stimmen aus Maria-Laach*, Freiburg in the Breisgau, 1902.

------ *The Discoveries of the Norsemen in America*, Basil Soulsby, tr., London, 1903.

------ 'Die Kartographische Darstellung der Entdeckungen der Normannen in Amerika,'*Proceedings*, 14th International Congress of Americanists 1904, 2 vols, Stuttgart, 1906.

Fitzhugh, William W., 'A Review of Paleo-Eskimo Culture History in Southern Quebec, Labrador and Newfoundland,' *Inuit Studies* 4: 1–2 (1980).

Fitzhugh, William W., 'Iron blooms, Elizabethans, and politics: The Frobisher Project 1974–1995,' pp. 12–21 in *The Review of Archaeology* 17: 2 (1997).

Fitzhugh, William W., and Jacqueline Olin, eds, *Archeology of the Frobisher Voyages*, Washington, D.C., 1993.

Fitzhugh,William W., and Elisabeth I. Ward, eds, *Vikings: The North Atlantic Saga*, Washington and London, 2000.

Foote, Peter G., 'Icelandic *sólarsteinn* and the medieval background,' pp. 140–54 in Michael Baranes, Hans Bekker-Nielsen, and Gerd Wolfgang Weber, eds, *Aurvandilstá*, Odense: 1984.

-------- ed., *Olaus Magnus: A Description of the Northern Peoples, 1555*, 3 vols, London: 1996–98.

Foote, Peter G., and David M. Wilson, *The Viking Achievement*, London and New York, 1970.

Fredskild, Bent, 'Paleobotanical investigations of some peat bog deposits of Norse age at Quagssiarssuk, South Greenland,' pp. 1–41 in *Meddelelser om Grønland* 204: 5 (1978).

-------- 'Agriculture in a marginal area: South Greenland from the Norse landnam (AD 985) to the present (1985),' pp. 381–84 in Hilary H. Birks, H.J.B. Birks, Peter Emil Kaland and Dagfinn Moe, eds, *The Cultural Landscape: Past, Present and Future*, Cambridge (England), 1988.

Gad, Finn, 'Grønlands tilslutning til Norgesvældet 1261,' pp. 259–72 in *Grønland* 12 (1964).

Gelsinger, Bruce, *Icelandic Enterprise: Commerce and Economy in the Middle Ages*, Columbia (South Carolina), 1981.

Gosch, C. C. A., ed., *Danish Arctic Expeditions 1605 to 1620*, 2 vols, London, 1887.

Graah, W. A., *Narrative of an Expedition to the East Coast of Greenland Sent by Order of the King of Denmark, in Search of the Lost Colonies*, London, 1837 (1976 reprint of the original used for this book).

Gulløv, Hans Christian, ed., *Grønlands forhistorie* (Greenland's Pre-History), Copenhagen, 2004.

Gunnarsson, Gísli , 'Given good time, legs get shorter in cold weather,' pp. 184–93 in Sigurðsson and Skaptason, *Aspects*.

Hakluyt, Richard, *The Principal Navigations Voyages Traffiques & Discoveries of the English Nation*, Glasgow: James MacLehose and Sons, 1904 (12 vols based on 1589 ed.).

Hall, Charles Francis, *Life with the Esquimaux: The narrative of Captain Charles Francis Hall of the Whaling Barque 'George Henry' from the 29th May, 1860, to the 13th September, 1862*, London, 1864.

Halldórsson, Ólafur, *Grœnland í miðaldaritum*, Reykjavík: Sögufélag, 1978.

Hamre, Lars, *Erkebiskop Erik Valkendorf: Trekk av hans liv og virke*, Oslo, 1943.

Hansson, Pär, ed., *Novgorod-Örebro-Lübeck after 700 years 1295–1995*, Örebro (Sweden), 1995.

Harrisse, Henry, *The Discovery of North America*, 2 vols, London, 1882.

Harley, J. B., and David Woodward, eds, *The History of Cartography*, vol. 1: *Cartography in Prehistoric, Ancient, and Medieval Europe and the Mediterranean*, Chicago and London, 1987.

Harp, Elmer, 'A Late Dorset Copper Amulet from Southeastern Hudson Bay,' pp. 33–44 in Folk 16/17(1975).

Hatcher, John, *Plague, Population and the English Economy, 1348–1530*, London, 1977.

Hedeager, Lotte, 'Centerdannelse i et langtidspersektiv; Danmarks jernalder,' pp. 89–95 in Egil Mikkelsen and Jan Henning Larsen, eds, *Økonomiske og politiske sentra i Norden ca. 400–1000 e. Kr.*, Oslo: 1992.

Helgason, Agnar, Sigrun Sigurdardóttir, Jeffrey R. Gulcher, Ryk Ward, and Kari Stefánsson, 'mtDNA and the origin of the Icelanders: Deciphering signals of recent population history,' pp. 999–1016 in *American Journal of Human Genetics* 66 (2000).

Helgason, Jón, *Islands Kirke fra dens Grundlæggelse til Reformationen*, Copenhagen, 1925.

Helle, Knut, *Kongssete og Kjøpstad, Fra opphavet til 1536. Bergen bys historie*, vol. 1, Bergen/Oslo/Tromsø, 1982.

Henschen, Folke, *The history of diseases*, London: 1966.

Hermannsson, Halldor, ed. *The Book of Icelanders*, Ithaca: Cornell University Library, 1930.

Hertz, Johannes, 'The Newport Tower,' p. 376 in Fitzhugh and Ward, *Vikings*.

Hildebrand, Bror, ed., *Diplomatarium Suecanum*, vol. 5 (1341–1347), Stockholm, 1856.

Hødnebø, Finn, and Hallvard Magerøy, eds, *Norges kongesagaer*, 4 vols, Oslo, 1979.

Holm, Gustav F., and V. Garde, 'Den østgrønlandske expedition udført i aarene 1883–1885 under ledelse af G. Holm,' *Meddelelser om Grønland* 9, 10 (1888–89).

Holm, Poul, 'Ireland, Norse in,' pp. 323–25 in Pulsiano, *Medieval Scandinavia*.

Holm Olsen, Inger Marie, 'The Helgøy Project: Evidence from farm mounds: Economy and settlement pattern AD 1350–1600,' *Norwegian Archaeological Review* 14, (1981).

Hreinsson, Víðar, gen. ed., *The Complete Sagas of the Icelanders*, 5 vols, Reykjavík, 1997.

Ingstad, Helge, 'Vinland ruins prove Vikings found the New World,' pp. 708–35 in *National Geographic Magazine* 126 (Nov. 1964).

--------- *Land under the Pole Star*, London, 1966.

Jansen, Henrik M., 'Critical account of the written and archaeological sources' evidence concerning the Norse settlements in Greenland,' *Meddelelser om Grønland* 182 (4), 1972.

Jóhannesson, Jón, 'Reisubók Bjarnar Jorsalafara,' pp. 68–96 in *Skirnir* 119 (1945).

------- *Íslendinga saga: A History of the Old Icelandic Commonwealth*, Haraldur Bessason, tr. , Winnipeg, 1974.

Jones, Gwyn, *Norse Atlantic Saga*, Oxford, 1986 (2nd ed.).

Jónsson, Arngrim, *Grönlandia: Eller Historie om Grønland af Islandske Haandskrevne Historie-Bøger …og først i det Latinske Sprog forfatted af Arngrim Jonsson*, tr. from Latin into Icelandic by Einar Eyjolfsson (1688), reprinted Copenhagen 1732.

Jónsson, Finnur, 'Grønlands gamle Topografi efter Kilderne, Østerbygden og Vesterbygden,' *Meddelelser om Grønland* 20 (1899).

------- ed., Ivar Bárðarson, *Det gamle Grønlands Beskrivelse udgiven efter Haandskrifterne*, Copenhagen, 1930.

Kahle, B., ed., *Kristnisaga, Tháttr Thorvalds ens Vidförla, Tháttr Ísleifs Biskups Gissurarsonar, Hungrvaka*, (Altnordische Saga-Bibliothek 11), Halle, 1905.

Karlsson, Gunnar, *The History of Iceland*, Minneapolis (Minnesota), 2000.

Karlsson, Stefán, *Islandske originaldiplomer indtil 1450*, Copenhagen: 1963.

Kellogg, Robert, 'Introduction,' in Hreinsson, ed., *Complete Sagas*.

Keyser, R., and P. A. Munch, eds, *Norges gamle Love*, 5. vols, Oslo, 1846–95.

Keyser, R., P.A. Munch and C.R. Unger, eds, *Speculum Regale*, 1848.

Kisbye Møller, J., 'Isaac de la Peyrère: Relation du Groenlande,' pp. 168–84 in *Grønland* 29 (1981).

Kristínsson, Axel, 'Productivity and population in pre-Industrial Iceland,' pp. 270–78 in Sigurðsson and Skaptason, *Aspects*.

'Kristni saga' see B. Kahle, *Kristnisaga*.

Krogh, Knud, *Viking Greenland*, Copenhagen, 1967.

------- 'Om Grønlands middelalderlige kirkebygninger,' pp. 294–310 in *Minjar og Menntir: Festskrift til Kristján Eldjarn*, Reykjavík, 1976.

Kulturhistorisk leksikon for nordisk middelalder, 21 vols, Copenhagen: 1956–78.

Kurlansky, Mark, *Cod: A Biography of the Fish that Changed the World*, Penguin Books: 1997.

Lainema, Matti, and Juha Nurminen, *Ultima Thule: Arctic Explorations*, Helsinki, 2001.

Landsverk, Ole G., *The Kensington Runestone: A Reappraisal of the Circumstances under which the Stone was Discovered*, Glendale (California), 1961.

Larsen, Sofus, *The Discovery of North America Twenty Years Before Columbus*, London, 1925.

Larson, Laurence Marcellus, tr., *The King's Mirror*, New York, 1917.

Larsson, Lars J., 'Sören Norby, Moskva och Grönland,' pp. 67–81 in *Scandia* 45: 1 (1979).

Lattimore, Richard, tr., *The Iliad of Homer*, Chicago, 1951.

Lebel, Serge, and Patrick Plumet, 'Étude Technologique de l'Exploitation des Blocs et des Galets en Métabasalte par les Dorsétiens au Site Tuvaaluk (DIA.4, JfEI–4),' pp. 143–70 in *Journal canadien d'archéologie* 15 (1991).

Lehn, Waldemar H. , 'Skerrylike mirages and the discovery of Greenland,' pp. 3612–19 in *Applied Optics* 39: 21 (2000).

Liestøl, Aslak, 'Runes,' in Alexander Fenton and Hermann Pálsson, eds, *The Northern and Western Isles in the Viking World*, Edinburgh, 1984.

(Lintot, Henry, and John Osborn, eds), *A Collection of Voyages and Travels*, 2 vols, London, 1744.

Logan, F. Donald, *The Church in the Middle Ages*, London and New York, 2002.

Lucas, Frederic W., *The Annals of the Voyages of the Brothers Nicolo and Antonio Zeno in the North Atlantic… and the Claim Founded thereon to a Venetian Discovery of America*, London, 1898.

Lynnerup, Niels, 'The Norse settlers in Greenland: The physical anthropological perspective,' *Acta Borealia* 1 (1991).

----- 'The Greenland Norse: A biological-anthropological study,' *Meddelelser om Grønland, Man & Society* 24 (1998).

------- 'Life and death in Norse Greenland,' pp. 285–94 in Fitzhugh and Ward, *Vikings*.

Lyschander, Claus Christopherse, *Den Grønlandske Chronica*, original 1608 ed. reprinted Copenhagen, 1726.

Magnusson, Magnus, and Hermann Pálsson, trs., *The Vinland Sagas: The Norse Discovery of America*, ['The Saga of the Greenlanders' and the 'Saga of Eirik the Red'], Penguin Classics, first pub. 1965.

Magnusson, Magnus, and Werner Forman, *Viking: Hammer of the North*, London, 1976.

Major, Richard Henry, tr. and ed., *The Voyages of the Venetian Brothers, Niccolò & Antonio Zeno, to the Northern Seas, in the XIVth Century, Comprising the Latest Known Accounts of the Lost Colony of Greenland; and of the Northmen in America before Columbus*, London: Hakluyt Society, 1873.

------- *The Voyages of the Venetian Brothers Zeno to the Northern Seas in the Fourteenth Century*, Boston: Massachusetts Historical Society, 1875.

Mallet, Paul Henry, *Introduction à l'histoire de Dannemarc*, Copenhagen: L.H. Lillie, 1755–56.

----- *Northern Antiquities. A Translation of 'Introduction à l'Histoire de Dannemarc' [1755–56, 2 vols]*, T. Percy, tr., London: 1770.

Mattox, William G., 'Fishing in West Greenland 1910–1966: The development of a new native industry,' *Meddelelser om Grønland* 197:1 (1973).

Menzies, Gavin, *1421: The Year China Discovered America*, New York. 2003 (2002 British ed. entitled *1421: The Year China Discovered the World*).

McCullough, Karen, and Peter Schledermann, 'Mystery Cairns on Washington Irving Island,' pp. 289–98 in *Polar Record* 35 (1999).

McGhee, Robert, 'Contact between Native North Americans and the medieval Norse: A review of the evidence,' *American Antiquity* 49 (1984).

------ 'The Skraellings of *Vínland*' in Clausen, *Viking*.

------ 'A new view of the Norse in the Arctic,' *Scientific American: Discovering Archaeology* 2 : 4 (2000).

-------- 'Radiocarbon dating and the timing of the Thule migration,' pp. 181–91 in Appelt et al., *Identities*.

McGovern, Thomas H., 'Economics of Extinction in Norse Greenland,' pp. 404–34 in T.M. Wrigley, M.J. Ingram and G. Farmer, eds, *Climate and History: Studies in Past Climates and Their Impact on Man*, Cambridge (England), 1980.

------- 'Bones, buildings, and boundaries: Palæoeconomic approaches to Norse Greenland,' pp. 193–230 in Christopher D. Morris and D. James Rackham, eds, *Norse and Later Settlement and Subsistence in the North Atlantic*, Glasgow, 1992.

------- 'The economics of landnám. Animal bone evidence from Iceland and Greenland,' Report at conference on 'The North Atlantic Saga,' Reykjavík, 9 – 11 August 1999.

McGovern, Thomas H., and G.F. Bigelow, 'Archaezoology of the Norse site Ø17a Narssaq District, Southwest Greenland,' pp. 85–101 in *Acta Borealia* 1 (1984).

McGovern, Thomas H., Gerald F. Bigelow, Thomas Amorosi, James Woollett and Sophia Perdikaris, 'The zooarchaeology of Ø17a,' pp. 58–74 in C.L. Vebæk, 'Narsaq – a Norse landnáma farm,' *Meddelelser om Grønland, Man & Society* 18, Copenhagen, 1993.

McNeill, William H., *Plagues and Peoples*, New York, 1976.

Mikkelsen, Egil, *Fangstprodukter i vikingtidens og middelalderens økonomi: Organiseringen av massefangst av villrein i Dovre*, Oslo, 1994.

Morison, Samuel Eliot, *The European Discovery of America: The Northern Voyages*, New York: 1971.

Munch, Peter Andreas, *Pavelige Nuntiers Regnskabe*, Christiania, 1864.

Nicolet, C., *Space, Geography, and Politics in the Early Roman Empire*, Ann Arbor (Michigan), 1991.

Nørlund, Poul, 'Buried Norsemen at Herjolfsnes,' *Meddelelser om Grønland* 67 (1), Copenhagen: 1924.

Nörlund, Poul, and Mårten Stenberger, 'Brattahlid,' *Meddelelser om Grönland* 88 (1), 1934.

Nørlund, Poul, and Aage Roussell, 'Norse ruins at Gardar, the episcopal seat of mediaeval Greenland,' *Meddelelser om Grønland* 76 (1), Copenhagen, 1929.

Norris, Kenneth S., and Flip Nicklin, 'Beluga: White whale of the North,' pp. 2–31 in *National Geographic* 185:6 (1994).

Nytt fra Norge (Oslo) 44: 3 (1998).

Oddsson, Gísli, 'Annalium in Islandia farrago' (Halldór Hermannsson, ed.), in *Islandica* 10 (1917).

Ortelius, Abraham, *Theatrum Orbis Terrarum*, Antwerp, 1570.

Pálsson, Hermann, and Paul Edwards, *Landnámabók*, Winnipeg: University of Manitoba Press, 1972.

Parker, John, ed., *Merchants and Scholars: Essays in the History of Exploration and Trade*, Minneapolis, 1965.

Pastor, Ludwig, *The History of the Popes*, 2 vols, London, 1891.

Philbert, Poul-Erik, 'Man er hvad man spiser,' pp. 12–13 in *Polarfronten* 2 (2002).

Pliny, *Natural History*, H. Rackham, tr., Cambridge (Massachusetts), 1999 (reprint of 1942 ed. in Latin and English).

Plumet, Patrick, 'Le Site de la Pointe aux Bélougas (Qilalugarsiuvik) et les maisons longues dorsétiennes,' *Archéologie de l'Ungava* (Montréal) 18 (1985).

------- 'Les maisons longues dorsétiennes de l'Ungava,' pp. 253–89 in *Géographie Physique et Quaternaire* 36: 3(1982).

------- 'L'Esquimau: Essai de synthèse de la préhistoire de l'arctique esquimau,' *Revista de Arqueología Americana* 10 (1996).

Pohl, Frederick J., *The Vikings on Cape Cod: Evidence from Archaeological Discovery*, Pictou, Nova Scotia, 1957.

Pontoppidan, Erik, *Norges Naturlige Historie*, Copenhagen, 1752.

--------- *The Natural History of Norway*, London, 1755.

Pulsiano, Phillip, ed., *Medieval Scandinavia*, New York, 1993.

Purchas, Samuel, *Hakluytus Posthumus or Purchas his Pilgrimes*, Glasgow: James MacLehose and Sons, 1905 (20 vols based on original 1625 ed.).

Qubs-Mrozewicz, Justyna, *Traders, Ties and Tensions: The Interaction of Lübeckers, Overrijsslers and Hollanders in Late Medieval Bergen*, Hilversum (The Netherlands), 2008.

Quinn, David Beers, *England and the Discovery of America*, London, 1974.

--------- *North America from Earliest Discoveries to First Settlements: The Norse Voyages to 1612*, London, 1977.

Quinn, David Beers, Alison M. Quinn and Susan Hillier, eds, *New American World: A Documentary history of North America to 1612*, 5 vols, New York: 1979.

Rafn, Carl Christian, and Finn Magnusen, comps. and eds, *Antiquitates Americanae*, Hafniæ: Regia Antiquarium Septentrionalium, 1837.

---------- *Grønlands historiske Mindesmærker* (Historical Monuments of Greenland), 3 vols, Copenhagen, 1838–45.

Rahn Phillips, Carla, 'The growth and composition of trade in the Iberian empires, 1450–1750,' pp. 34–101 in James D. Tracy, ed., *The Rise of Merchant Empires*, New York, 1990.

Rask, Rasmus, and Finn Magnusen, 'Efterretning om en i Grønland funden Runesteen…,' pp. 309–43 (with an addendum by P. Kragh, pp. 367–79) in *Antikvariske Annaler* (Copenhagen) 4: 2 (1827).

Ravenstein, E.G., *Martin Behaim: His Life and His Globe*, London, 1908.

Regesta Norvegica, Oslo: Norsk Historisk Kjeldeskriftfond,1889–1979.

Rey, Louis, 'Gardar, the "Diocese of Ice,"' pp. 324–33 in *Arctic* 37: 4 (1984).

Rogers, Penelope Walton, 'The raw materials of textiles from GUS – with a note on fragments of fleece and animal pelts from the same site,' pp. 66–73 in Arneborg and Gulløv, *Man, Culture.*

Roussell, Aage, 'Sandnes and the neighbouring Farms,' *Meddelelser om Grønland* 88: 2 (1936).

------- 'Farms and churches in the mediaeval Norse settlements of Greenland,' Meddelelser om Grønland 89(1), 1941.

Ruddock, Alwyn A., 'John Day of Bristol and the English voyages across the Atlantic before 1497,' pp. 177–89 in *The Geographical Journal* 132: 2 (1966).

--------- 'The Reputation of Sebastian Cabot,' pp. 95–9 in *Bulletin of the Institute for Historical Research* 47 (1974).

Russell, Jeffrey, *Inventing a Flat Earth: Columbus and Modern Historians*, New York: Praeger, 1991.

Ryder, C., 'Tidigere expeditioner til Grønlands nordkyst nordfor 66° N. br.,' *Geografisk Tidsskrift* 11 (1891–92).

Sabo, George and Deborah 'A possible Thule carving of a Viking from Baffin Island N.W.T.,' pp. 33 –42 in *Canadian Journal of Archaeology* 2 (1978).

Sawyer, Birgit and Peter, *Medieval Scandinavia: From Conversion to Reformation circa 800–1500*, Minneapolis (Minnesota), 1993.

(Saxo Grammaticus), *Saxonis Grammatici Danorvm Historiæ*, Paris, 1514.

---------- *Saxonis Grammatici Danorvm Historiæ*, Basel, 1536.

---------- *Den danske Krønike* (Anders Sørensen Vedel, tr.), Copenhagen, 1851.

Schledermann, Peter, 'Preliminary results of archaeological investigations in the Bache Peninsula region, Ellesmere Island, NTW,' pp. 459–74 in *Arctic* 31(1978).

-------- 'Ellesmere Island: Eskimo and Viking Finds in the High Arctic,' pp. 574–601 in *National Geographic* 159: 5 (1981).

------- 'Nordbogenstande fra Arktisk Canada,'pp. 222–25 in Clausen, *Viking.*

------- 'Ellesmere: Vikings in the Far North,' pp. 238–56 in Fitzhugh and Ward, *Vikings.*

------- 'A.D. 1000: East meets west,' pp. 189–92 in Fitzhugh and Ward, *Vikings*;

Schledermann, Peter, and Karen McCullough, 'Western Elements in the Early Thule Culture of the Eastern High Arctic,' *Arctic* 33: 4 (1980).

------ *Late Thule Culture developments on the central east coast of Ellesmere Island*, Copenhagen, 2003.

Schofield, J. Edward, Kevin J. Edwards and Charlie Christensen, 'Environmental impacts around the time of Norse landnám in the Qorlortoq valley, Eastern Settlement, Greenland,' pp. 1643–57 in *Journal of Archaeological Science* 35 (2008).

Scoresby, William, the Younger, *An Account of the Arctic Regions with a History and Description of the Northern Whale-Fishery*. 2 vols, Edinburgh, 1820.

Scott, G. Richard, Carrin M. Halffmann and P.O. Pedersen, 'Dental Conditions of Medieval Norsemen in the North Atlantic,' pp. 183–207 in *Acta Archaeologica* 62 (1991/1992).

Seaver, Kirsten A., *The Frozen Echo: Greenland and the Exploration of North America ca. A.D. 1000–1500*, Stanford, California, 1996.

------- '"A Very Common and Usuall Trade": The Relationship Between Cartographic Perceptions and Fishing in the Davis Strait c.1500–1550,' pp. 1–26 in Karen Severud Cook, ed., *Images and Icons of the New World: Essays on American Cartography*, London, 1996.

------- 'Norumbega and *Harmonia Mundi* in Sixteenth-Century Cartography,' *Imago Mundi* 50 (1998).

------- Seaver, Kirsten A. 'Baffin Island mandibles and iron blooms,' in pp. 563–74 in Symons, *Meta Incognita*, vol. 2.

------- Seaver, Kirsten A., 'How strange is a stranger? A survey of opportunities for Inuit-European Contact in the Davis Strait before 1576,' pp. 523–52 in Symons, *Meta Incognita*, vol. 2.

-------- 'Land of wine and forests: The Norse in North America,' *Mercator's World* 5: 1 (2000), pp.18–24.

-------- 'Renewing the quest for Vínland: The Stefánsson, Resen and Thorláksson maps,' pp. 42–9 in *Mercator's World* 5: 5 (2000).

-------- 'Far and yet near: North America and Norse Greenland,' pp. 3–5, 23 in *Viking Heritage Newsletter* 1, no. 1 (2000), Visby (Sweden).

------- 'Olaus Magnus and the "compass"on Hvitsark,' pp. 235–54 in *The Journal of Navigation* (London), May 2001.

-------- *Maps, Myths, and Men: The Story of the Vinland Map*, Stanford (California): Stanford University Press, 2004.

-------- 'Walrus pitch and other novelties: Gavin Menzies and the Far North,' 2006, on <http://www.1421exposed.com>.

-------- 'Ettertraktete tenner: Middelalderens handel med hvalrosstann og afrikansk elfenbein,' pp. 231–50 in *Historisk Tidsskrift* (Oslo, 2006, no. 2).

-------- 'Thralls and queens: Aspects of female slavery among the medieval Norse,' in vol. 1, pp. 147–67, Gwyn Campbell, Suzanne Miers, and Joseph C. Miller, eds, *Women and Slavery*, Athens (Ohio) Ohio University Press, 2007.

-------- 'Pygmies of the Far North,' pp. 63–87 in *Journal of World History* 19:1 (2008).

Seller, John, *The English Pilot: The First Book, Published by the Special Licence and Approbation of His Royal Highness the Duke of York*. London: John Darby, 1671.

Sigurðsson, Gísli, 'The quest for Vínland in saga scholarship,' pp. 232–37 in Fitzhugh and Ward, Vikings.

Sigurðsson, Ingi, and Jón Skaptason, eds, *Aspects of Arctic and Sub-Arctic History: Proceedings of the International Congress on the History of the Arctic and Sub-Arctic Region, Reykjavík, 18–21 June 1998*, Reykjavík, 2000.

Skaaning Høegsberg, Mogens, 'A reassessment of the development of the cathedral at Garðar, Greenland,' pp. 74–96 in *Archaeologica Islandica* 6 (2007).

Skaare, Kolbjørn, 'En norsk penning fra 11. årh. funnet på kysten av Maine, U.S.A.,' pp. 2–17 in *Meddelelser fra Norsk Numismatisk Forening*, May 1979.

Skelton, Raleigh A., Thomas E. Marston, and George D. Painter, *The Vinland Map and the Tartar Relation*, New Haven (Connecticut), Yale University Press, 1965.

Sköld, Tryggve, articles on the Kensington Rune Stone and Edvard Larsson's runes in *DAUM-katta*, winter 2003, winter 2004, June 2005 and spring 2007, <http://www.sofi.se/daum/>.

Skovgaard-Petersen, Inge, 'Islandsk egenkirkevæsen,' pp. 230–96 in *Scandia* 26 (1960).

Skre, Dagfinn, ed., *Kaupang in Skiringssal*, Aarhus (Denmark) and Oslo, 2007.

Slack, Paul, *The Impact of Plague in Tudor and Stuart England*, London, 1985.

Smith, Brian, 'Earl Henry Sinclair's fictitious trip to America,' *New Orkney Antiquarian Journal* 2 (2000), read as prepublication typescript.

Smith, Kevin P., 'Who Lived at L'Anse aux Meadows?' in Fitzhugh and Ward, *Vikings*.

Sørensen, Ingrid, 'Pollenundersøgelser i møddingen på Niaqussat,' pp. 296–304 in *Grønland* 30 (1982).

Spies, Marijke, *Arctic routes to Fabled Lands: Oliver Brunel and the Passage to China and Cathay in the Sixteenth Century*, Amsterdam, 1997.

Stefánsson, Vilhjalmur, and Eloise McCaskill, *The three voyages of Martin Frobisher*, 2 vols, London: Argonaut Press, 1938.

Storm, Gustav, *Monumenta historica norvegiæ latine conscripta*, Kristiania [Oslo]: A.W. Brøgger, 1880.

------- ed., *Islandske Annaler Indtil 1578*, Oslo, 1977 (repr. of 1888 ed.).

------- 'Den danske Geograf Claudius Clavus eller Nicolaus Niger,' pp.129–46 in *Ymer* 9: 1– 2, (Stockholm, 1889).

------- 'Ginnungagap i Mytologien og i Geografien,' in Axel Koch, ed., *Arkiv för nordisk Filologi* 6: 2 (1890).

Sutherland, Patricia D., 'The Norse and Native Norse Americans,' pp. 238–47 in Fitzhugh and Ward, *Vikings*.

------- 'Strands of culture contact: Dorset-Norse interactions in the Eastern Canadian Arctic,' pp.159–69 in M. Appelt, J. Berglund, and H.C. Gulløv, eds, *Identities and Cultural Contacts in the Arctic*, Copenhagen, 2000.

Sutherland, Patricia D., and Robert McGhee, 'Arktisk kontakt,' pp. 12–15 in *Skalk* 3 (1983)

Symons, Thomas H.B., ed., *Meta Incognita: A Discourse of Discovery. Martin Frobisher's Arctic Expeditions, 1576–1576*, 2 vols, Hull, Québec, 1999.

Taylor, Eva G. R., 'A letter dated 1577 from Mercator to John Dee,' pp. 56–68 in *Imago Mundi* 13 (1956).

Taylor, Michael, *The Lewis Chessmen*, London, 1978.

Thirslund, Søren, 'Sailing directions of the North Atlantic Viking Age (from about the year 860 to 1400),' pp. 55–64 in *The Journal of Navigation* 50: 1 (1997).

------- *Viking Navigation: Sun-compass guided Norsemen first to America*, Skjern (Denmark): 1997.

Thorsteinsson, Björn, 'Henry VIII and Iceland,' pp. 67–101 in *Bulletin of the Institute for Historical Research* 15 (1957–59).

------- 'Íslands- og Grænlandssiglingar Englendinga á 15. öld of fundur Norður-Ameríku,' pp. 3–71 in *Saga* 4–5 (1965–67).

------- *Enska öldin í sögu íslendinga*, Reykjavík: 1970.

Thorsteinsson, Ingvi, 'The environmental effects of farming in South Greenland in the Middle Ages and the twentieth century,' pp. 258–263 in Sigurðsson and Skaptason, *Aspects*.

Torfæus, Tormod, *Gronlandia antiqua*, tr. by the author as Det gamle Grønland, Copenhagen, 1706, reissued Oslo, 1947.

Vebæk, Christen Leif, 'The church topography of the Eastern Settlement and the excavation of the Benedictine convent at Narsarsuaq in the Uunartoq fjord,' *Meddelelser om Grønland: Man & Society* 14, Copenhagen, 1991.

------- 'Vatnahverfi: An Inland District of the Eastern Settlement in Greenland,' *Meddelelser om Grønland: Man & Society* 17 (1992).

------- 'Narsaq – a Norse *landnáma* farm,' *Meddelelser om Grønland, Man & Society* 18, Copenhagen, 1993.

Vebæk, Christen Leif and Søren Thirslund, *The Viking Compass Guided Norsemen First to America*, Skjern (Denmark), 1992.

Vésteinsson, Orri, 'Settlement in Light of Recent Archaeological Investigations,' address given on 16 September, 2000, at the Viking Millennium International Symposium in St. John's, Newfoundland.

Vigfússon, Guðbrandr, and Theodor Möbius, eds, *Fornsögur: Vatnsdælasaga, Hallfreðarsaga, Flóamannasaga*, Leipzig, 1860.

Vollan, Odd, 'Torskefiske,' *Kulturhistorisk leksikon for nordisk middelalder* 18 (1974): cols. 506–10.

Wahlgren, Erik, *The Vikings and America*, London, 1986.

Wallace, Birgitta, 'L'Anse aux Meadows, the western outpost,' in Clausen, *Viking Voyages*.

------- Wallace, Birgitta L., 'The Vikings in North America: Myth and reality,' pp. 206–12 in Ross Samson, ed., *Social Approaches to Viking Studies*, Glasgow, 1991.

------- 'The Norse in the North Atlantic: The L'Anse aux Meadows settlement in Newfoundland,' pp. 486–500 in Sigurðsson and Skaptason, *Aspects*.

Wallis, Helen, F.R. Maddison, G.D. Painter, D. B. Quinn, R. M. Perkins, G. R. Crone, A. D. Baynes-Cope and Walter C. and Lucy B. McCrone, 'The strange case of the Vinland Map: A Symposium,' pp. 183–217. *The Geographical Journal* 140: 2 (1974).

White, Paul A., *Non-Native Sources for the Scandinavian Kings' Sagas*, New York, 2005.

Willerslev, Eske, et al., report 7 July 2007, accessed 10 July 2007 at http://news.nationalgeographic.com/news/2007/07/070705-oldest-dna.html

Williamson, James A., *Cabot Voyages and Bristol Discovery under Henry VII*, Cambridge (England), 1962.

Wroth, Lawrence E., *The Voyages of Giovanni da Verrazzano 1524–28*, New Haven and London, 1970.

Index

Please Note: For Nordic names prior to about AD 1500, the Christian name comes first, followed by the patronym.

INDEX